THE ESSENTIAL MICKEY ROONEY

THE ESSENTIAL MICKEY ROONEY

James L. Neibaur

ROWMAN & LITTLEFIELD
Lanham • Boulder • New York • London

Published by Rowman & Littlefield
A wholly owned subsidiary of The Rowman & Littlefield Publishing Group, Inc.
4501 Forbes Boulevard, Suite 200, Lanham, Maryland 20706
www.rowman.com

Unit A, Whitacre Mews, 26-34 Stannary Street, London SE11 4AB

All photos from the author's collection

British Library Cataloguing in Publication Information Available

Library of Congress Cataloging-in-Publication Data

Neibaur, James L., 1958–
The essential Mickey Rooney / James L. Neibaur.
pages cm
Includes bibliographical references and index.
ISBN 978-1-4422-6095-5 (hardback : alk. paper) — ISBN 978-1-4422-6096-2 (ebook) 1. Rooney, Mickey. 2. Actors—United States—Biography. I. Title.
PN2287.R75N45 2016
791.4302'8092—dc23
2015033910

∞™ The paper used in this publication meets the minimum requirements of American National Standard for Information Sciences—Permanence of Paper for Printed Library Materials, ANSI/NISO Z39.48-1992.

Printed in the United States of America

CONTENTS

ACKNOWLEDGMENTS

Thanks for the help, encouragement, assistance with research materials, interviews, and other such support: Mickey Rooney, Katie Carter, Terri Lynch, Ted Okuda, Tony Bensley, Rick Greene, Ann Rutherford, Scott McGee, Richard Lertzman, Scott Rivers, Allan Ellenberger, Cliff Aleperti, Jerry Beck, James Zeruk, Jerry Lewis, Eddie Deezen, Turner Classic Movies, and GetTV.

INTRODUCTION

Approaching the mammoth project of discussing Mickey Rooney's eighty-eight-year film career causes one to prioritize the most important aspects of his screen work for the most attention. Mickey Rooney was in films from early childhood until only weeks before his death in 2014 at age ninety-three, with a couple of feature appearances being released posthumously. His film career went from silent movies into the second decade of the twenty-first century, numbering hundreds of roles.

As a result, this is *The Essential Mickey Rooney*. We will first discuss, in survey form, his earlier pre-stardom films during the end of the silent era and the first half of the 1930s, and then go film by film for the remainder of the filmography. Since this period covers 1936–2014, and over three hundred titles, we will zero in on the essential films of his long career. But what makes a Mickey Rooney movie essential? This does not mean only good movies, nor does it mean only starring roles.

Making an impact with his acclaimed performance in *The Devil Is a Sissy* (1936), Rooney went into the popular Andy Hardy series the following year; he also began costarring with Judy Garland in a series of equally popular musicals and appeared in top moneymaking MGM hits like *Boys Town* (1938) and *Young Tom Edison* (1940). He was among the top five box office stars from 1938 to 1943, achieving the number one spot in 1939, 1940, and 1941 amid incredible competition.

In 1944, shortly after completing work on the film *National Velvet* opposite Elizabeth Taylor, Rooney enlisted in the armed forces. He served more than twenty-one months, until shortly after the end of World War Two. He entertained the troops in America and Europe, including in combat zones, and was awarded the Bronze Star Medal, the Army Good Conduct Medal, the American Campaign Medal, the European-African-Middle Eastern Campaign Medal, and World War II Victory Medal for his military service.

Upon returning to Hollywood in 1946, Rooney discovered that his home studio of MGM, where he had appeared in movies that made millions, had little interest in his return. After a failed attempt to resurrect the Andy Hardy series and a few films that failed to click at the box office, Rooney was released from his MGM contract. His final film there, *Words and Music* (1948), received terrible notices, and his performance as songwriter Lorenz Hart was singled out as especially wrongheaded.

Nearly all of the Mickey Rooney features from *The Devil Is a Sissy* until the end of the 1940s are considered essential and will get full chapter-by-chapter coverage in this book. These films present his rise to stardom, his having achieved major stardom, his attempt at a comeback after the war, and his being dropped by longtime studio MGM and investigating opportunities at other studios.

Rooney spent the 1950s working hard to recapture the stardom he had enjoyed before the war. While continuing to secure leading roles and always approaching each project with talent and enthusiasm, Rooney was no longer the box office champion he had been. Not every starring film he made was essential. There is little to be said about the forgettable *My Outlaw Brother* (1951), *The Twinkle in God's Eye* (1955), or *Magnificent Roughnecks* (1956). But impressive films like Nicholas Ray's *Drive a Crooked Road* (1954) or Don Siegel's *Baby Face Nelson* (1957) are certainly among the actor's more essential movies of this period. And, although they are not particularly good films, *Francis in the Haunted House* (1956) and *Andy Hardy Comes Home* (1958) are worthy of some discussion as examples of Rooney's attempts to revive his career by continuing or resurrecting old series. The same goes for films like *Sound Off* (1952), *A Slight Case of Larceny* (1953), or *The Atomic Kid* (1954), which were attempts to turn Rooney into a comedian.

By the 1960s, he was no longer leading man material and settled into character roles and small parts. Due to a gambling problem, as well as several well-documented divorces and alimonies, Rooney was perpetually short on money, so he took whatever parts came his way. Chapter-length studies will cover highlights like *Requiem for a Heavyweight* (1962); *It's a Mad, Mad, Mad, Mad World* (1963); and *Ambush Bay* (1966). Much of Rooney's work in the 1960s was unremarkable, including a cameo in *Breakfast at Tiffany's* (1961) that he regretted for the rest of his life. *Everything's Ducky* (1961) tried to create a team dynamic between Rooney and Buddy Hackett. However, these films and others, such as *The Comic* (1969), are essential representations of the era and/or of this period in his career.

By the 1970s and into the twenty-first century, Rooney spent more time doing television work than film work. And often his movie appearances were in throwaways like *The Godmothers* (1975) and *Silent Night, Deadly Night 5* (1991). What is most impressive is that this once major box office sensation, who had started in silent films as a child, continued working throughout his life. And while much of his work continued to make little real impact (Rooney would quip, "Some of my pictures weren't released, they escaped!"), he did enjoy some highlights during these years. His performance in *The Black Stallion* (1979) received an Oscar nomination, and he won an Emmy for his portrayal of the real-life title character in the TV movie *Bill* (1981). He also triumphed on Broadway in the 1980s in the burlesque throwback musical *Sugar Babies*, which earned him a Tony nomination.

Mickey Rooney is one of the most durable, important, and fascinating performers in American film history. His career reached the very height of stardom and plummeted to where he had to take whatever opportunities were available. Despite the circumstances, Rooney's innate sense and genuine talent were always evident. His perseverance, continuing to try to make it work in a field that wasn't always particularly kind to him, is probably the most impressive and admirable aspect of his personality. In a career that spanned vaudeville, silent movies, Hollywood classics, Broadway, radio, television, cartoon voice-overs, and even the Internet, Mickey Rooney's accomplishments are quite impressive.

PROLOGUE

From Joe Yule Jr. to Mickey McGuire and Early Supporting Roles

The story of Mickey Rooney's early life has been told many times and many different ways, often by Rooney himself. His first appearance in show business is usually claimed to be as a six-month-old toddler during his parents' vaudeville act. Rooney was born Joe Yule Jr. on September 23, 1920, to parents Joe Yule and Nell Carter Yule. According to Rooney, he became a part of their act before he was two years old, singing "Pal O' My Cradle." Rooney has recalled the devastation he felt when his father left the family in 1924, after which Rooney and his mother moved to California. Rooney made his film debut in the 1926 short film *Not to Be Trusted*, which was released in October. The following March he appeared opposite Colleen Moore in *Orchids and Ermine*. Footage that exists on *Orchids and Ermine* shows the six-year-old Rooney playing a dapperly dressed, cigar-chomping midget, who eyes the pretty ladies as they walk by, confidently approaches Ms. Moore's character, and starts flirting.

After this decidedly odd introduction to movies, Rooney's mother saw an ad in the trades looking for a child to start in a proposed movie version of the Toonerville Trolley comic strip series. The role of brash young Mickey McGuire seemed perfect for Rooney, so his mother bought some inexpensive black hair dye[1] to make her son look like the raven-haired cartoon character. Rooney got the part, and filming began on the first short in 1927. In 1931, Mickey had his name legally changed to Mickey McGuire at the suggestion of film producer Larry Darmour, who hoped to avoid paying the

$1,000 royalties to comic strip creator Fontaine Fox by indicating that that was the actor's actual name. The comic creators sued, with success, in 1930.

The Mickey McGuire comedies were producer Darmour's attempt to compete with the Hal Roach Studios, which had been producing the Our Gang comedies to great success. But while there was a natural, creative flair to the Our Gang films, the Mickey McGuire comedies were broader and slapdash in their style. Rooney recalled in an interview,

> Most of the Mickey McGuire pictures were directed by a guy named Al Herman.[2] There was a lot of running, a lot of falling, and a lot of stunts. I was just a kid so I didn't realize the danger of some of the things we did. I remember in the first Mickey McGuire picture[3] there was a fella chasing me on a bicycle and he rode it into a lake. I also remember we were putting on a circus so there were all kinds of animals on the set. Dogs, cats, horses, goats, just about every animal you can think of. Animals, kids, and dangerous stunts! What could possibly go wrong? But the pictures were popular, and it was a steady job that lasted several years. I know the first ones were silent but I had no trouble once they started making them as talkies. I was a kid, so my squeaky voice fit the character.[4]

Rooney played Mickey McGuire in seventy-eight two-reel comedies released from 1927 to 1934. Others in Mickey's gang included Hambone Johnson, usually played by Jimmy Robinson, the black juvenile who was the counterpart to Farina, Stymie, or Buckwheat in the Roach series; Billy McGuire, Mickey's little brother, played by dwarf actor Billy Barty, who had a long career in films and television; and Tomboy Taylor, the only girl in the gang, played by Delia Bogard until 1933, then by Shirley Jean Rickert for the final year (Rickert had been a member of Our Gang). Mickey's rival was Stinky Davis, played variously by Douglas Fox, Doug Thomas, and Kendall McComas (who had been Breezy in the Our Gang comedies).

The Mickey McGuire films were successful rivals to the Our Gang comedies, especially since they also managed to transition with success from silent movies to talkies. Although new to films, Rooney already demonstrated charisma and a confident manner and would grow discernibly throughout the series. While there was little room for any real acting challenges in these quickly produced comedies, they allowed Rooney to create a foundation for his later acting prowess. Rooney recalled in an interview,

> Those pictures were good training for later on. Whenever I had to do slapstick, whenever I had to be angry, whenever I had to be bossy, whenever I had to cry, I had done it at one time or another in one of the McGuires.[5]

The Mickey McGuire comedies ceased production in 1932, although new shorts continued to be released as late as 1934. Nell had her son take a few stage dates to continue the needed steady income. Mickey would trade off his new-found movie popularity, singing and dancing as he had before he got a break in the McGuire comedies. In one 1932 appearance, Rooney (billed as Mickey McGuire) appeared in a show that also featured Ted Healy and his Stooges, Moe, Larry, and Curly. This is particularly significant as it was the first appearance of Moe Howard's younger brother, Curly Howard, in the Stooges act. (Older brother Shemp had left to work as a solo comic. He would return to the act years later when illness forced Curly's retirement.)

On this show there are advertisements where Rooney is billed as Mickey (himself) McGuire, as that was his legal name. However, the owners of the comic strip were successful in refusing to allow Rooney to continue using the Mickey McGuire name in personal appearances. At first Rooney and his mother considered simply using his real last name of Yule, but their estrangement from Mickey's father made them decide against that. Rooney's mother came up with the name Mickey Looney, but they soon arrived upon Rooney and that became the actor's name for the remainder of his life.

Rooney had enough notoriety from the Mickey McGuire comedies to pick up small parts in movies elsewhere. Rooney costarred with western action performer Tom Mix in *My Pal the King* (1932); appeared in the classic gangster drama *Beast of the City* (1932), which featured a cast that included Walter Huston and Jean Harlow; and supported Douglas Fairbanks Jr. in *The Life of Jimmy Dolan* (1933), which also featured an early appearance by a young John Wayne.

Most of the freelancing Rooney did between 1932 and 1934 is of little consequence, except for the fact that Rooney was sometimes billed as Mickey McGuire, and would occasionally get as high as third billing. A lot of these movies were made on the infamous poverty row, where small independent studios cranked out features with very low budgets. Studios like Allied Pictures and Eagle Pictures were among the production companies whose films Rooney worked on during this period. The filmmaking at such studios has its own interest, and books have been written about their methods of production and distribution in an era when film companies came and went almost as often as actors did. In one low-budget movie, *Sin's Pay Day* (1932), Rooney worked for the first time with director George Seitz, who would later helm nearly all the Andy Hardy movies. This movie was distributed by Action Pictures via the states rights system, but once Rooney's star began to rise in 1938, it was rereleased as *Slums of New York* to capitalize on his fame.

By 1934, Rooney's occasional appearances in Metro-Goldwyn-Mayer (MGM) films like *Beast of the City* were impressive enough that he was frequently asked back to play juvenile roles. By the time he played Clark Gable as a boy in *Manhattan Melodrama* (1934), he had become fairly well established at the studio. He was then offered a contract by Louis B. Mayer to make films for MGM.

EARLY SUPPORTING ROLES (1934–1936)

Mickey Rooney had been receiving $250 per week while making the Mickey McGuire comedies, but that rate increased to $500 per week once he was under contract to MGM. Throughout 1934, Rooney kept busy in a variety of small roles; some gave him reasonable screen time, while others were veritable walk-ons.

In the fall of 1934, Mickey Rooney was cast as Puck in Max Reinhardt's stage presentation of Shakespeare's *A Midsummer Night's Dream.* Reinhardt had been a top stage director in his native Germany and was trying to resume his career after fleeing to America to escape the rule of the Third Reich. *A Midsummer Night's Dream* was performed in the Hollywood Bowl in September of 1934. According to the Los Angeles Philharmonic Association's program designer/annotator John Mangum,

> It was [a] spectacular production. The shell was removed and replaced by a "forest" planted in tons of dirt hauled in especially for the event, and a trestle was constructed from the hills to the stage for the wedding procession between Acts IV and V. Reinhardt's son Gottfried later recalled, "He worked out a torch parade for the last act, stepping to Mendelssohn's Wedding March, from the heights of the Hollywood Hills to the bottom of the valley. . . . It did not concern him that in Southern California's tinder-dry vegetation, that constituted a fire hazard of the first order."[6]

When Warner Bros. decided to film the show in 1935 they were taking a real chance. Douglas Fairbanks and Mary Pickford had produced a film version of *The Taming of the Shrew* in 1929 that flopped at the box office. Films based on Shakespeare's plays were still considered box office poison. Furthermore, Warner Bros. wanted to fill the cast with its own contracted stars, like James Cagney, Dick Powell, and Joe E. Brown. The only actors hired from the Hollywood Bowl performance to appear in the film were

Rooney and Olivia de Havilland. This resulted in a contract at Warner Bros. for Olivia de Havilland. For Rooney, it was greater recognition. Rooney recalled,

> Other studios wanted me to be in their pictures and paid MGM a fee to loan me out. The fee was much more than the $500 a week I was making. I was just a kid and didn't care. I do now. But back then, during the Depression, I was making a lot of money doing something I loved.[7]

Rooney also recalled the hazards of attempting to live a normal child's life outside of the studio when, during production on *A Midsummer Night's Dream*, he broke his leg in a tobogganing accident. Rooney recalled,

> Jack Warner wasn't just mad, he was furious. He threatened to break my other leg! They shot around me, covered my cast with leaves, pushed me around on a bicycle, all kinds of things to keep the picture going. I don't think I cost them any time. But I was sure careful after that.[8]

Rooney's own studio also realized by his acclaimed performance as Puck that they had a rather formidable young actor under contract. They tried him out initially in more prestigious supporting parts to see if he could meet the challenge of these roles. One of Rooney's more prestigious films at this time was *Ah, Wilderness!* (1935), based on Eugene O'Neill's play. Rooney enjoyed working with top-drawer MGM actors Lionel Barrymore and Wallace Beery as well as one of the studio's top directors, Clarence Brown. Rooney recalled,

> When you're a kid and you're starting to work in bigger pictures, with bigger parts, you learn a lot. You take everything in. I would watch actors like Lionel Barrymore and Wallace Beery and learn more about acting.[9]

Many younger actors recall Beery negatively, including Jackie Cooper and Margaret O'Brien, but Rooney became quite fond of him in their first movie together. Cooper claimed in his autobiography[10] that Beery was cold and aloof, making their frequent screen teamings in classics like *The Champ* (1931) and *Treasure Island* (1934) difficult experiences. O'Brien stated in an interview on Turner Classic Movies[11] that Beery would pinch her in their scenes together to distract from her performance. But Rooney recalled in his autobiography,

> Wallace Beery (was) a lovable, shambling kind of guy who never seemed to know that his shirttail belonged inside his pants, but always knew when a little kid actor needed a smile and a wink, or a word of encouragement.[12]

Rooney was also quite enamored with actress Jean Harlow, with whom he had worked a couple of years earlier in *Beast of the City* (1932). Rooney had a role in *Riffraff* (1936), which was one of the actress's last movies. She died in June of 1937 at the age of only twenty-six. Rooney recalled,

> Jean Harlow's death was like losing a member of the family. That's what MGM was back then. Louis B. Mayer's extended family. He paid for a huge funeral at the studio, with a banquet. We all attended. It was very sad.[13]

Now that the MGM executives were taking notice, Mickey Rooney's role in *Little Lord Fauntleroy* opposite Freddie Bartholomew made enough of an impact to consider him for larger costarring roles. Though his role was small, Rooney's performance as Dick, a shoeshine boy, is a noticeable contrast to the refined Fauntleroy played by Bartholomew. Fauntleroy's affected British accent, telling a group of ruffians, "That's none of your affair," is combined with Dick's American street slang with lines like "Why'd the cops come? We woulda had 'em licked!" Any European separation of class and status that might have existed between these two boys at this time did not occur in America. Dick is impressed with Fauntleroy's fancy bicycle, about which the other kids had been chiding him. Fauntleroy is quite willing to engage in the fight that erupts with these neighborhood bullies, even before Dick jumps in to help. The wide gap between their respective social upbringings is overlooked as Dick longs for the privileges Fauntleroy enjoys, and the young lord wishes to be just another ordinary boy. The scene where Fauntleroy must take on his duties as a royalty and say goodbye to his old friend Dick is an emotional highlight of the film, with Rooney effectively showing the vulnerable side of the tough street kid he was portraying.

Freddie Bartholomew had made quite an impact in the title role of MGM's film version of Charles Dickens's *David Copperfield* (1934), just as Rooney had in *A Midsummer Night's Dream*. Their success in another literary adaption impressed MGM executives, so they wanted to try them together in another project, though not necessarily from classic literature. They wanted to instead explore the dynamic between the disparate characters the two actors played in *Little Lord Fauntleroy*, but from the perspective of a more modern story with a contemporary setting. Warner Bros. was enjoying some success with Depression-era social dramas, but MGM wasn't the studio to do gritty stories about the streets.

After some research, MGM chose a story by Rowland Brown, who specialized in writing about crime and tough street characters. His past story credits included the gangster movie *The Doorway to Hell* (Warner Bros.,

1930), featuring an early appearance by James Cagney, and an especially brutal prison drama titled *Hell's Highway* (RKO, 1932). While Brown's usual gritty dramas were not the forte of the refined MGM, this story dealt with a young British lad who moves to Manhattan to live with his father and must prove himself to the rough street kids who react negatively to his English-bred refinement. Naturally Freddie Bartholomew was a shoo-in for the lead role. Mickey Rooney was hired to play Gig Stevens, a tough kid whose father is soon going to the electric chair. MGM also cast another of their top younger stars, Jackie Cooper, to further help ensure box office. A former Our Gang star, Cooper had already made quite an impact in the MGM dramas *The Champ* (1931) and *Treasure Island* (1934).

A screenplay by John Lee Mahin and Richard Schayer was written from Brown's story, giving it the indelible MGM stamp of refinement, just desserts, family strength, and a happy conclusion. W. S. Van Dyke was selected to direct (with an uncredited contribution by Brown himself). Rooney would be able to draw from the various roles he'd already played as far back as the silent movie days in order to define the sort of tough street kid that best fit the production's intent. And while the part would be in support, Rooney turned it into the most interesting character in the movie, and one in which he could truly exhibit the depth of his talents even if only in a few isolated scenes. The title chosen for the movie was *The Devil Is a Sissy*.

THE DEVIL IS A SISSY

(MGM, 1936)

Director: W. S. Van Dyke with Rowland Brown
Screenplay: John Lee Mahin, Richard Schayer. *Story:* Rowland Brown
Producer: Frank Davis. *Cinematographers:* Harold Rosson, George Schneidermann. *Editor:* Tom Held
Cast: Freddie Bartholomew (Claude), Jackie Cooper ("Buck" Murphy), Mickey Rooney ("Gig" Stevens), Ian Hunter (Jay Pierce), Katharine Alexander (Hilda Pierce), Gene Lockhart (Mr. Murphy), Kathleen Lockhart (Mrs. Murphy), Peggy Conklin (Rose), Jonathan Hale (Judge Holmes), Etienne Girardot (Principal), Frank Puglia (Grandma), Sherwood Bailey (Bugs), Buster Slaven (Six Toes), Grant Mitchell (Paul Krumpp), Harold Huber (Willie), Stanley Fields (Joe), Etta McDaniel (Molly), George Davis (Charley), John Kelly (Shivvy), Myra Marsh (Joe's Mother), Dorothy Peterson (Jennie Stevens), John Wray (Priest), Charles Trowbridge (Doctor), Ian Wolfe (Pawnbroker), Andrew Tombes (Muldoon), Christian Rub (Tombstone Mason), David Thursby (Court Clerk), William Gould (Court Clerk), Wally Maher (Taxi Driver), Buddy Messinger (Elevator Operator), Lester Dorr (Intern), Richard Powell (Football Salesman), Charles Coleman (Doorman), George Guhl (Detective), Stanley Andrews (Doctor), Don Brodie (Chauffeur). The following actors are in the studio records and casting call lists as appearing in this movie, but they are not identifiable: Rollo Lloyd, Mary Doran, Jason Robards Sr., Harry Tyler, Ben Hendricks Jr.
Released: September 18, 1936
Specs: 92 minutes; black and white
Availability: DVD (Warner Archive Collection)

Stories about tough street people were Warner Bros.' territory, as they boasted actors like James Cagney, Edward G. Robinson, and Humphrey Bogart in films that explored the gangster lifestyle that was permeating the newspapers during the Depression. Racketeers like Al Capone and bank robbers like John Dillinger became folk heroes in popular culture. Warner films like *Little Caesar* (1930) and *The Public Enemy* (1931) were gritty dramas that made a real impact on American cinema and were quite popular with moviegoers. Even the Broadway stage responded to this dark appetite as seen in Sidney Kingsley's massively successful play *Dead End* about a group of tough street kids functioning within the limited parameters of their income level.

Dead End opened to rave reviews on Broadway on October 31, 1935. Six days later, MGM announced to the trades their plans to make a film out of Roland Brown's story *The Devil Is a Sissy*, with Brown directing. However, unlike the gritty, realistic Warner Bros. movies, or even Sidney Kingsley's play, MGM had a rather distinct approach to the material. There were certain moral standards that the studio steadfastly maintained, and somebody as evil as Rico Bandello in *Little Caesar* or as sinister as Tom Powers in *The Public Enemy* would simply not fit into MGM's perspective.

One thing the studio did seem to like was a story about tough kids realizing the error of their ways. Learning a lesson was a staple of MGM films featuring young people in the central roles. A year after the release of *The Devil Is a Sissy*, MGM would inherit Hal Roach's Our Gang series, transforming it from something clever and funny to something preachy and moralistic. As a result, despite good performances and a writer like Brown, who would go on to pen the quintessential juvenile gangster drama *Angels with Dirty Faces* (Warner Bros., 1938), *The Devil Is a Sissy* is a prototypical example of how MGM approached such tawdry subject matter.

Claude (Freddie Bartholomew) is the child of divorced parents. His mother (Katharine Alexander) is wealthy and lives among the privileged. His father (Ian Hunter) is a struggling artist more comfortable in an urban area. When Claude goes to stay with his father, he must prove himself to his rough-edged peers, who perceive him as effete and different. The film presents Claude as genuinely interested in the urban lifestyle, not spoiled by his mother's pampering or his privileged lifestyle. He takes boxing lessons so he can win a fight. He purchases a football so he can learn to play. He stands up to bigger boys and is not above using what he'd learned from his boxing instructor. Eventually, he is accepted.

The two boys to whom Claude is closest are Buck (Jackie Cooper) and Gig (Mickey Rooney). Buck comes from a strict disciplinarian father who boasts of his wartime adventures, believing his service should net him some entitlement. Gig is the son of a long-suffering mother and a crooked father who sits on death row. Such circumstances are completely alien to Claude.

MGM takes this promising situation and gives it the studio treatment, making it far less effective than its potential. There are tangential interludes

Jackie Cooper, Mickey Rooney, and Freddie Bartholomew

such as a visit to Gig's rich aunt (Peggy Conklin) that results in an impromptu song-and-dance number that seems out of character for all involved. With all of the calculated street slang in the screenplay, there are many "Gee, that'd be swell" moments where the dialogue doesn't ring true to the characters. Rooney and Cooper both seem to be clean-cut boys who enjoy exploring the seamy underbelly of society, unlike the juveniles in Warner movies like *Wild Boys of the Road* (1933), where the Depression forces teenagers to run away from home and form their own egalitarian society down by the railroad tracks. Buck and Gig are good boys in bad circumstances. There is no fight-to-survive ethos as found in such films from other studios.

That said, *The Devil Is a Sissy* was still a major opportunity for Mickey Rooney. His Gig character is confident and fast-talking, which is a role that Rooney could play expertly. He comes off better than his costars.

There is a scene during the first ten minutes of the film when Gig is standing outside the rooming house where he lives on the night his father is about the die in the electric chair. The streetlights dim, and he realizes it's been done. His head shakes, his eyes tear up, and his voice catches in his throat. The experience completely overwhelms him. It is one of the finest pieces of acting in Rooney's entire long career. Jackie Cooper recalled in his autobiography,

> That was the first time I felt one of my peers was stealing a scene from me, and I didn't like my reaction to that. But there wasn't much I could do about it. . . . So I watched Rooney go to town and steal the scene and the whole picture.[1]

While Cooper and Freddie Bartholomew were the clear stars of the movie, earning $2,000 per week next to Rooney's $500, they were not the ones singled out by most critics. Frank Nugent stated in the *New York Times*,

> Freddie Bartholomew is naturally meant for the role of Limey. Jackie Cooper does a workmanlike job with Buck. But it is Mickey Rooney, the Puck of *A Midsummer Night's Dream*, who penetrates beyond the script and emerges as a living study of Gig, the son of a murderer. His is, without question, one of the finest performances of the year.[2]

Rowland Brown began directing the film but was replaced by W. S. Van Dyke after less than a week. Van Dyke reshot what Brown had completed. Mickey Rooney recalled,

> Woody Van Dyke was a popular director at MGM and he liked working with us kids. He was like a kid himself, always horsing around with us on the set. He'd have us over to his house for parties. He was a really great guy and a lot of fun.[3]

Van Dyke was recognized for inspiring actors to explore their role in greater depth, resulting in especially strong performances. He was also known for efficiency, never one to waste time and money doing endless retakes. Riding high after receiving Academy Award nominations for *The Thin Man* (1934) and *San Francisco* (1936), Van Dyke was the perfect director for this material.

Although he was billed third, Mickey Rooney emerged as the real star of *The Devil Is a Sissy*, and despite the film's shortcomings, it is an important movie in Rooney's career. MGM would continue to use him in various situations, gauge his effectiveness and box office appeal, and watch him very quickly become the biggest star in movies.

2

DOWN THE STRETCH

(Warner Bros., 1936)

Director: William Clemons
Story and Screenplay: William Jacobs. *Dialogue Director:* Gus Shy
Producer: Bryan Foy. *Cinematographer:* Arthur L. Todd. *Editor:* Louis Hesse
Cast: Patricia Ellis (Patricia Barrington), Mickey Rooney (Snapper Sinclair), Dennis Moore (Cliff Barrington), Willie Best (Noah), Gordon Hart (Judge Adams), Gordon Elliott (Robert Bates), Virginia Brissac (Aunt Julia), Charles C. Wilson (Tex Reardon), Joseph Crehan (Secretary Burch), Mary Treen (Nurse), Robert Emmett Keane (Nick), Jonathan Hale (Secretary Lyon), Charles Foy (Arnold), Crauford Kent (Sir Oliver Martin), Edward Keane (Fred Yates), Frank Faylen (Ben), James Eagles (Sonny Burnett), Hal Dawson (Mr. Watson), George Beranger (William J. Cooper), Raymond Brown (Colonel Carter), Lowden Adams (Butler), Glen Cavendar (Race Track Tout), Ralph Dunn (Race Starter), Cliff Saum (Detective), David Thursby (Groom), Emmett Vogan (Lawyer), Stuart Holmes (Official), Milton Kibbee (Vet), Charles Marsh (Photographer), Anne Nagel (Hat Check Girl), John Richardson (Jockey), Tom Wilson (Policeman), Bob Tansill (Butch)
Released: September 18, 1936
Specs: 66 minutes; black and white
Availability: Not on DVD

Prior to starting work on *The Devil Is a Sissy*, Mickey Rooney had been loaned to Warner Bros. for the B-level horse racing drama *Down the Stretch*. Second billed after actress Patricia Ellis, Rooney's stature from his previous roles was notable enough to secure some attention in a B movie. In what appears to be a complete coincidence, *Down the Stretch* reached theaters the very same day that MGM released *The Devil Is a Sissy*. While Warners had produced this quickie as a proposed second feature, once the reviews and word of mouth about the MGM feature began circulating, *Down the Stretch* was elevated to A-picture status, securing bookings at the top of the double bill.

Mickey Rooney recalled,

> Of course it's obvious to cast a short actor as a jockey. Warners liked my work in *Midsummer Night's Dream* and wanted me for the role. Bryan Foy, of *The Seven Little Foys*,[1] was in charge of Warners' B picture unit. So this was just a B picture that we did in a few weeks. They paid MGM a lot more for my services than I was getting.[2]

The story features Rooney as Fred "Snapper" Sinclair, a homeless boy about to go to the reformatory for stealing out of necessity. The Barringtons happen to be in court and recognize his name as being the same as that of a once-great jockey. They discover that the jockey was young Snapper's father. He is now deceased, and Snapper is alone. The Barringtons take custody and plan to train him to become a jockey for their stables.

Snapper is an outcast who is looked down upon due to an unsavory reputation his father left behind. Snapper's father would purposely lose races for an easy payoff, and the resentment young Snapper receives from the established jockeys results in a few fistfights. Noah, a black stable worker (Willie Best), recognizes Snapper's status as an outcast and befriends him. Snapper welcomes the friendship, and the two are a mutually supportive team.

When Snapper is the only jockey able to tame Faithful, the wildest and most unruly horse at the stable, he is elevated to being the lead jockey and rides him to victory in the Kentucky Derby. However, when he is preparing to ride another horse, Blue Boy, in an important race, he is framed by gamblers and officials force him to forfeit. Blacklisted in America, Snapper goes to England and achieves success there; he is scheduled to ride a horse from the king's stable in an important race. However, when he discovers that Faithful is also entered, he throws the race by purposely falling, seriously injuring himself and destroying his career due to his love for the horse he had tamed and trained and for its owner, Mrs. Barrington, who had given him his first chance.

The dynamic between Snapper and Noah represents a relationship that was almost never explored in films during this period, especially at the major studios (even in their B-picture units). Warners did occasionally have black actors extending beyond their stereotype (e.g., Sam McDaniel as the head waiter at an upscale café in *The Public Enemy* [1931], exhibiting a position of management rather than straight servitude).

However, Willie Best was a comedian who played the black stereotype for laughs in the same manner as Stepin Fetchit, Mantan Moreland, and other comic actors of color during the same era. The difference here is that Best is elevated to a veritable costarring role with Rooney. When Snapper starts to achieve success as a jockey, Noah continues to work for him, being given a nice suit of clothes and a solid paycheck.

Mickey Rooney, Willie Best

Mickey Rooney recalled,

> Willie was a talented guy and we became pretty good friends on that picture. He was also a talented musician, so between takes he'd play his guitar and we'd sing. He did what he had to with those roles like a lot of black actors back then. He had to act like he was afraid, and he made it funny, but he wasn't afraid of anything.[3]
>
> Best earned $65 a week. However, RKO, which had Best under contract, got $130 for Best's work. At the same time Warners paid $50 a day to rent a mechanical horse to stand in for my ultra-speedy colt. I guess black kids were in greater supply than mechanical robots![4]

The character of Noah is never mistreated and is well liked. The film does not investigate any situations where Noah is not welcome. No segregation is evident in the story. However, the film does explore Noah's status when gamblers hand him a stack of expensive betting tickets at the track. A security officer takes the confused Noah to see a racing official as Noah innocently reveals who he is, and his status, which links the tickets to Snapper. The gamblers (and the film's narrative) play on the black character's stereotypical naïveté to frame the jockey.

Willie Best was given fourth billing in the credits, which was much higher than most other black actors of the period. But the film strikes a strange balance between giving him the credit he deserves and not giving him payment equal to the white actors', while the posters for *Down the Stretch* referred to him as "the newest dark cloud of comedy."

The other interesting dynamic is Rooney's response to working with horses, as he would do so frequently and in some of his higher profile films (including *The Black Stallion* as late as 1979, earning him an Oscar nomination). Rooney's ability to project real passion as an actor helps greatly in the scenes where Snapper connects with the wild Faithful. Snapper recognizes that Faithful is the same sort of outcast at the stable, and the two outcasts respond to each other at a level much different than that between Snapper and Noah. In the end, when Snapper is lying in a hospital bed due to the injuries he sustained on the track, he is asked why he threw the race and lost everything. "I've lost nothing," he replies. There's a wonderful irony about the ending of this film, as Snapper, who tried so hard to escape his father's shadow, ends up throwing a race just as he did, although for more selfless reasons.

Down the Stretch is a fast-paced, solid B movie from a studio that produced some of the strongest films of the 1930s. All of the performances are top drawer, and Rooney maintains solid charisma throughout the film's duration. It was given little notice by the critics, having been eclipsed by the more predominant *The Devil Is a Sissy*, which had box office stars in the lead roles. But the success of the MGM film caused this B drama for Warners to achieve greater box office dividends than the studio expected. Even today, *Down the Stretch* is among the least known Mickey Rooney features of the 1930s.

Mickey Rooney would be loaned out a few more times over the next year, but once massive stardom was thrust upon him, MGM preferred to keep him active at the home studio. And, while *Down the Stretch* would not be his final appearance in a B movie, Mickey Rooney would very soon be the top-selling actor in A pictures at what was considered the biggest and most important studio of the era.

3

A FAMILY AFFAIR

(MGM, 1937)

Director: George B. Seitz
Screenplay: Kay Van Riper, Hugo Butler, based on the play *Skidding*, by Aurania Rouverol
Producers: Lucien Hubbard, Sam Marx. *Cinematographer:* Lester White. *Editor:* George Boemler
Cast: Lionel Barrymore (Judge [James K.] Hardy), Cecilia Parker (Marian Hardy), Eric Linden (Wayne Trent [III]), Mickey Rooney (Andy Hardy), Charley Grapewin (Frank Redmond), Spring Byington (Mrs. [Emily] Hardy), Julie Haydon (Joan Hardy [Martin]), Sara Haden (Aunt Milly), Allen Vincent (Bill Martin), Margaret Marquis (Polly [Benedict]), Selmer Jackson (Hoyt Wells), Harlan Briggs (Oscar Stubbins), Robert Emmett Keane (J. Carroll Nichols), William Soderling (Adams), Erville Alderson (Dave), Joe Caits (Delegate), Pat West (Delegate), O. G. "Dutch" Hendrian (Delegate), Al Hill (Delegate), Sam Hayes (Radio Announcer), Guy Usher (Chairman), James Donlan (Reporter), Virginia Sale (Social News Editor), George Chandler (Waiter), Don Barclay (Drunk), Arthur Housman (Drunk), Sam McDaniel (Chauffeur)
Released: March 12, 1937
Specs: 69 minutes; black and white
Availability: DVD (Warner Archive Collection: *The Andy Hardy Film Collection: Volume 2*)

A Family Affair is the first of the Hardy family series with Mickey Rooney playing all-American teenager Andy Hardy. However, this first film was not produced with the intention of becoming a series. Sam Marx, a story editor at MGM, had seen Aurania Rouverol's play *Skidding* when it premiered at the Bijou Theater in May 1928. Marx recalled the play fondly and suggested MGM's B unit purchase it. However, Lucien Hubbard, the head of the studio's B unit, was skeptical. Marx had to coproduce with Hubbard in order to get the film made.

Box office was ensured by hiring most of the actors who had appeared in the studio's 1935 hit *Ah, Wilderness!* including Lionel Barrymore, Spring Byington, Cecilia Parker, Eric Linden, and Mickey Rooney. Barrymore's star status allowed *Skidding*, retitled *A Family Affair*, to secure billing at the top of double bills. *Ah, Wilderness!* is very similar to *A Family Affair*, also being about a small-town American family.

The ingredients of *Skidding* contained a lot of elements that appealed to studio head Louis B. Mayer's interest in a wholesome family product. It was set in a small town, it dealt with the problems of a typical American family, and a minor update from the screenwriters penning the adaption placed the family in the throes of the Depression. However, unlike other Depression-era movies, this dealt with a well-to-do family whose response to the surrounding community is from a loftier financial perspective, but a somewhat less engaged one. There are lessons each character is forced to learn during the course of the narrative.

Lionel Barrymore plays James K. Hardy, a judge in the small town of Carvel. Newspaper editor Nichols (Emmett Keane) creates a petition to investigate contractor Hoyt Wells (Selmer Jackson) regarding the construction of an aqueduct. Judge Hardy must cease production while the investigation is in process, but this puts many citizens out of work during the cessation. Meanwhile at home, the judge's oldest daughter, Joan (Julie Haydon), is going through a divorce and gets involved in a scandal of her own that the reporter threatens to print if the judge does not cooperate with some corrupt public works plans. Judge Hardy's second-oldest daughter, Marian (Cecilia Parker), is falling in love with Wayne (Eric Linden), a man she just met who happens to also be an engineer on the viaduct project and might lose his job. What the film attempts to emphasize is Judge Hardy's stern control over the matters and a calm, pragmatic approach to the situations. But from the first scene, he is shown frequently taking antacids to calm a nervous stomach.

Mickey Rooney's role as the judge's son Andy Hardy is decidedly tangential to the other, more serious conflicts. His problems are comparatively marginal, but it is his situation that is more attractive because it is the lighter counterpart to the narrative's heavier base. Andy is going to his first boy-girl party, and his comical grumbling about dressing up and having to take a girl is an amusing distraction to the more dramatic proceedings. Rooney offers his usual enthusiasm, being totally committed to the role of this typical small-town boy whose problems seem so tiny next to what is going on elsewhere within his own family, but seem every bit as important to him.

Rooney recalled in his autobiography,

> I knew *A Family Affair* was a B picture, but that didn't stop me from putting my all into it.[1]

While Rooney's smaller role is more noticeable to a greater degree than the larger portions of the story, most of the highlights involve other actors. One of the more stirring ones features daughter Marian and boyfriend Wayne having car trouble, and being towed to a gas station by two comical drunks (Don Barclay, Arthur Housman). The drunks hook the cars together with a rope and begin pulling Marian and Wayne's vehicle, but soon forget all about them and pass service stations without pulling over. When Wayne starts beeping his horn, the drunks believe they are being chased and take off at breakneck speed. Despite some obvious rear projection, the editing is

Mickey Rooney, Lionel Barrymore, and Cecilia Parker

tight and director George Seitz does a good job switching from long shots of the speeding cars to close-ups of the participants' reactions. However, this scene does not seem to know if it wants to play as comical or serious and harrowing. In any case, it is perhaps the most exciting scene in the movie.

Critics were generally pleased with *A Family Affair*, understanding it as a B movie that offers pleasant, harmless entertainment. *Variety* stated,

> *A Family Affair* is wholesome entertainment, well done by a capable cast and superbly directed. Picture is a triumph for Lionel Barrymore. As the honest country-town judge, and again as the family-loving father, he is in his element. It is one of those meaty roles that is Barrymore's dish. Cecilia Parker and Eric Linden are successfully teamed as the youthful romantic interest, as is Mickey Rooney, as the kid, in his puppy-love affair with Margaret Marquis. Young Rooney's interpretation is true boy stuff, and good for the best laughs. George B. Seitz directs with skill and sincerity, getting the maximum tempo out of a wordy piece [from the play *Skidding* by Aurania Rouverol].[2]

Frank S. Nugent of the *New York Times* stated,

> Lionel Barrymore wears the mantle of justice and the crown of thorns with his usual dignity and patience. . . . Mr. Barrymore knows how to handle these things, and so do the other members of the cast. Spring Byington invariably is a model of wifely and motherly understanding. Mickey Rooney is the epitome of all 14-year-olds who hate girls until they see a pretty one in a party dress. They all have taken their *Family Affair* rather seriously and, although it was not that important, we rather enjoyed our eavesdropping at Judge Hardy's home.[3]

Usually a fixture in top-level A productions, Lionel Barrymore was between pictures, so MGM placed him in this B drama, which was shot in about seventeen days (February 3–20, 1937). Barrymore anchors the proceedings as only he can, as his Judge Hardy character is supposed to be the most important figure in the narrative. His performance presents the judge as a no-nonsense purveyor of society's ways and responsibilities, as well as having the strength of a quintessential patriarch at home. He is introspective, pragmatic, and suffering inside, resulting in an occasional crotchetiness that seems to fit the character comfortably. But Mickey Rooney steals the movie.

A *Family* Affair was made for the low-budget cost of $178,000 and grossed over $500,000. MGM was not quite prepared for the reaction moviegoers gave *A Family Affair* and Mickey Rooney's performance. Exhibitors commented in the trades and sent personal letters to Mayer himself indicating that they wanted more movies like *A Family Affair* and more with "that kid Rooney." Rooney recalled,

> *A Family Affair* was the picture that made me. I had been in pictures for ten years and suddenly I was discovered in *Devil Is a Sissy* and celebrated in the first Hardy picture. They kept me even busier, and eventually my movies made millions for the studio, but only thousands for me.[4]

According to the book *MGM: When the Lion Roars* by Peter Hay,

> The response to *A Family Affair* and to Rooney was so positive that Mayer asked Hubbard to produce another Hardy picture—this time concentrating on the relationship between the judge and his son—with the intention of making it a series. When Hubbard left the studio, Mayer placed the production in the hands of J. J. Cohn and director George B. Seitz. Mayer's growing enthusiasm for the subsequent Hardy films almost became a personal crusade for him. He would sit through previews next to Carey Wilson, the veteran producer-writer, in order to transmit his criticisms directly.[5]

Watching *A Family Affair* in the twenty-first century, with some knowledge of the Hardy series to follow, it is significant how different this film feels in comparison to the later movies. The cast changes a bit, and the focus is later shifted almost entirely to Andy. *A Family Affair* is much more serious in tone with the Depression being a major issue and peoples' jobs at stake, whereas the future films are much more lighthearted.

Mayer's response to wholesome entertainment was effective for the Hardy series, but detrimental to a lot of comedies made at the studio. The anarchic spirit of the Marx Brothers when they moved from Paramount to MGM in 1935 was diluted by this process, as were the Our Gang/Little Rascals short comedies when they set up shop at the studio after leaving Hal Roach productions in 1937. Just like scenes in *The Devil Is a Sissy* were missing the discernible edge that permeated similar productions from Warner Bros., the MGM approach cleaned up any similar edge that comedy might have. Romantic comedy, drama, literary adaptions, and wholesome family entertainment were the studio's forte. Thus, creating a series from characters in a little-known play property after the movie adaption had made a strong profit for the studio was a sound business idea.

However, MGM was not about to let Mickey Rooney wait around while they prepared a sequel to *A Family Affair*. Rooney continued to be very active—mostly at MGM, especially after the box office returns for *A Family Affair* solidified his burgeoning stardom. For his next project, Rooney was reunited with his *Ah, Wilderness!* costar Wallace Beery as the two were loaned out to 20th Century Fox for *Slave Ship*.

SLAVE SHIP

(20th Century Fox, 1937)

Director: Tay Garnett
Screenplay: Sam Hellman, Lamar Trotti, Gladys Lehman. *Story:* William Faulkner, based on a novel by George S. King
Producer: Darryl F. Zanuck. *Associate Producer:* Nunnally Johnson. *Cinematographer:* Ernest Palmer. *Editor:* Lloyd Nosler
Cast: Warner Baxter (Jim Lovett), Wallace Beery (Jack Thompson), Elizabeth Allen (Nancy Marlowe), Mickey Rooney (Swifty), George Sanders (Lefty), Jane Darwell (Mrs. Marlowe), Joseph Schildkraut (Danelo), Miles Mander (Corey), Arthur Hohl (Grimes), Minna Gombell (Mabel), Billy Bevan (Atkins), Francis Ford (Scraps), J. Farrell MacDonald (Proprietor), Paul Hurst (Drunk), Holmes Herbert (Commander), Edwin Maxwell (Auctioneer), Douglas Scott (Boy), Jane Jones (Ma Belcher), J. P. McGowan (Helmsman), DeWitt Jennings (Snodgrass), Dorothy Christy (Blonde), Charles Middleton (Slave Dealer), Dewey Robinson (Bartender), Tom Kennedy (Bartender), James C. Morton (Waiter), Herbert Heywood (Old Man), Winter Hall (Minister), Marilyn Knowlden (Girl), Arthur Aylesworth (Stranger), Matthew "Stymie" Beard (Black Boy on Pier), Scott Becket (Boy), James Burtis (Waiter), John Burton (Officer), Russ Clark (Laborer), Lon Chaney Jr. (Man Killed at Ship's Launch), John Biefer, Sven Hugo Borg, Jack Byron, Bull Anderson, John Wallace, Dale Van Sickel, Lee Powers, Robert St. Angelo, Jack Stoney, Remington Olmstead, Jack Low, Frank Meredith, Art Dupuis, Bobby Dunn, Richard Clarke, Larry Dods, George Du Count (Crew Members)
Released: June 16, 1937
Specs: 92 minutes; black and white
Availability: DVD (Fox Video Archive)

Slave Ship is one of the most brutally accurate films about the slave trade, and, as a result, among the least seen. It was made at 20th Century Fox, a major studio that did not feel the need to present essentially family entertainment with the same passion as Metro-Goldwyn-Mayer.

A ship known as *Wanderer* gets the reputation of being a "blood ship" when a worker is killed upon its launch. Three years later it is purchased at an auction by Jim Lovett (Warner Baxter), who renames it the *Albatross* and uses it for the slave trade. The ship goes to West Africa, purchases black men and women, and sails them to the United States. By 1860, slaving has become illegal, so Jim and his crew risk hanging for large profits, as their slave ship is one of only three still operating. Jim meets and marries Nancy (Elizabeth Allen) and brings her aboard to travel to Jamaica, where he plans to buy a plantation and settle down. Jim orders his partner, Thompson (Wallace Beery), to discharge the crew—except for Swifty, the cabin boy (Mickey Rooney)—and to hire new men who are not slavers.

Once at sail, Jim discovers the crew is the same, including Thompson and Swifty, and they mutiny to take the ship to Africa, planning to continue in the slave trade. They arrive in Africa and select their slaves, who board the ship, but leave Jim ashore without paying the slave trader. The trader tries to kill Jim, who escapes, reaches the ship, and takes control. Thompson orders the chained slaves thrown overboard, weighted with an anchor, so that no evidence will exist to convict him. A lantern falls and the boat catches fire, so Jim frees the slaves, allowing them to swim to safety. Jim is knocked out as the crew abandons ship. Thompson cannot leave Jim to hang and puts him in a boat with Swifty and Nancy before he dies as the ship explodes. At the trial, Nancy explains that Jim freed the slaves even though he knew their existence would be proof against him. He is found not guilty and retires to a plantation in Jamaica with Nancy and Swifty.

The screenplay for *Slave Ship*, based on the novel by George S. King, went through many treatments, including some doctoring by novelist William Faulkner, before a script was ready to shoot. The film was originally set to be directed by John Ford, who turned down the project and took a vacation after having helmed three feature films in quick succession. Howard Hawks was then approached before producers settled on Tay Garnett.

Wallace Beery's and Mickey Rooney's services were secured by 20th Century Fox from MGM, but Fox's attempt to use Clark Gable for the role of Jim was turned down. Warner Baxter being cast in the role might have been why John Ford was the first choice to direct, as Ford had directed Baxter to a brilliant performance in *The Prisoner of Shark Island* (1936).

Several cast changes occurred during preproduction, including Peter Lorre as a slave trader (the role instead went to Joseph Schildkraut) and Mary Rogers (daughter of humorist Will Rogers) as Nancy (who was replaced by Elizabeth Allen due to illness). Servants and chauffeurs of Hollywood stars played slaves.

Although Mickey Rooney exhibits exuberance and confidence in his role, he is clearly in support. Rooney has a few scenes of his own, including some nice, pensive moments standing alone on deck in the dark, but it is really Baxter's and Beery's film. But what is most interesting, and also unsettling, about *Slave Ship* is how it approaches the idea of slavery without exploring or investigating how wrong it is. Jim has second thoughts about continuing in the slave trade because it has become illegal. He does not want to hang for being engaged in illegal activity. He does not consider the human element at all; he simply wants to avoid hanging. Even when he frees the slaves, it is more a natural human instinct to not want any of them to burn to death—almost like freeing horses. The slaves are products, livestock; they are never considered human beings. In the film they are extras. There is no character development for any of them. We are not allowed to explore the situation from their perspective. When Thompson throws slaves overboard, anchored, to drown, he is merely disposing of illegal matter to avoid hanging. None of the slaves are allowed dialogue. They are disposed of without remorse. Such is the brutal accuracy indicated at the outset of this chapter. Because of this harsher tone, *Slave Ship* is a film that is rarely revived in the twenty-first century. Rooney is an amusing distraction, but overall it is difficult to embrace any character as the hero.

Tay Garnett's direction is particularly impressive in scenes where a great deal of action is occurring within the frame. For instance, a long overhead shot of many scantily clad slaves chained closely together and struggling is a striking, disturbing image. The editing during the violent scenes keeps up the pace.

One interesting bit of trivia is Lon Chaney Jr.'s nonspeaking bit role as the crew member who is killed when the boat first launches at the beginning of the movie. Chaney had been in films for about a half-dozen years by this time, with several speaking roles to his credit, so this is a rather curious appearance.

A very interesting production at several levels, *Slave Ship* had little impact on Mickey Rooney's career other than to act as something of a catalyst for his being cast in an MGM production about living on board a ship. However, *Captains Courageous*, based on Rudyard Kipling's novel, had nothing to do with the slave trade.

5

CAPTAINS COURAGEOUS

(MGM, 1937)

Director: Victor Fleming
Screenplay: John Lee Mahin, Marc Connelly, Dale Van Every, based on the novel by Rudyard Kipling
Producer: Louis D. Lighton. *Cinematographer:* Harold Rosson. *Editor:* Elmo Veron
Cast: Freddie Bartholomew (Harvey), Spencer Tracy (Manuel), Lionel Barrymore (Disko), Melvyn Douglas (Cheyne), Charley Grapewin (Uncle Salters), Mickey Rooney (Dan), John Carradine (Long Jack), Oscar O'Shea (Cushman), Jack LaRue (Priest), Walter Kingsford (Dr. Finley), Donald Briggs (Tyler), Sam McDaniel (Doc), Bill Burrud (Charles), Art Berry (Captain Anderson), Leo G. Carroll (Burns), Charles Coleman (Butler), Roger Gray (Nate Rogers), Katherine Kenworthy (Mrs. Disko), Myra Marsh (Chester's wife), Charles Trowbridge (Dr. Walsh), Jay Ward (Pogey), Dave Wengren (Lars), Kenneth Wilson (Alvin Savage), Gene Reynolds (Boy in print shop), Wally Albright (Boy), Wade Boteler (Blue Gill skipper), Tommy Bupp (Boy on Boat), Jimmy Conlin (Martin), Dora Early (Appleton's wife), Norman Ainsley (Robbins), Christian Rub (Old Clement), C. E. Anderson (Fisherman), William Arnold (Reporter), Don Brodie (Reporter), David Kerman (Reporter), Bobby Watson (Reporter), Lester Dorr (Steward), Billy Gilbert (Soda Jerk), Lloyd Ingraham (Skipper), Gladden James (Secretary), Jack Kennedy (Captain of *Flying Swan*), Murray Kinnell (Minister), Boots Lebaron (Boy), William Stack (Elliott), Frank Sully (Taxi Driver), Gertrude Sutton (Nate's Wife), Bill Fisher, Larry Fisher, Richard Howard, James Kilgannon, Stubby Krueger, Philo McCullough, Gil Perkins, Edward Peil Sr., Jack Sterling (Crewmen), Lee Van Atta (Boy), David Thursby (Tom), Reggie

Streeter (Boy), Goldie Sloan (Black Woman), Dennis O'Keefe, Mira McKinney, Sherry Hall, Henry Hanna, Betty Alden (Bits)
Released: June 25, 1937
Specs: 117 minutes; black and white
Availability: DVD (Warner Home Video)

Mickey Rooney is billed sixth in *Captains Courageous* and has very little to do in the film. It is really a showcase for Freddie Bartholomew and Spencer Tracy. Rooney recalled,

> *Captains Courageous* and *Slave Ship* were practically made on top of each other. Two ship movies and for a while I was going back and forth from studio to studio and working on both. *Captains Courageous* is one of the best pictures I was ever in, and I am hardly in it. Freddie Bartholomew was the best actor of all us kids. Spencer Tracy won an Oscar, but I think Freddie should have been nominated.[1]

The story concerns a spoiled rich boy, played by Bartholomew, who falls overboard while on a luxury liner with his wealthy father. He is fished out of the water by a Portuguese fisherman (Spencer Tracy) and must live and work on a fishing boat until they finish their voyage and return to shore. Through the course of the film, the young rich boy eventually learns values to which he'd heretofore not been exposed, and leaves the voyage with a greater maturity and more positive character.

Rooney plays the son of the skipper, who is portrayed by Lionel Barrymore. His contribution to the film is a veritable cameo. His character shows up every so often to punctuate a scene, but he is never central to the narrative or significant to any of the characters. Perhaps his role can be considered a counterpart to the one Freddie Bartholomew is playing, in that the Rooney character is a part of this world, which is far different than the wealth and privilege the rich boy understands. The relationship between the Barrymore-Rooney father-son characters is without the sort of social privilege the Bartholomew character is accustomed to having, but it does have a genuine emotional connection—something the Bartholomew character lacks with his own father (Melvyn Douglas).

Captains Courageous was quite an expensive production, with a budget of nearly $1.7 million. However, it grossed over $3 million, and continued to be a hit long after its initial release. It also has the distinction of being the first MGM-produced movie to play on television (in 1955). In the *New York Times*, critic Frank Nugent stated,

Metro's *Captains Courageous*, which had its premiere at the Astor last night and will be shown henceforth on a two-a-day basis, is another of those grand jobs of moviemaking we have come to expect of Hollywood's most prodigal studio. With its rich production, magnificent marine photography, admirable direction and performances, the film brings vividly to life every page of Kipling's novel and even adds an exciting chapter or two of its own. In tailoring the narrative to the starring dimensions of Freddie Bartholomew, the trio of adapters (John Lee Mahin, Marc Connelly, and Dale Van Every) had to trim several years from the age of Harvey Cheyne, changing him from a spoiled nineteen-year-old to a spoiled twelve-year-old. Except for that and a few pardonable additions, they have steadfastly followed the Kipling tale of an imperious and detestable young scamp who toppled from a liner's rail off the Grand Banks, was picked up by a Portuguese doryman, and became a regular fellow during an enforced three-months fishing cruise. Interesting as the early sequences are, with their telling revelation of Harvey's character, the picture does not really come alive until the cameras turn upon the (fishing boat). Then, in its depiction of the men and methods of the old Gloucester fleet, it takes on almost the quality of a documentary film, enriched by poetic photography of schooners spanking along under full sail, of dories being lowered into a running sea, and shading in, quite deftly, the human portraits of the fishermen with their quiet heroism and resignation, their Down East humor, and their stern code of decency.[2]

Variety stated,

Spencer Tracy is a Portuguese fisherman with an accent and a flair for singing songs of the briny. Lionel Barrymore is the happy-go-lucky but stern captain of a fishing schooner while Bartholomew, of course, is the boy. Bartholomew's transition from a brat to a lovable child is done with convincing strokes. His performance is matched by Tracy, who also doesn't seem right doing an accent and singing songs, but he, too, later gets under the skin of the character. Barrymore is himself, as usual. As the father of the boy, Melvyn Douglas gives a smooth, unctuous performance. One of the fishermen is deftly portrayed by John Carradine.[3]

Spencer Tracy objected to many things during the making of this movie, including having to curl his hair and affect an accent for the role. It wasn't until he received critical acclaim and awards for his performance that he reacted positively to the experience. Freddie Bartholomew would soon be eclipsed by Rooney as the top young star on the MGM lot (Jackie Cooper left MGM shortly after finishing *The Devil Is a Sissy*), but he was clearly the star of this movie along with Tracy. Their performances are among the best in either's career.

Lionel Barrymore was in the throes of the arthritis that would soon cripple him. *Captains Courageous* is one of the last films in which he is walking without assistance. By the following year, in Frank Capra's Oscar-winner *You Can't Take It with You* (Columbia, 1938), Barrymore was on crutches. A year later he was confined to a wheelchair and would be for the rest of his life.

One of the rooms on the ship set doubled as a classroom for Rooney and Bartholomew. A lot of the filming had to be scheduled around their lessons.

Captains Courageous is a very good film—one of the finest MGM productions of the 1930s—and an enduring classic. But in a study on Mickey Rooney's work, it is of less significance in that Rooney has roughly twenty minutes (or less) of footage in the entire feature. However, Rooney said in an interview,

> Even though my part was small, *Captains Courageous* was a big picture with a lot of stars that people wanted to see. So when you are in a major motion picture that everyone goes to see, you get more recognition. They remember they saw you in something else, and they recognize you the next time they see you.[4]

While he would soon be the leading box office star in the nation, Mickey Rooney was, at this time, slowly building a name for himself by appearing in many movies, in both large and small roles. One of those small roles was in this classic feature that gave him enormous exposure.

HOOSIER SCHOOLBOY

(Monogram, 1937)

Director: William Nigh
Screenplay: Robert Lee Johnson, based on the novel *Hoosier Schoolmaster*, by Edward Eggleston
Producer: Ken Goldsmith. *Cinematographer:* Paul Ivano. *Editor:* Roy Livingston
Cast: Mickey Rooney (Shockey Carter); Anne Nagel (Mary Evans); Frank Shields (Jack Matthews Jr.); Edward Pawley (Captain Fred Carter); William Gould (John Matthews Sr.); Dorothy Vaughan (Miss Hodges); Anita Deniston (Elvira); Harry Hayden (Mr. Townsend); Bradley Metcalfe (Roger Townsend); Walter Long (Riley); Cecil Weston (Teacher); Mary Field (Secretary); Fred Kelsey (Crowder); Lester Dorr (Hotel Manager); Maude Philby (Mrs. Townsend); Elaine Koehler, June Parkes, Mildred Kornman, Doris Rankin, Helena Grant, Zita Moulton (Schoolgirls); Junior Hughes, Buddy Londelius, Martin H. Pawley (Schoolboys)
Released: July 7, 1937
Specs: 62 minutes; black and white
Availability: DVD (Alpha Home Video)

Monogram studios, a low-budget studio that specialized in B movies, released several lucrative second features from 1931 to 1935. Rooney had worked in a Monogram picture, *The Healer*, in 1935. Once a star is established with a major studio, the lower budget studios often would utilize the talents of a bankable name by paying the larger studio a fee along with the star's salary. Thus, MGM would allow for Rooney's services if they were paid a substantial fee.

Monogram had merged with Mascot pictures under the umbrella of Republic Pictures in 1935. However, a couple of stockholders broke away from this arrangement and in 1937 re-formed Monogram. They commissioned Rooney from MGM to appear in the screen adaption of Edward Eggleston's novel *Hoosier Schoolmaster.* Often major studios would send a bankable star to a lower budget company as a punishment. Rooney, however, was not being punished. MGM executives were still investigating what they could do with him and allowed the smaller studio to utilize his services. Fortunately, *Hoosier Schoolboy* turned out to be a positive experience for Rooney on several levels.

The story deals with a rough kid named Shockey Carter (Rooney) from the wrong side of the tracks who is integrated with wealthier kids in a public school. Because he is poor and his father (Edward Pawley), a shell-shocked war veteran, is a noted town drunk, Shockey is often teased by the others and gets into a lot of fights. A new teacher in town (Anne Nagel) understands Shockey and befriends both him and his father. A young man in town (Frank Shields), whose father (William Gould) owns a dairy, is interested in the teacher but at odds with his father, who is giving too little money to the farmers for their milk, thus causing a strike. The son gets Shockey's father a job, but while driving the dairy truck, Shockey's father is haunted by battlefield visions, crashes down a mountain, and is killed. Shockey plans to leave town, but the owner of the dairy takes him in, telling him his father's death ended the strike and he died a hero.

Cheap sets and tentative performances abound in *Hoosier Schoolboy*, with amateurs like Frank Shields (who made very few films) blended with the more capable Edward Pawley and Anne Nagel. Nagel at the time was trying to get over the January 1937 suicide of her husband, actor Ross Alexander.

Rooney liked the script and was also pleased with director William Nigh. In later years, he would look back on *Hoosier Schoolboy* and realize an even greater importance:

> This was a cheap picture, but it had a good script with a good role for me. William Nigh let me play the character my way, so I had more freedom than I did on my other pictures. I liked that. Nigh would guide me when I needed it, but he never told me how to play a scene. He would ask me what I thought and let me try it that way. I had a lot to do in that picture and it really helped me as an actor. Later when I did *Boys Town*, I used what I learned playing the same kind of tough kid in this picture.[1]

Perhaps the only really fascinating thing about *Hoosier Schoolboy* is Rooney's performance. Given room to explore the character, Rooney takes what could have been a very basic role by any other actor, and gives Shockey Carter some real depth. Rooney walks with his shoulders drooped, his head lurched forward, showing tension but not fear. When he is with his father, his eyes soften. In the scene where his father is killed, he explodes with gut-wrenching sobs. Everything Rooney does with this role stands out. It is completely his movie.

Along with the tough dramatic scenes, there are a few tangential ones that are softer and more amusing. At a school social, Shockey is attracted to Elvira (Anita Deniston) and the attraction is mutual. She asks if he can dance, and he gets up and shows her some impressively difficult tap steps, which net applause from others nearby.

Cinematically, there are a lot of problems with *Hoosier Schoolboy*. The script is uneven, many performances are lackluster, it ends a bit too pat and abrupt, and there is a very discernible cheapness to the entire production. However, Mickey Rooney enjoyed being first billed (above the title), having a large role that allowed for some real acting, and being given so much creative freedom from the director. In his later years, Mickey Rooney saw *Hoosier Schoolboy* as a stepping-stone toward the massive stardom he would soon achieve.

7

THOROUGHBREDS DON'T CRY

(MGM, 1937)

Director: Alfred E. Green
Screenplay: Eleanore Griffin, J. Walter Ruben, Lawrence Hazard
Producer: Harry Rapf. *Cinematographer:* Leonard Smith. *Editor:* Elmo Veron
Cast: Ronald Sinclair (Roger Calverton), Judy Garland (Cricket West), Mickey Rooney (Timmie Donovan), C. Aubrey Smith (Sir Peter Calverton), Sophie Tucker (Mother Ralph), Forrester Harvey (Mr. Wilkins), Charles D. Brown (Click Donovan), Frankie Darro (Dink Reid), Henry Kolker (Doc Godfrey), Helen Troy (Hilda), Elisha Cook Jr. (Boots), George Chandler (Jim, the usher at the racetrack), Douglas Wood (Mr. Sloan), Bob Tansill (Bones), Buster Slaven (Hoot), Edgar Norton (Mr. Fox), Louis Natheaux, Donald Kerr (Click Donovan's Cohorts), Lionel Belmore (Butler), Marie Blake (Operator), Francis X. Bushman (Steward), James Flavin (Agent), Edward Gargan (Policeman), Edgar Dearing (Police Sergeant at Track), Chuck Hamilton (Guard), Don Brodie (Teller), Ernie Alexander (Usher), Chester Clute (Man with Toupee), Edward Earle (Bettor), Harry Depp (Racetrack Official), Robert Homans (Officer Higgins), Wilbur Mack (Bettor), Bert Moorhouse (Bettor), Cliff Nazarro (Tubby), Jack Norton (Monocled Man), Russ Powell (Diner Counter Worker), Eddie Shubert (Taxi Driver), Pierre Watkin (Racetrack judge), Frank Whitbeck (Racetrack Announcer), Charles Wilson (Horse Owner)
Song: "Got a Pair of New Shoes" (music by Nacio Herb Brown, lyrics by Arthur Freed; played as background music and sung by Judy Garland

during the opening credits; reprised by Judy Garland again on piano, on guitar, and as background music at the end)
Released: December 3, 1937
Specs: 80 minutes; black and white
Availability: DVD (Warner Home Video)

Upon returning to the MGM lot after his appearance at Monogram in *Hoosier Schoolboy*, Rooney first did a cameo in the romantic comedy *Live, Love and Learn*. It does not require a separate chapter because the film hardly registers at all as a Mickey Rooney movie. *Live, Love and Learn* is about an artist who marries a society girl and their attempt to adjust to each other's lifestyles. Rooney plays the landlady's son in a rooming house. In his only scene in the film, he bursts into the apartment of the newlyweds and shows the man his new pitch, almost falling down in the process. Rooney recalled,

> Sometimes you'd be doing two pictures at once in those days. I'd be rehearsing for one movie and they'd ask me to run in and do a scene or two on another. We all had to do that.[1]

As this was another movie featuring popular stars, Rooney having a cameo did add something to his visibility and, ultimately, his reputation. The sheer quantity of Mickey Rooney's appearances resulted in his becoming more recognized by audiences when he would show up fleetingly as he did in *Live, Love and Learn*.

Thoroughbreds Don't Cry is Mickey Rooney's first film with Judy Garland, but the only one of their ten movies together where she was billed ahead of him. While she would achieve her own level of stardom, Rooney would continue to be the bigger star and the stronger box office draw. Ronald Sinclair is actually billed first in the credits. The opening credit for the three of them shows them walking toward the camera, arm in arm, with Sinclair on the far left, Judy in the middle, and Rooney on the right; thus the billing is presented in that order. Sinclair's role was originally to be played by Freddie Bartholomew, but salary disputes and the adolescent peril of voice changing were among the factors that caused young Sinclair to be cast instead.

Sinclair is Roger Calverton, who travels from England to America with his grandfather (C. Aubrey Smith) to race his horse Pookah. Rooney is Timmie Donovan, the jockey chosen to ride Pookah. Garland is Cricket, whose aunt (Sophie Tucker) runs a rooming house for jockeys. Because the jockeys are a bit rough, Cricket is enamored with Roger's refined British manner. Roger has a hard time fitting in with the jockeys until he holds his own in a fistfight with Timmie.

The relationship among the three leads forms the underlying basis of the plot. Judy Garland had been in several films, but she often came off as awkward and unsure of herself. Playing opposite the confident Rooney (they were friends off screen) seemed to inspire a more anchored performance. Cricket is confident, understanding, and unflinching at the characters or situations with which she is confronted. And while Garland's on-screen interest is in Sinclair's character, sparks are discernible in her scenes opposite Rooney. They are fairly adversarial and argumentative within the context of the narrative, but the chemistry between them is still quite evident.

Judy Garland was also at an awkward age around this time, making her hard to cast, which is why this, a film starring other young people, was kind of her breakout movie. She comes off as much younger than Rooney despite there being only a two-year age difference; maybe that's why she wasn't cast as his love interest in their first couple films together despite the obvious chemistry.

When Timmie's estranged father convinces the boy that he is dying and needs money for medical treatment, the young jockey is talked into throwing the race. When Pookah does not win, the stress causes Roger's grandfather to suffer a heart attack and die. This puts Roger in the unhappy situation of having to sell the horse for enough money to return to England. Cricket tells Timmie, who goes to his father for a loan, believing he is owed such reciprocation. The father refuses, and Timmie realized his illness was a ruse. He steals his father's wallet, runs to Roger, gives him the $1,000 entry fee to put Pookah in the race, and plans to ride him. However, Timmie has been banned from riding, so Roger must ride the horse himself, with Timmie's instructions leading him to victory.

Judy Garland was not pleased with being cast in *Thoroughbreds Don't Cry* because she was added after the script had been written. But her performance in the 1937 musical *Broadway Melody of 1938* singing a version of "You Made Me Love You" to Clark Gable ("Dear Mr. Gable") had a strong impact on moviegoers, so MGM wanted her in a vehicle that featured their younger actors in the lead. Curiously, she only has one song in the entire movie, and it is not a major scene. *Thoroughbreds Don't Cry*

The ad for *Thoroughbreds Don't Cry* gave Judy Garland top billing.

allowed Garland to exhibit some stronger acting ability and allowed viewers, and executives, to discover the chemistry she had with Mickey Rooney.

Another singer, Sophie Tucker, billed as "the last of the red hot mamas" on stage, was also in the movie as the aunt who runs the boarding house, and she gets no songs at all. Marie Dressler, a top MGM actress, had died a few years earlier and the studio wanted to groom Ms. Tucker as another Dressler type. Around the same age as Dressler, and the same heavyset physical type, Tucker was given the late actress's old costumes and roles that were similar to what she might play. Tucker recalled in her autobiography,

> I didn't particularly like my part. It was a part any fifty-dollar character actress could do better than I. Producer Harry Rapf kept telling me, "Here's your chance to be another Marie Dressler!" I said to L.B. [Mayer] and to everyone on the lot, "Judy, if carefully handled and groomed, will be the big MGM star in a few years."[2]

Ronald Sinclair's real name was Ra Hould, and he was originally from New Zealand. He had already played a few parts in films at other studios before being cast as a replacement for Freddie Bartholomew in *Thoroughbreds Don't Cry*. As an adult, he remained in the film business as an editor.

Critics were not exactly blown away by *Thoroughbreds Don't Cry*, but they found it amusing enough. Marguerite Tazelaar of the *New York Herald Tribune* stated,

> An appealing picture, especially for children. The story has to do with a racetrack. Mickey is a vain young jockey who has never lost a race and Ronald is the son of a titled Englishman who has brought his horse to America not only to recoup his waning fortunes but because of his genuine love and belief in Pukka [*sic*], his horse. The introduction of the two boys by Judy Garland, who is the niece of the keeper (Sophie Tucker) of the boarding house where Mickey and the other jockeys live is especially enlivening. All except Judy make fun of his English speech and gentlemanly manners. . . . Miss Garland does several imitations nicely. . . . Miss Tucker, in a rather small role, plays it with sympathy and not too much emphasis. Mickey Rooney gives a really fine performance . . . and Robert Sinclair is genuinely appealing.[3]

Both Mickey Rooney and Judy Garland were on the cusp of stardom when they appeared in *Thoroughbreds Don't Cry*, which was made on a $503,000 budget and grossed $731,000. There was some talk of a sequel, to be titled *Thoroughbreds Together*, but it never went past the initial planning stage.

Thoroughbreds Don't Cry was the sixth film Rooney appeared in during 1937. It's follow-up, *You're Only Young Once*, would be the second film in which Rooney would play Andy Hardy, and the changes in the cast and characters from the earlier *A Family Affair* would reflect how the series would be presented thereafter. Although the initial films centered more on the character of Judge Hardy, it soon became evident that Andy should be the focal point. This all would happen in 1938 when Rooney would steadily rise in stature at the box office and continue to show, in a variety of roles, his natural ability and versatility as an actor.

8

YOU'RE ONLY YOUNG ONCE

(MGM, 1937)

Director: George B. Seitz
Screenplay: Kay Van Riper. *Characters:* Aurania Rouverol
Producer: Carey Wilson. *Cinematographer:* Lester White. *Editor:* Adrienne Fazan
Cast: Lewis Stone (Judge Hardy), Mickey Rooney (Andy Hardy), Cecilia Parker (Marian Hardy), Fay Holden (Mrs. Hardy), Frank Craven (Frank Redmond), Ann Rutherford (Polly Benedict), Eleanor Lynn (Jerry Lane), Sara Haden (Aunt Milly), Ted Pearson (Bill Rand), Charles Judels (Capt. Swenson), Selmer Jackson (Hoyt Wells), Robert Wayne (Ed Carter), Wilson Benge (Francois), Ruth Hart (Mary), Mary Gordon (Mary's Mother), Spec O'Donnell (Drowsy), Norman Phillips Jr. (Fish Face), Jack Baxley (Court Clerk), Billy Dooley (Postman), Oscar O'Shea (Sheriff), Garry Owen (Guide), Phillip Terry (Pilot)
Released: December 10, 1937
Specs: 78 minutes; black and white
Availability: DVD (Warner Archive Collection: *The Andy Hardy Film Collection: Volume 1*)

After the massive success of *A Family Affair*, Louis B. Mayer and other MGM executives held a meeting in which they expressed some concern that a low-budget movie about a folksy small-town family could net such a large sum at the box office. Were the days of stars like Clark Gable, Myrna Loy, and Spencer Tracy over? Was this a new trend? A decision was made to have a series based on these characters, set in a small town, and retaining the original movie's folksy charm. Louis B. Mayer had a real sentimental streak and was attracted to that aspect of the series.

Technically, the second movie about the Hardy family, *You're Only Young Once*, is also the first movie in the series as established by MGM based on the characters created by Aurania Rouverol. Mickey Rooney is back as Andy Hardy, Cecilia Parker as sister Marian, and Sara Haden as Aunt Milly, but veteran actor Lewis Stone takes over the role of Judge Hardy, and Fay Holden plays Mrs. Hardy. Stone and Holden, taking the roles Lionel Barrymore and Spring Byington had played in the first film, would remain with the series for its duration.

Judge Hardy, tired and overworked, wants to take the family on their first vacation in seven years. He chooses two weeks on Catalina Island, where he wants to try and catch a swordfish. Daughter Marian meets a handsome, flirtatious lifeguard (Ted Pearson), who turns out to be married. Andy meets a girl named Jerry (Eleanor Lynn), whose mother is in Reno ending a fourth marriage, leaving her daughter on her own. When the Hardys return home to their small town of Carvel, they discover that a note of endorsement the judge signed for newspaper owner Frank Redmond (Frank Craven) has come due, and the family is in danger of losing their home to Hoyt Wells (Selmer Jackson), who intends to collect on the debt.

You're Only Young Once was made on a small budget and is mostly interesting for how it establishes what would be the basis for the remainder of the Hardy family series. Rooney's character of Andy Hardy was not yet the focal point of the story. This is more of an ensemble piece, with the judge, Marian, and Andy each having their own situations and conflicts to confront.

When one considers the folksy charm and quaint innocence of the subsequent Hardy movies, *You're Only Young Once* deals with some rather sophisticated material. Marian is courted by a man who admits he is married and says he intends to get a divorce and marry her. This is merely a ploy to get what he can from the naive small-town girl in what Mrs. Hardy later refers to as a "vacation romance." In true MGM fashion, the man fesses up to the entire family, admits he loves his wife, and apologizes for being a "four flusher."

Andy's dalliance with the more sophisticated Jerry Lane thrusts him into a life of late nights, speedboats, cigarettes, and easy romance. Judge Hardy sees right through the girl and tries to convince Andy that she is not for him, but Andy reacts angrily. He finally realizes on his own that the judge's assessment was accurate, and upon leaving the girl for the last time, tells her, "You can have your 'sophisticated'; I'll take football!"

The judge's problem is more serious, but he uncovers that due to an old government statute, the land in question (which had been earmarked for a viaduct in the previous film, a plot element carried over to this movie) is rightfully his, and the promissory note is without grounds.

Mickey Rooney, Lewis Stone, and Cecilia Parker

One of the more fascinating things about *You're Only Young Once* is an epilogue delivered by Lewis Stone, in character as Judge Hardy, after the end credits roll. The judge states, "Ladies and gentlemen. I hope you have enjoyed the adventures of the Hardy family. I hope that we meet very soon. Thank you." It is followed by a title card that reads, "Watch for the new adventures of Judge Hardy's children." Screenwriter Kay Van Riper was already penning the script for the next Hardy movie, titled *Judge Hardy's Children*, while *You're Only Young Once* was being filmed.

Lewis Stone's performance as Judge Hardy was different than Lionel Barrymore's. Stone was more gallant and steady, and he exuded greater confidence. His voice was deep and strong, his convictions were evident, his strength was discernible. He did not seem stressed; he appeared to be more aware of his surroundings, more focused with his decisions. His performance was so good that Louis B. Mayer promised the actor a home at MGM for the remainder of his career. And while this film does give his character some attention, even the scene where he finally does catch his swordfish seems to be a distraction from the more interesting scenes featuring Andy.

Fay Holden perfectly played the loving, understanding matriarch who followed the era's stereotype perfectly. Taking care of the household, her husband, and the children, she had no real understanding of the outside world and depended on the judge for such matters. While dated when seen in the twenty-first century, her portrayal and her character are both accurate for their era.

Ann Rutherford makes her first appearance as Polly Benedict in this movie, a role she would continue for the remainder of the series. Rooney commented,

> Ann and I didn't like each other. We went to school together on the studio lot, and didn't get along well. She didn't want to do the movie. But she ended up doing it, and we ended up becoming good friends.[1]

It should also be noted that the title song for this movie, also called "You're Only Young Once," became the theme music over the credits for all subsequent Hardy family films.

Audiences were once again pleased with the exploits of the Hardy family. The *Motion Picture Herald* had a section for exhibitor comments titled "What the Picture Did for Me." In its May 14, 1938, issue, an exhibitor commented on *You're Only Young Once*, stating,

> There was more audience reaction and good comments received after showing this picture than we've enjoyed in some time. It's the sort of homey American type story that always pleases. Mickey Rooney once again adds up to 75 percent of the fun. I wonder if Mickey is the next Clark Gable.[2]

While critics understood the popularity, especially among moviegoers in the heartland, Howard Thompson of the *New York Times* stated,

> The average American family (if, indeed, there is such a thing) has been so frequently libeled by the average program film it is a surprising experience and occasion for relief to come upon a fictional group which can reasonably be accepted as such, and the group to which credit is given with thankful approval this morning is that in *You're Only Young Once* now playing at the Rialto. Here, at least, is a "series" family (for that is what MGM intends it to be) in which the individual members react like human beings instead of like third-rate vaudevillians. The idea, of course, is the old one—domestic trials and comic tribulations of a family in which there are growing children. Hollywood has long since learned that there is no place like home for a program picture. Without any trepidation, indeed, we can look forward to future reunions with Judge Hardy's family.[3]

You're Only Young Once still doesn't have all the hallmarks of a classic Andy Hardy film—some of the content is a bit too serious—and less of the focus is on Andy. But with this movie you slowly start to see all the pieces coming together as the filmmakers figure out what works best for this series, and casting Stone and Holden is a big step forward.

By the end of 1937, Mickey Rooney had appeared in seven feature films, most of them at his home studio of MGM and usually in supporting roles. The popularity of the Hardy series and the chemistry with Judy Garland had now been established. Building upon both of these would catapult Mickey Rooney to the very top.

LOVE IS A HEADACHE

(MGM, 1938)

Director: Richard Thorpe
Screenplay: Marion Parsonnet, Harry Ruskin, William R. Lipman
Producer: Frederick Stephani. *Cinematographer:* John Seitz. *Editor:* Conrad A. Nervig
Cast: Gladys George (Carlotta "Charlie" Lee); Franchot Tone (Peter Lawrence); Ted Healy (Jimmy Slattery); Mickey Rooney (Mike O'Toole); Frank Jenks (Joe Cannon); Virginia Weidler (Jake O'Toole); Ralph Morgan (Reggie ODell); Jessie Ralph (Sheriff Janet Winfield); Fay Holden (Mary); Barnett Parker (Hotchkiss); Julius Tannen (Hillier); Ernie Alexander (Johnson); Marie Blake (Hillier's Secretary); Edgar Dearing (Pinch Reardon); Sarah Edwards (Mrs. Warden); Sam Ash (Waiter); Sidney Bracey (Waiter); Georgie Billings (Mike's Friend); June Brewster (Betty Bartholomew); Henry Koker (Sam Ellinger); Don Brodie (Reporter); Cyril Ring (Reporter); Gil Patrick (Reporter); Chester Clute (Salesman); Richard Cramer (Process Server); Leigh De Lacey (Neighbor); Jim Farley (Plainclothesman); Jules Cowles (Dorrman); Chaster Gan (Louie); Leyland Hodgson (Chauffeur); Buster Slaven, Leonard Kibrick, Sidney Kibrick (Mike's friends); Robert Middlemass (Police Commissioner); Lillian Read (Hat Check Girl); Phillip Terry (Club 44 Radio Man); Bea Nigro (Woman at Dock); Jack Norton (Bartender)
Released: January 14, 1938
Specs: 74 minutes; black and white

Love Is a Headache is a fast-talking comedy, the type that was quite popular during the 1930s, and although Mickey Rooney has only a supporting role, it is much larger than those he had in *Slave Ship* or *Captains Courageous* the year before. This is the first Rooney film to be released in 1938, which would turn out to be a pivotal year in his career with the continued success of the Hardy series and a few more high-profile films.

The plot of *Love Is a Headache* centers on haughty actress Carlotta Lee (Gladys George) and a reporter named Peter Lawrence (Franchot Tone), who has known her since they were kids. Since he is aware of Carlotta's background and sees through the publicity surrounding her, Peter offers revealing information on the actress in his column, much to her chagrin.

While this conflict is essentially the center of the film's narrative structure, it is augmented with a subplot where Peter must sadly inform two kids from a rough area of town that their father, a window washer, fell to his death. The children are Mike and Jake O'Toole (Mickey Rooney and Virginia Weidler), and despite their gruffness, Peter takes a liking to them and tries to find them a home. Carlotta takes them in, having something of a gruff exterior and rough background herself, but Peter believes it to be a publicity stunt and is concerned about the welfare of the children.

Although the adults are supposed to be the axis of this film, the biggest laughs in *Love Is a Headache* come from the scenes with Rooney and Weidler. This is where tough kid characters at MGM and at, say, Warner Bros. or Paramount differ. The kids in the other studio films were genuinely tough, and their toughness ran deep. If they were entrusted into the care of a wealthy benefactor, they'd likely steal from them. A tough kid at MGM appreciated the wealth and privilege and wanted to do good. So when the O'Toole children accidentally knock over fragile knick-knacks in the movie star's expensive home, the scene is played for laughs and they are genuinely sorry. At one point Jake says, "Maybe we oughta behave different from now on."

This is not a melodrama like the low-budget *Hoosier Schoolboy* where an understanding adult tries to reach a surly punk. This is a woman of privilege who wants to reach out, and the adjustment between the characters is played for comedy. Carlotta sleeps with Jake, whose tossing and turning result in enough kicks and nudges to keep the actress awake. Carlotta goes out into the living room and tries to get comfortable on two chairs, but Mike is asleep on the couch and the boy's snoring disturbs her.

The kids are taken aback at such mundane things as "a separate room just to eat in," being unfamiliar with this level of privilege. Carlotta asks the kids, "Are those the only clothes you have?" Mike replies, "No, we have hats!" During a scene where Carlotta attempts to buy them new clothes,

Mickey Rooney and Virginia Weidler

Mike balks at being dressed by the pants salesman, while Jake and Carlotta engage in the following dialogue:

Carlotta: Your brother's rather headstrong isn't he?

Jake: Strong? On Tenth Avenue they call him one-punch O'Toole.

Carlotta: Do you like your new things?

Jake: Yes. I've never been in an apartment store before.

Carlotta: Department store.

Jake: Yeah, I always wondered what they was like.

Carlotta: What they *were* like.

Jake: We're gonna have a hard time understanding each other, ain't we?

Carlotta: *Aren't* we.

Jake: You said it!

Rooney recalled,

> The scene I did with the pants salesman [Chester Clute] when I was trying on the pants was really difficult. He had that expression on his face that kept making me break up. I would yell at him, and he'd stand there and fidget with that expression and I would bust up laughing. One of my shortest scenes in the picture, and one of the hardest to do.[1]

The sequences involving Rooney and Weidler are such highlights that it is the scenes with the leading stars, Tone and George, that are comparatively less interesting. Even Frank Nugent of the *New York Times* noticed, stating in his review,

> Somebody had better do something about his boy Mickey Rooney—quick!—before the little rascal runs away with every picture he appears in. . . .The kid has that natural faculty of making everything he plays seem real, which throws into the most unfortunate light those lesser and cardboard characters who are fictitiously involved with him. . . . Whatever breath of life there is in *Love Is a Headache* must be attributed to . . . Rooney, with an able—though obviously restrained—assist from little Miss Weidler.[2]

The chemistry between Mickey Rooney and ten-year-old Virginia Weidler resulted in their appearing together a few more times over the next five years. While never reaching the height of stardom Rooney was to enjoy, before 1938 the young actress was popular enough to promote a line of children's hats, each one featuring a label with her name and likeness. Rooney fondly recalled Virginia Weidler during an interview:

> Virginia Weidler was terrific, always knowing her lines and she delivered them with perfect timing. She could play tough, but she was really a sweet, vulnerable girl. I remember she had to get a bit rough with me a few times on this

picture, and she had trouble doing it. I took her aside and said, "Don't be afraid to hit me, Ginny, I can take it." She got over it, because she really got me good a few times! [*Rooney laughs*][3]

There is a great deal of funny dialogue in *Love Is a Headache*, the sort that happens a lot in 1930s comedies. Ted Healy, a vaudeville veteran who had been doing character roles in films for a few years, has a supporting role and engages in this dialogue:

Healy: Sometimes I wish I was born a woman.

Secretary: With that face it wouldn't do you any good.

Healy: You oughta know.

Sadly, this was Ted Healy's final film. In December of 1937 he went out drinking to celebrate the birth of his son, but his surly manner got him into a series of fights that upset an already bad kidney and heart condition from heavy drinking. He died the same night. Healy's greatest fame involved his bringing the Three Stooges into show business. First it was just Moe Howard and Shemp Howard. Larry Fine joined later. When Shemp left the act to work as a single, Moe suggested his brother Jerome take Shemp's place. Ted disliked Jerome and said the only way he'd hire him is if he shaved his head and called himself Curly. Jerome did it and was hired in the act. When the Stooges split from Healy and got a job doing short comedies for Columbia Pictures, Curly quickly became a much bigger star than Ted Healy ever was.

Other members of the cast included such welcome supporting players as Frank Jenks, Jessie Ralph, the aforementioned Chester Clute, Ralph Morgan, and, interestingly enough, Fay Holden, who was concurrently engaged in the long-running role of Ma Hardy in the Hardy series.

Love Is a Headache is not a Mickey Rooney movie per se, but he is easily the most interesting and dynamic performer in the film. He received fourth billing in a cast of (mostly) adult stars, so that gives more evidence of his growing stardom. And the fact that reviewers were singling him out as stealing the movie from its established grown-up leading players further demonstrates how Rooney was on the fast track to greater stardom. With each film, Mickey Rooney's impact became just a bit more noted by moviegoers, critics, and MGM executives.

JUDGE HARDY'S CHILDREN

(MGM, 1938)

Director: George B. Seitz
Screenplay: Kay Van Riper. *Characters:* Aurania Rouverol
Producer: Carey Wilson. *Cinematographer:* Lester White. *Editor:* Ben Lewis
Cast: Lewis Stone (Judge Hardy), Mickey Rooney (Andy Hardy), Cecilia Parker (Marian Hardy), Fay Holden (Mrs. Emily Hardy), Ann Rutherford (Polly Benedict), Betty Ross Clarke (Aunt Milly), Robert Whitney (Wayne Trenton), Ruth Hussey (Margaret "Maggie" Lee), Jonathan Hale (Mr. Lee), Leonard Penn (Steve Prentiss), Jacqueline Laurent (Suzanne Cortot), Janet Beecher (Miss Budge), Boyd Crawford (Radio Announcer), Don Douglas (J. O. Harper), Edward Earle (Peniwill), Charles Peck (Tommy MacMahon), Georges Renavent (Mr. Cortot), Sarah Edwards (Miss Adams), Hal LeSuer (Chauffeur), Alphonse Martell (Maître d'hôtel), John T. Murray (Waiter), Sunny Brooks (Orchestra Leader), Erville Alderson (Deputy Sheriff)
Released: March 26, 1938
Specs: 78 minutes; black and white
Availability: DVD (Warner Archive Collection: *The Andy Hardy Film Collection: Volume 2*)

The third Hardy family movie is an improvement on the first and second. The first, *A Family Affair*, seems more like a movie unto itself and not part of the series. The second, *You're Only Young Once*, seemed to be initially establishing the characters and their situations. *Judge Hardy's Family* is an establishing film as well, but it progresses from where the previous movie left off. The formula for the Hardy films is already starting to become familiar at this point: the kids get into trouble, the judge imparts some wisdom to help them out of it, and all ends well.

Judge Hardy has been offered $200 per day by the United States government to hear a case involving utility company monopolies. This was a topical subject in the late 1930s when private companies sued the Tennessee Valley Authority (the Supreme Court eventually ruling that government control of utilities was constitutional). While Judge Hardy's situation once again anchors the proceedings, daughter Marian is unwittingly duped into causing him some serious trouble. Although she has a boyfriend back in Carvel, Marian gets caught up with a fast-talking Washington, DC, type and provides information about her father's exploits, which she picked up from casual dinner conversation at home. Her small-town innocence ends up causing a problem for her and her father's reputations, as well as the outcome of an important federal case.

Attention on these characters in a discussion of Mickey Rooney's films is significant despite the fact that this particular area of the narrative does not involve his Andy character. It shows that the judge is still the central figure of the story (it is his name in the title), while Marian remains a focal point of the main plot. This is important on several levels. First, it shows how the writers initially perceived the series. It also presents Andy as comic relief to lighten up the more serious proceedings that involved others in the cast. However, a tangent to the plot involving Andy in a more serious situation is also introduced.

The most diverting portion of *Judge Hardy's Children* is Andy's situation. Rooney plays Andy as sufficiently wide-eyed and amusingly cocky as he struts through the DC area with a pretty young French student, who is being carefully chaperoned by a woman her father has hired. She invites Andy to a cotillion dance, and the highlight of the entire film is when she and Andy dance the Big Apple, disrupting the staid affair where tuxedoed boys and formally dressed girls are boringly waltzing with unsmiling expressions.

The serious portion in which Andy is involved first occurs at the very outset of the movie. Judge Hardy chastises some high school boys in his court for distributing anti-authority leaflets protesting the removal of the star football player from the team due to bad grades. The judge responds angrily, and one boy states, "This is 1938; times have changed," perhaps alluding to other areas of civil disobedience that might have been topical at the time. Judge Hardy responds, "The rules of civilized behavior have not changed. I have no patience for anyone, young or old, who live in a democracy and try to wreck its underpinnings." He sentences the boys to write "a twenty-thousand-word essay on the American system of free education." One of Andy's friends warns him that his father better never find out that Andy was actually the one who spearheaded this activity. The judge does find out while also dealing with other troubles in DC, and responds with hurt and disappointment. He takes Andy to Mount Vernon, home of George Washington, and offers an explanation for American patriotism. As this film is prewar, this portion comes off rather naturally and does not appear to be blatant flag-waving as can be found in some wartime movies. It is effectively presented as a naive teenager being counseled by a benevolent father that his actions were misguided.

However, the context of the film and its era help this particular portion of the narrative's conflict play somewhat better. In the pre–civil rights era, before rock and roll and Vietnam, the American way of thinking was more naturally conducive to elements of progress that were scientific and technological rather than sociocultural. Throughout the subsequent series, the staid old judge would be impressed at advancements in technology (e.g., a ham radio set allowing communication across the nation in a later film), but "civilized behavior" would always be expected.

Civilized behavior is expected of Andy at the cotillion dance as well. When he upsets the dullness of the party by getting the band to do a swing number and then starts dancing the Big Apple with the French girl, the other young people join in and attempt to copy the steps. Everyone is having a good time, when one of the chaperones in another room wonders what the noise is, and another spits out the answer—"Jazz!"—in a manner that exudes real disgust. The dance is stopped, the tearful French girl is told by her chaperone she has to leave, and Andy is forbidden to see her again, the chaperone telling him, "You simply do not understand how to conduct yourself at these affairs." However, the film does not embrace this situation. Andy is pleased to later discover that the French girl's father is happy to have his daughter immerse herself in American culture and learn the new swing dances, much to the chagrin of the chaperone, whom Andy dismisses as a "stuffed shirt."

The manner in which women are presented in this movie is especially intriguing. Ruth Hussey plays a sharp operator who works with a couple of men to dupe Marian, whose small-town innocence does make sense, into revealing information that could be detrimental to her father's case. Mrs. Hardy, however, is all aflutter about the goings on, even though she is carefully sheltered from the most serious aspects. She is strictly a housewife and knows nothing of current events, which might be acceptable for someone playing a small-town woman in a 1930s movie. But at one point, when Andy wants to absorb some culture before a museum trip with the French girl, he asks, "Mom, who is Leonardo Da Vinci?" Mrs. Hardy responds, "I don't know. I don't think we had any Da Vincis living in Carvel." The judge laughs aloud. So Mrs. Hardy is not only naive to the ways of the world on a newsworthy level, she is also ignorant of basic cultural history that she might have learned in school. The judge does not laugh at her in a derisive manner. His is more of a "Isn't that cute?" response, which could be considered just as insulting.

Judge Hardy's Children may feature some archaic sociocultural ideas, but it is progressive within the context of the series, as it continues to explore the characters and their importance. While the judge is the central character and Marian is the more sympathetic one, it is Andy and his cheerful situations that stand out. While the main portion of the film deals with scandal and blackmail, Andy is courting a pretty girl, dancing to popular big band music, and getting the last laugh with a "stuffed shirt." Moviegoers responded best to his situation, resulting in studio executives suggesting that he, not the judge, be the central figure of the next Hardy family movie.

11

HOLD THAT KISS

(MGM, 1938)

Director: Edwin L. Marin
Screenplay: Stanley Rauh, Jane Hall, Ogden Nash. *Story:* Stanley Rauh. *Dialogue:* Bradbury Foote
Producer: John W. Considine Jr. *Cinematographer:* George Folsey. *Editor:* Ben Lewis
Cast: Maureen O'Sullivan (June "Junie" Evans); Dennis O'Keefe (Tommy "Tom" Bradford); Mickey Rooney (Chick Evans); George Barbier (Mr. J. Westley Piermont); Jessie Ralph (Aunt Lucy McCaffey); Edward S. Brophy (Al); Fay Holden (Mrs. Emily Evans); Frank Albertson (Steven "Steve" Evans); Phillip Terry (Ted Evans); Ruth Hussey (Nadine Piermont Kent); Barnett Parker (Marcel Maurice—Couturier); Evelyn Beresford (Mrs. Thornley); Charles Judels (Otto Schmidt); Leonard Carey (Gibley); Ernie Alexander (Mickey); Tully Marshall (Mr. Lazarus); Jack Norton (Mallory); Brent Sargent (Noel); Ray Turner (Fred); Morgan Wallace (Mr. Wood); E. Alyn Warren (Sam); Edgar Dearing (Policeman); Martin Faust (Taxi Driver); Billy Benedict (Boy Delivering Suit); David Horsley (Chauffeur); Mary Howard (Nurse); Eleanor Lynn (Theater Cashier); Edwin Maxwell (Theater Manager); Buddy Messinger, Billy Taft (Theater Ushers); Frank McClure (Man in Travel Agency Office); Tom O'Grady (Bartender); Oscar O'Shea (Pop); Tom Quinn (Horse Parlor Cashier); Ben Taggart (Apartment Doorman); Eric Wilton (Butler); Dale Van Sickel, Russell Wade, Betty Blythe, Betty Ross Clarke (Wedding Guests); Forbes Murray, William Worthington (Dog Show

Judges); Jack Luden, Edmund Mortimer, Suzanne Ridgeway, Cyril Ring, Larry Steers (Dog Show Attendees)
Released: May 13, 1938
Specs: 79 minutes; black and white

Hold That Kiss is yet another cute, disarming romantic comedy with an ensemble cast of which Rooney is a fairly major part. The focus of the narrative is on the characters played by Maureen O'Sullivan and Dennis O'Keefe, who meet at a society wedding. Each believes the other to be among the wealthy guests, but both are there to simply make a delivery. They each maintain the façade after they start dating.

Mickey Rooney appears as O'Sullivan's clarinet-playing brother and exhibits his usual enthusiasm and charisma whenever he is on screen. Even when the focus is not on him directly, Rooney's character is on the sidelines, loudly practicing his clarinet for his jazz band's next gig. This does not distract from the scene that is supposed to get most of our attention, but it enhances a comic element from the sidelines. His performance is amusing, and his character is likable. While only a supporting player, Rooney is singled out in this review from *Variety*:

> Its drawing ability is limited to the pull in the names of Maureen O'Sullivan, Mickey Rooney and Dennis O'Keefe, who impressed recently in *The Bad Man of Brimstone* [1937]. . . . It's all been done before with variations but Edwin Marin in his direction carries the thin thread of plot to a satisfactory finish. Good supporting performances by George Barbier, Jessie Ralph and Frank Albertson hold up the interest over the weak spots. Film could have profited with more of Mickey Rooney, who is coming along fast with each succeeding appearance. Boy has something for the customers and knows how to sell it. . . . *Hold That Kiss* will get by with audiences that like light entertainment.[1]

At face value, *Hold That Kiss* appears to be yet another romantic comedy that has little consequence in Rooney's development. However, Rooney recalled,

> I learned a lot in pictures like *Hold That Kiss*. We were all working together, all playing off each other, and even if the picture was a little simple, it is what audiences wanted. I was being used a lot, getting noticed, and on my way up.[2]

Perhaps *Hold That Kiss* could be considered another pivotal film in Rooney's career, but on its own, it now comes off as amusing fluff and little more. The cast is filled with welcome old pros like Jessie Ralph and Ed Brophy, as well as Fay Holden appearing as Rooney's mother, as she was now doing in the Andy Hardy series. The script may not be quite as sharp and witty as other MGM romantic comedies, such as *Libeled Lady* (1936), but it has a relaxed confidence that is entertaining enough.

Even in smaller roles, Rooney was gaining in popularity as 1938 wore on, and *Hold That Kiss* would be the last time Mickey Rooney would not be given star billing. In his next film, he would be given above-the-title billing, alongside Freddie Bartholomew, even though he was playing a supporting role.

LORD JEFF

(MGM, 1938)

Director: Sam Wood
Screenplay: James Kevin McGuinness, Bradford Ropes, Endre Bohem, Frank Davis, Walter Ferris, Sam Wood. *Story:* Val Burton
Producer: Frank Davis, Sam Wood. *Cinematographer:* John Seitz. *Editor:* Frank E. Hull
Cast: Freddie Bartholomew (Geoffrey Braemer), Mickey Rooney (Terry O'Mulvaney), Charles Coburn (Captain Briggs), Herbert Mundin (Bosun "Crusty" Jelks), Terry Kilburn (Albert Baker), Gale Sondergaard (Doris Clandon), Peter Lawford (Benny Potter), Walter Tetley (Tommy Thrums), Peter Ellis (Ned Saunders), George Zucco (James "Jim" Hampstead), Matthew Boulton (Inspector Scott), John Burton (John Cartwright), Emma Dunn (Mrs. Briggs), Monty Woolley (Jeweler), Gilbert Emery (Magistrate), Charles Irwin (Mr. Burke), Walter Kingsford (Superintendent), Evan Thomas (Captain Wilson), David Thursby (Milk Cart Driver), Norman Ainsley (Assistant Purser), Frank Baker (Inspector), Wilson Benge (Chauffeur), Lionel Braham (Constable), Charles Coleman (Hotel Desk Clerk), Alec Craig (Gardener), Jack Deery (Clerk), Johnny Douglas and Vernon Downing (Lift Boys), Tommy Hughes (Page Boy), Olaf Hutten (Instructor), P. J. Kelly (Bailiff), Richard Lancaster (Host of Party), Doris Lloyd (Hostess of Party), Dan Maxwell (Postman), Versey O'Davoren (*Queen Mary* Steward), C. Montague Shaw (Magistrate), Claire Verdera

(Maid), Eric Wilton (Mate), Red Evans (Doorman), Helena Grant (Woman Magistrate), Ramsay Hill (Jewelry Clerk), Keith Hitchcock (Transportation Clerk), Lon McCallister and Dick Chandlee (Bits)
Released: June 17, 1938
Specs: 85 minutes; black and white

Perhaps the most interesting thing about *Lord Jeff* is that it shows Mickey Rooney clearly in support of the film's star, Freddie Bartholomew, as Rooney's star was rising and Bartholomew's was descending. Despite Rooney's supporting role, he is given equal billing above the title with Bartholomew. The studio realized that Rooney's stature was growing, while Bartholomew's adolescence, with his changing voice and gangly features, was becoming less effective. The change in Bartholomew's appearance, even since *Captains Courageous* the year before, is surprising.

The story deals with haughty young Geoffrey (Bartholomew), who is working with two adults in a jewel theft ring. Geoffrey gets caught by authorities, but rather than send him to reform school, they allow him to train to become a seaman at a nautical academy. Feeling superior to the others, Geoffrey is tolerated for just so long, until his insolence results in him being alienated by his classmates. He eventually proves himself and realizes his opportunities in the academy are genuine. When the adults return to arrange another heist, he helps authorities capture them.

MGM liked using the idea of an insolent brat learning good values and becoming a better person in the end. Bartholomew did this in *Captains Courageous*, so the studio felt he would be effective in *Lord Jeff* doing much the same thing. However, in *Captains Courageous*, Rooney's part is so small he barely registers, while in *Lord Jeff* he shares most of Bartholomew's scenes as one of the classmates who reaches out to the newcomer.

As the film is set in England, the cast includes young British actors like Peter Lawford and Terry Kilburn (who would be a smash this same year in MGM's production of Charles Dickens's *A Christmas Carol*). Radio actor Walter Tetley is also one of the boys, and is American, but he was adept at dialect and plays an English student effectively. Rooney plays an Irish boy, and thus affixes an Irish accent throughout the film. One would assume MGM had dialogue coaches to assist the American actors with proper inflection. The result is another enthusiastic performance by Rooney, and he pairs well with Bartholomew.

However, despite his being prominent in the film, *Lord Jeff* does not require much assessment in a study of Mickey Rooney's movies. The film, despite the aforementioned actors and such fine performers as Charles Coburn and Gale Sondergaard, is pretty standard fare that achieved average results from moviegoers. Its chief interest in this study is how Mickey Rooney and Freddie Bartholomew were costarring, but Rooney was eclipsing Bartholomew's star status despite being cast in a supporting role. When they would appear in a film together for the fifth and last time a couple of years later, Rooney would be the star and Bartholomew among the supporting players.

Bartholomew and Rooney had been personal friends since appearing together in *Little Lord Fauntleroy* a couple of years earlier. Even as late as 1991, when being interviewed for Peter Hay's book *MGM: When the Lion Roars*, Freddie Bartholomew recalled Rooney fondly:

> I will say this about Mickey: of the whole group of us, my personal opinion is that he was the very best actor. He could do anything. Tear your heart out, make you laugh, he could sing, dance, juggle, play any instrument you could name. To this day I have a feeling of awe about his talent.[1]

Lord Jeff would be the last time Mickey Rooney would play a supporting role for the remainder of his time at MGM. With his next film, *Love Finds Andy Hardy*, he is reteamed with Judy Garland, resulting in what might be the best movie in the entire series. The Andy Hardy series, already popular, soared to the top of the box office. And Mickey Rooney's ascension is just as remarkable and rapid.

LOVE FINDS ANDY HARDY

(MGM, 1938)

Director: George B. Seitz
Screenplay: William Ludwig. *Story:* Vivien R. Bretherton. *Gag Consultant:* Buster Keaton
Producers: Lou L. Ostrow, Carey Wilson. *Cinematographer:* Lester White. *Editor:* Ben Lewis
Cast: Mickey Rooney (Andrew "Andy" Hardy), Lewis Stone (Judge James K. Hardy), Fay Holden (Mrs. Emily Hardy), Cecilia Parker (Marian Hardy), Judy Garland (Betsy Booth), Lana Turner (Cynthia Potter), Ann Rutherford (Polly Benedict), Mary Howard (Mrs. Tompkins), Gene Reynolds (Jimmy MacMahon), Don Castle (Dennis Hunt), Betty Ross Clarke (Aunt Milly), Marie Blake (Augusta), George P. Breakston (Beezy), Raymond Hatton (Peter Dugan), Jay Ward (Gene), Rand Brooks (Man at Bandstand), Jules Cowles (Court Attendant), George Noisom (Western Union Boy), Erville Anderson (Court Attendant)
Songs: "In Between" (performed by Judy Garland); "It Never Rains but What It Pours" (performed by Judy Garland); "Meet the Beat of My Heart" (performed by Judy Garland)
Released: July 22, 1938
Specs: 91 minutes; black and white
Availability: DVD (Warner Archive Collection: *The Andy Hardy Film Collection: Volume 1*)

There is a shot in *Love Finds Andy Hardy* where the doorbell rings, Andy looks to the front door, and he sees the face of Betsy Booth smiling admiringly through the window. This image of Judy Garland, who plays Betsy, is one of many moments that season the proceedings of *Love Finds Andy*

Hardy, making it not only among the best films in the entire Hardy family series, but also the movie that sent both Mickey Rooney and the series near the top of the box office.

Love Finds Andy Hardy is set in the month of December, and Andy Hardy is all set for the Christmas Eve dance. He is even planning to buy his first car for a mere twenty dollars. Such an amount is not easy for a teenage boy to acquire in 1938, so Andy puts a twelve-dollar down payment on a used vehicle and needs to get the other eight dollars by December 23. There is a bit of a problem, as girlfriend Polly informs Andy she will be visiting her grandmother for the next three weeks and will not be able to attend the Christmas Eve dance with him. Planning to go stag, Andy gets an opportunity when his friend Beezy asks Andy to take his girlfriend, Cynthia, to the dance. Beezy will also be out of town for the holidays and doesn't want other boys distracting his girl, so he decides to hire Andy to be her beau, with the plan that he will dump her once Beezy returns home. Andy asks for eight dollars plus expenses, and Beezy reluctantly agrees. This way Andy can get the money for his car and have an attractive date for the dance in Polly's absence.

The innocence of small-town life before America got involved in a second world war sometimes offers a skewed response to social situations from a twenty-first-century perspective. Andy and Beezy are obviously using these women in a most dishonest manner—Andy for money and Beezy because he is insecure about dating above his status, having landed a very beautiful girl. Andy tries in vain to interest Cynthia in activities like swimming and tennis, but discovers all she really wants to do is make out. At first this seems great, but eventually it is overwhelming. He seems to prefer the more reticent Polly to the easily accessible Cynthia. But he has to keep her happy because he won't be paid if he doesn't "date her up" until Beezy's return.

Betsy Booth is simply a thirteen-year-old girl who is visiting her grandmother next door to the Hardy home. Quickly developing a worshipful crush on Andy, she settles for being his supportive confidante. Their scenes together are charming, as the younger girl comes off as the more mature pragmatist as Andy tries to maintain his plans to attract Cynthia, get the money, and obtain his car.

Not only is Polly conveniently removed from the body of the film, so are Mrs. Hardy and Aunt Milly. The Hardy family receives a telegram indicating that Mrs. Hardy's mother has suffered a stroke. She and her sister, Aunt Milly, rush to their mother's side. Andy's sister, Marian, is given some responsibility as woman of the house, but a cook is also hired. Judge Hardy continues to maintain his controlled, understanding balance to all

Poster for *Love Finds Andy Hardy*

that is going on with his family, remaining home while his wife tends to her mother. However, unlike the previous Hardy films, the judge is important as support rather than as the central figure, the writers having realized that Andy is whom moviegoers connect with as the central figure. Marian has a weepy opening scene about yet another problem with boyfriend Wayne and a conflict with the wise-cracking cook Judge Hardy hires in his wife's absence, but otherwise she is pretty much in the periphery.

The new dynamic here is between Andy and Betsy. Judy Garland lends her formidable presence to the movie by continuing to support and care for Andy while he struggles through girl problems. Distracted by those, Andy does not completely realize what a great partner Betsy is. Coming from wealth, Betsy purchases a fancy new radiator cap for his car, and Andy talks about how much Cynthia will like it and how much Polly will admire it afterward. Betsy's face falls, while Andy has no idea he's hurt her. After he leaves, Judy Garland performs the number "In Between," which allows the Betsy character to project, through song, her limited status of being wealthy, mature, intelligent, but too young to be noticed. In the hands of Judy Garland, Betsy Booth's wealth and privilege never appear indulgent. The character uses her more privileged status to help Andy, even at her own expense.

While the judge serves as a reliable figure for advice and support, Andy needs a friend closer to his age to confide in, especially with all the craziness happening in his life. Betsy is strong and also admirable because, while she loves Andy, she recognizes that he doesn't feel the same way about her and is still willing to help him sort out his girlfriend troubles. Without Betsy, this movie would not be nearly as great.

Polly writes Andy to indicate she will be returning in time to attend the dance. Committed to Cynthia for Beezy's money, he tells Polly he can't take her due to "another engagement," believing he can explain to her later. Shortly thereafter, Beezy sends a note indicating he has found another girl while he was away, so he is no longer interested in Cynthia and the whole deal is off. Now Andy is without the car money, is stuck with Cynthia, and has upset Polly, whom he does care for.

The way the story has Andy acquire the money for his car is especially clever as it neatly ties the family plot elements together. The judge wants to find out how the situation is with Mrs. Hardy's mother, but there is no telephone there and he does not want to upset his wife with a telegram. Andy tells his father about a young friend, Jimmy MacMahon, who is a ham radio operator. Jimmy gets a message to Mrs. Hardy and receives the response that her mother has "passed her crisis" and is on the road to recovery. Impressed with Andy's ingenuity and what modern technology allows, the judge gives Andy the money he needs to get his car. The film spends a bit of time with the scene involving the ham radio. Jimmy must send out a message to the designated area, and it sometimes takes hours to get a response. They all wait patiently when suddenly another young boy is able to take a message to the address.

While this system may seem crude in the Internet era, actor Lewis Stone does a brilliant job of effectively conveying Judge Hardy's astonishment at how this communication can exist. Earlier in the film, as Andy is attempting to get money for the car, he talks to his father about how technology has advanced. He mentions airplanes not having been a part of his dad's childhood, to which the judge responds, "I was quite grown before men began to fly." Andy then states that cars were also not around until the judge had reached adulthood, but they are now a necessity. This ploy fails to get the money, but it does a nice job of setting up the scene with the ham radio and the eventual success Andy has in obtaining the funds. The judge, who grew up having to travel by horseback, now lives in a world with cars and airplanes and has been introduced to a method of communication, conducted by mere children, that allows him to contact his wife up in Canada. The judge gives Andy the car money partly due to a realization that his son is very much a part of this modern world of advancing technology.

Without telling Andy, Betsy informs Cynthia that the car Andy plans on driving to the dance is a real wreck. The haughty, pretentious Cynthia calls Andy and says she refuses to go with him. Andy is pleased and calls Polly to reinvite her. But she has found out about Cynthia and indicates she has plans to attend with a college boy. Andy is dejected until Betsy comes over wearing an evening gown. She is the one Andy takes to the dance.

Unlike *Judge Hardy's Children*, this film doesn't show off Mickey Rooney's dancing prowess, but instead displays Judy Garland's singing skills. The bandleader at the dance recognizes her as the daughter of a famous singer, and knows she can sing also. Judy performs two songs—"It Never Rains but What It Pours" and "Meet the Beat of My Heart." Betsy Booth and Andy Hardy lead the dance's grand march.

Everything wraps up nicely. Polly's college boy date turns out to be her cousin. Betsy explains the situation between Andy and Cynthia, and Polly somehow understands. Mother Hardy surprises the family by coming home in time for Christmas. Polly's handsome cousin introduces himself to a smitten Marian.

Love Finds Andy Hardy was filmed in nineteen days and released two months after production wrapped. It was the catalyst for the burgeoning popularity of Mickey Rooney, Judy Garland, and the Hardy series itself. Produced on a budget of $212,000, the film grossed $2,247,000 and placed ninth in the movie trade magazine *Film Daily*'s annual poll of the top films of 1938. Rooney's salary would increase from $500 per week to $5,000 per film, and he would hereafter have star billing on all of his movies. Judy Garland was involved in a car accident just as production was about to begin, suffering three broken ribs. The Betsy Booth character was almost written out of the script, but trooper Judy was back to work three weeks later and sang her songs as her ribs were still healing.

This was Betty Ross Clarke's second and final performance as Aunt Milly. Sara Haden, who'd played the role in the first two movies, would return to the series and remain with it until the end. Lewis Stone would maintain his role as Judge Hardy, Fay Holden as Mrs. Hardy, and Ann Rutherford as Polly Benedict. But soon they would be characters in support of Andy, who would be even more of a focal point with each successive effort. Cecilia Parker's role as sister Marian Hardy would be shunted to the background so much that she would be absent from some of the films. Lana Turner played Cynthia in one of her first big movie roles, and from here on the series would often serve as a showcase for up-and-coming young actresses.

Silent-screen comedian Buster Keaton, who had produced some of the great classic comedies during the silent era, was, at this time, serving as an adviser on comedy scenes in MGM movies. In one scene, an enthusiastic Andy goes running up the steps, stumbles, and falls back down. According to Rooney, it is Buster Keaton who showed him how to properly do that fall.

Critics were generally pleased with *Love Finds Andy Hardy*, realizing what the series had to offer was connecting with its audience. *Variety* certainly noticed the impact Judy Garland had on the film, stating in its review,

> Newcomer to the Hardy group of players . . . is Judy Garland, who tops off a slick performance by singing three good songs. . . . Based on her showing, they will have to find a permanent place for Miss Garland in the future Hardys.[1]

Exhibitors were also pleased with the box office receipts. The *Motion Picture Herald* had a section for exhibitor comments titled "What the Picture Did for Me," and in its November 12, 1938, issue, one exhibitor raved,

> And what a grand small town picture it is. Patrons ask why we don't get more pictures like this. We certainly would if we could. It's swell. Judy Garland was a fine addition. And let's not forget Ann Rutherford and Lana Turner. Who

> can blame Andy for falling for these swell girls? Mickey Rooney is an absolute riot. This will easily rank among the ten best of 1938.[2]

Along with its importance to the careers of both Rooney and Garland, and to the success of the Hardy series, it is significant as being the first film for which MGM recorded part of the soundtrack in stereo. It was awarded a special Academy Award "for its achievement in representing the American way of life." In 2000, *Love Finds Andy Hardy* was selected for preservation in the United States National Film Registry by the Library of Congress as being "culturally, historically, or aesthetically significant."

What is finally impressive about *Love Finds Andy Hardy* is that Mickey Rooney was spending a lot of time working on this movie while simultaneously working on *Boys Town*, which was to be his next release. Playing two different characters in two of the best films of his entire career, Mickey Rooney met every challenge.

BOYS TOWN

(MGM, 1938)

Director: Norman Taurog
Screenplay: John Meehan, Dore Schary. *Story:* Dore Schary, Eleanore Griffin
Producer: John W. Considine Jr. *Cinematographer:* Sidney Wagner. *Editor:* Elmo Veron
Cast: Spencer Tracy (Father Edward Flanagan), Mickey Rooney (Whitey Marsh), Henry Hull (Dave Morris), Leslie Fenton (Dan Farrow), Addison Richards (The Judge), Edward Norris (Joe Marsh), Gene Reynolds (Tony Ponessa), Minor Watson (The Bishop), Jonathan Hale (John Hargraves), Bobs Watson (Pee Wee), Sidney Miller (Mo Kahn), Frankie Thomas (Freddie), Mickey Rentschler (Tommy), Jimmy Butler (Paul Ferguson), Martin Spellman (Skinny), Robert Emmett Keane (Burton), Victor Kilian (Sheriff), Arthur Aylesworth (Tim), King Baggott (Derelict), Wesley Giraud (Butch), Donald Haines (Alabama), John Hamilton (Warden), Al Hill (Rod), Murray Harris (Hillbilly), Roger Converse (Reporter), Barbara Bedford, Nell Craig, Helen Dickson (Nuns), Stanley Blystone (Guard)
Released: September 9, 1938
Specs: 96 minutes; black and white
Availability: DVD (Warner Home Video)

If *Love Finds Andy Hardy* gave a major boost to Mickey Rooney's film career, as well as to the Hardy series, *Boys Town* is the film that fully established him as one of the top movie actors in American cinema at that time. Rooney had shown areas of natural ability as far back as *The Devil Is a Sissy*, and over the next several movies he continued to hone that talent in various roles. *Boys Town* was something of a culmination. To further emphasize the vastness of Rooney's talent, much of this drama was filmed at the same time the actor was working on *Love Finds Andy Hardy*. Very long days that stretched into night were spent playing wholesome, amusing Andy on one set, and then tough, streetwise Whitey Marsh on another. (This was only during studio work on the latter movie. It was only when Rooney concluded work on *Love Finds Andy Hardy* that *Boys Town* production began filming the scenes that were shot on location in Nebraska.)

In 1917, Edward Flanagan, a Roman Catholic Priest, founded a home for homeless boys, ages ten to sixteen, in Omaha, Nebraska. In 1921, when the initial location was no longer adequate, Father Flanagan established Boys Town ten miles west of Omaha. Over the next decade, Father Flanagan's vision came to fruition in a manner that was impressive and inspiring. Boys Town became a student-run community with its own mayor, school buildings, post office, living areas, gymnasium, and so on.

By 1937, Father Flanagan's success was internationally known. MGM producer John Considine, who was of the Catholic faith, was intrigued by what he'd read of Boys Town, and asked screenwriter Dore Schary to write a story for Spencer Tracy and Freddie Bartholomew. Schary convinced Considine to instead feature Mickey Rooney as a troublesome new recruit, believing he would fit better in such a story than Bartholomew. Considine approved, and Schary went to visit Boys Town. Being of the Jewish faith, Schary needed to get a better understanding of Catholicism as well as a firsthand account of the operation.

As Flanagan and the students had been relying a great deal on donations, there were still areas of Boys Town where a lack of finances caused limitations. For instance, they had a winning basketball team, but the team uniforms consisted of tattered donated garments. Schary wanted to write a movie about Boys Town and approached Louis B. Mayer with the idea, who approved. Father Flanagan was reluctant to allow the rights to film until he saw and approved of the script. MGM gave Boys Town $5,000 and financed new uniforms for the sports teams as part of the rights deal.

The story is a fictional account of Flanagan (Spencer Tracy) being asked by a criminal in prison to watch over his younger brother Whitey Marsh (Mickey Rooney), who is only a teenager but on his own with no supervision. Flanagan agrees and takes a reluctant Whitey to Boys Town. At first Whitey is belligerent and defiant, but a series of events cause him to realize Flanagan's purpose and how it is best for him. And while by twenty-first-century standards much of the story seems a bit sentimental, its underlying strength, positive statement, and outstanding performances have sustained *Boys Town* as an enduring classic.

Mickey Rooney and Spencer Tracy

The role of Whitey Marsh is something of a tour de force for Rooney as well as a culmination of elements from previous roles. The elements of toughness he'd displayed in *The Devil Is a Sissy*, *Hoosier Schoolboy*, and *Love Is a Headache* are given more depth for the Whitey role, as this character is central to the film. Rooney did recall that a lot of what he did in *Hoosier Schoolboy*, despite being a poverty-row loan out, helped inform his work in this very important role.

In the film, it is Flanagan's job to reach Whitey, to bring out whatever heart this hardened adolescent may have. This appears daunting at first. Flanagan, whose motto is "There is no such thing as a bad boy," is confident, as nearly all of the many boys under his watch were pretty tough characters at one time. Whitey, however, is beyond that level. He has been toughened by the streets, hardened by experiences in petty crimes, made wise to criminal activities beyond the scope of the others. He struts through a tour of Boys Town with confidence, condescension toward the others, a defiant attitude. He plans to leave almost immediately, but the dinner bell goes off and he decides to stick around for a free meal. Eventually he becomes attracted to the parameters that allow him to flourish within the confines of a small community and sees the opportunity to be a big fish in a small pond. He manages to acquire a few friends who are attracted to his candor and runs for mayor.

The dynamic between Whitey and Flanagan is not initially explored. Most of the film deals with Whitey's relationships with the other boys, from the tumultuous friendship with Mo, to the begrudging respect crowding his rivalry with Freddie, to the hero worship he receives from Pee Wee, a smaller, younger boy. After losing a boxing match against Freddie, a humiliated Whitey angrily starts to leave Boys Town, followed by a weeping Pee Wee. As Whitey crosses the street, a speeding car hits Pee Wee and drives off. Flanagan and the others run to assist as Whitey sobs while holding the smaller child's body in his arms. It was one of the most emotionally uninhibited performances in Rooney's career to that point. He brings out the heart that Flanagan had been searching for with screaming, gut-wrenching sobs. Flanagan takes Pee Wee, who is seriously injured. As the other boys gather to pray for his recovery, Whitey joins them, feels out of place, and wanders off. The next scene shows him dazedly walking the city streets, unaware that he is bumping into others.

Meanwhile, Whitey's brother has escaped from prison. He and two others pull a bank robbery not realizing Whitey is hiding in a nearby alley. Whitey sees his brother, calls out to him, and his brother turns and shoots him in the leg. When Whitey identifies himself, his brother approaches him and insists he return to Boys Town. "Don't take my road, kid," he says. Whitey's brother calls Flanagan anonymously and tells of Whitey's whereabouts. However, Whitey's cap, with Boys Town knitted inside, is left behind, near the crime scene. Reporters link a member of Boys Town to the crime, and the subsequent stories threaten to close the institution. Whitey is torn between informing on his brother and forcing the closure of Boys Town. He sneaks out of the infirmary where his leg is being treated, and painfully limps his way to his brother's hideout. Once he arrives, he tearfully tells his brother that he can't let Boys Town close. Pleased that his brother is showing a heart, the criminal tells him to go back and do what he needs to do, that they will move on. However, the others in the gang disagree and hold Whitey and his brother at gunpoint. Word gets back to Flanagan via some boys who followed Whitey (at a distance) when he snuck away. A recovering Pee Wee overheard the boys planning to follow Whitey and informs Father Flanagan, stating, "Don't let anything happen to Whitey." A large contingent converges on the hideout and Whitey is rescued. The film concludes with a crying Whitey being honored as the next mayor of Boys Town. Father Flanagan has the last line: "There is no bad boy."

The relationship between Whitey and Flanagan is not what causes Whitey to have a heart. He continues to defy the priest throughout the film. However, the honesty of the other boys, and their integrity, slowly seems to seep through. After an altercation with Mo where the two boys are given the punishment of milking several cows a day, the two shake hands and walk away from the disciplinary meeting as friends. Whitey's rivalry with Freddie concludes with a humiliating loss in the boxing ring, but he is forced to realize who is the better man. Pee Wee's worship of him is so honest and sincere; it is probably the main factor in Whitey's emotional connection to these new surroundings. When Pee Wee is nearly killed, the emotions that have been suppressed come flowing out. Whitey's heart is now at the forefront. When Flanagan finds him in the alley after being tipped off by the brother's phone call, Whitey is praying that Pee Wee survives.

Spencer Tracy was initially reluctant to play the role of Flanagan. He had earned a Best Actor Oscar nomination for playing a priest in *San Francisco* (1936) and didn't want to play another one. Tracy was also a hard-drinking man, a factor the studio carefully covered up. Tracy finally agreed to the role, but first he had to recover from his most recent drinking binge. A man from MGM was hired to stay on the set of the film to keep Tracy away from the booze and Rooney away from the girls.

Once he committed to the role, Spencer Tracy spent a lot of time with Father Flanagan, studying his mannerisms. Tracy's performance is brilliant, anchoring each scene he is in with a relaxed confidence. He is the star of the film, and his role is most important. But it is the scenes involving Whitey that are responsible for the film's rhythm. Tracy was smart enough to realize that upon first seeing the script. Part of his reluctance to take the role was his belief that he was acting only as a straight man.

When the film was being shot on location in Nebraska, the June heat was so oppressive that some of the audio recordings melted, forcing crews to rerecord some of the film's sound. The filming also attracted a great deal of attention. While the administration of Boys Town was chagrined at how movie fans would trample flower beds to catch a glimpse of the filming, both Rooney and Tracy tried to be accessible and friendly to the crowds in hopes that giving them some attention would keep filming from being disrupted.

Costar Henry Hull recalled working with Tracy on the film in the biography *Spencer Tracy: Tragic Idol* by Bill Davidson:

> I don't remember Spence getting particularly close to any of the boys, including Rooney, but he put on the boxing gloves with the bigger kids one day, just fooling around, and one kid jabbed Spence's head off, and Spence got mad. Rooney was a lot like Spence. He kept to himself and they didn't have much truck with each other off-camera.[1]

Bobs Watson, who played Pee Wee, the Boys Town mascot in the film, was as enamored with Tracy off camera as he was on. As reported in James Curtis's book *Spencer Tracy: A Biography*, Watson remembered,

> Often, after a scene, he'd reach over and hug me and take me on his lap. I felt like a little puppy. I would follow along and stand close, hoping he'd call me over, and often he would. He'd say, "How're you doing?" and put his arm around me. I've heard that Tracy drank a lot, that he was a loner. I understand that he could be quite nasty, quite belligerent, but from my perspective, he was always a very kind man.[2]

Bobs Watson later grew up to be a Methodist minister and would frequently attribute his experience working on *Boys Town* as part of the inspiration for his choice of career.

It was then arranged that the movie's premiere would be held in Omaha, where the actual Boys Town resided. In an article for the *Omaha World-Herald*, writer Irving Green stated,

> Thirty thousand persons jam-packed all streets surrounding the Omaha Theater last night for a fleeting glimpse of a troupe of movie bigwigs who turned

> the city into Hollywood for a night. The city did more than imitate Hollywood for this—its first world movie premiere. It outdid Hollywood. Of the more than a score of persons introduced, the biggest applause was reserved for the movie principals. But loudest cheers of all went to the man who was introduced as "the one who made all this possible," Msgr. Edward J. Flanagan, director of Father Flanagan's home at Boys Town. The stars and their dignitaries made their entrances unobserved by many in the auditorium. Only a pattering of applause greeted some, but Mickey's profuse blushing when he entered with an Omaha girl brought him a hand, and the crowd rose as one in an ovation for Father Flanagan. When the film ended Mr. McDermott asked Father Flanagan to escort Tracy and Rooney to the stage. It was their first official appearance to the crowd in the theater. Tracy stood with his arm around Mickey's neck, a pose made familiar by his use of it in the film. "Words fail me for the first time," said young Mr. Rooney, who most decidedly didn't have that failing in the picture. He predicted another Academy award for Tracy, for his performance in *Boys Town*.[3]

Boys Town had been produced on a budget of $772,000 and took in $4,058,000 at the box office. This was great for the movie, but caused a problem with the actual Boys Town. The public got the impression that the movie's success was equal to the institution's success, not realizing that the actual Boys Town received only $5,000 and some athletic uniforms. Donations started to wane, so Spencer Tracy issued a statement asking the public to keep contributing, while MGM donated another $250,000 for a new dormitory.

The film received several Oscar nominations, including Best Picture, Best Director, and Best Screenplay, and it won for Best Actor (Tracy) and Best Original Story (Schary and Eleanore Griffin). Louis B. Mayer would often cite *Boys Town* as his favorite movie from his twenty-five-year tenure as head of MGM.

In February 1939, when he accepted his Oscar, Spencer Tracy responded graciously by spending all of his acceptance speech talking about Father Flanagan. An overzealous MGM publicity representative announced to the press that Tracy was donating his Oscar to Boys Town. Unfortunately, this PR move was not OK'd with the actor, who did indeed want the award his performance earned. The Academy hastily struck up another award for Flanagan to have on display, while Tracy kept his statuette.[4] As a further testament to his increasing star power, Mickey Rooney received a special Oscar at the same award ceremony (along with young Universal Studios actress Deanna Durbin, whose star was also on the rise).

Boys Town meant a lot to Mickey Rooney. It was his first fully formed dramatic role in a major MGM feature. It was his first time enjoying above-the-title billing alongside a star the caliber of Spencer Tracy. It was a role for which he was called upon to be funny, disarming, challenging, and emotional. The elements of the character Rooney played in *Boys Town* were so diverse, it took the very depths of his massive talent to portray a cocky, defiant character who was somehow endearing to the audience, even before his character's perspective changed by the end of the movie. It would remain one of the finest performances of his long career. Rooney recalled,

> By the time I did *Boys Town* I had been in pictures a long time and was learning from every picture I did and from everyone I worked with. So this wasn't just a job, this was something bigger and more important, and I realized that by just looking at my part. A lot of people tell me it is my best picture and my best performance. I agree it is a good picture and I am very proud of it. But as I look back on it now, I am wondering if it means that my career had peaked when I was seventeen years old.[5]

Boys Town was one of the biggest box office hits of 1938. A sequel, *Men of Boys Town*, was eventually made in 1941 featuring much of the same cast. And, nearly sixty years later, a TV movie titled *The Road Home* was produced, and one of the characters was Father Flanagan. To play the role of Flanagan, the producers cast Mickey Rooney.

In the meantime, Rooney continued with his career, and his stardom was maintained. His casting opposite Wallace Beery for *Stablemates* was another great success and, according to Rooney, "the most fun I ever had making a picture."[6]

15

STABLEMATES

(MGM, 1938)

Director: Sam Wood
Screenplay: Richard Maibaum, Leonard Praskins. *Story:* Reginald Owen, William Thiele
Producer: Harry Rapf. *Cinematographer:* John Seitz. *Editor:* W. Donn Hayes
Cast: Wallace Beery (Doc Thomas "Tom" Terry), Mickey Rooney (Michael "Mickey"), Arthur Hohl (Mr. Gale), Margaret Hamilton (Beulah Flanders), Minor Watson (Barney Donovan), Marjorie Gateson (Mrs. Shepherd), Oscar O'Shea (Pete Whalen), Al Herman (Merlin), Cliff Nazarro (Cliff), Sam McDaniel (Snowball), Frank Hagney (Poolroom Owner), Stanley Andrews (Track Steward), Spencer Charters (Choirmaster), James Quinn (Swipe), James C. Morton (Bartender), Scoop Martin (Danny), Charles Dunbar (Stable Hand), Phillip Hurlic (Boy)
Released: October 7, 1938
Specs: 89 minutes; black and white

If latter-day autobiographical accounts can be believed, not many younger actors liked Wallace Beery. He exuded a certain sloppy charm on screen, but off screen he apparently could be quite difficult. However, because he was one of MGM's biggest stars, they put up with any problems he might cause. Mickey Rooney, however, liked Beery a lot. As indicated in the chapter on *Slave Ship*, Beery was very kind and friendly to Rooney on the set of that film, which endeared Beery to the young actor. By the time Rooney worked with Berry again in *Stablemates*, his star had risen to where he was able to secure a costarring role, with his name above the title, alongside Beery's. And despite what anyone else might have said about Wallace Beery, Rooney would look back on this project with fondness for the rest of his life.

Beery plays Doc, a washed-up old veterinarian whose skills have been diluted by alcohol over the years. Rooney is a jockey named Michael (or Mickey), who loves Lady Q, the horse he rides. The horse is no longer performing on the track, so the owner wants to destroy the animal, even threatening to send the mare to a wildlife farm where she would be fed to lions. Mickey offers all of his savings and buys Lady Q himself. Mickey has no home, no family, and lives at the stable. There he meets Doc, a drifter who is bedding down in the stable. Mickey initially sees him as a possible troublemaker, but Doc calms him down and reveals that he recognizes a problem with the horse's gait. He checks the animal's hoof and discovers a tumor. Doc then reveals his identity to Rooney by referring to a past champion horse who had a similar tumor that he removed with an operation. Mickey pleads with him to do the same for this horse, so Doc operates. The horse recovers quickly, and Mickey and Doc become fellow drifters. Their relationship grows and Mickey starts referring to Doc as "Pop," which Doc encourages.

The film, at this point, fluctuates between sentiment, straight drama, and comedy. Beery's aw-shucks bumbling demeanor, pretending to be mad when he's really just a lovable old softy, responds to Rooney's usual portrayal of an earnest, enthusiastic adolescent. The humor increases when Mickey and Doc seek shelter in a barn on a farm owned by an old widow played by Margaret Hamilton, who would later achieve screen immortality as the Wicked Witch of the West. She is stern and unsmiling, but Beery turns on the charm to secure employment for himself and Mickey so they can raise money to enter Lady Q in a race. Beery and Hamilton are delightful in his attempts to charm her.

Doc: I'll bet you look nice when you're all gussied up.

Widow: I look the same wet or dry.

Doc: Don't you get lonely here living all alone?

Widow: I have a canary and a shotgun, that's all I need.

The sternness of Hamilton's character offsets the lovable buffoon that Beery projects, and their screen relationship is among the film's most delightful elements. When she has a choir party at her house and Beery is recruited to join, his off-key warbling is somehow accepted, while his initial reluctance to join in evolves into enthusiasm and enjoyment.

Mickey goes to enter the horse in an important race. When he does so, one of the officials starts asking him about Doc, whom the official recognized from somewhere. Mickey learns that Doc was once forced by gangsters to fix a race by surgically altering the leg of the presumed winner. This resulted in the horse falling to his death during the race and killing the jockey. Mickey acts very vague with the official and quickly leaves the track. When Mickey returns to the farm, he does not want to reveal to Doc what he knows, so he pretends to no longer be interested in traveling with him. The two friends get into an argument, and Mickey hits Doc. The youngster leaves in tears, while Doc stands befuddled, unable to understand this sudden change in personality.

The strength of this pivotal scene in the movie rests completely on the talent of the actors, both of whom open up completely and effectively. As their relationship has developed thus far in the movie, there is a palpable affection that exudes from their characters. Each is fulfilling a need in the other's life, so they engage in chores on the farm, continue to work with Lady Q, and have exciting plans once she wins her next race. Mickey's sudden change hurts Doc more than it angers him.

Rooney's chemistry with Wallace Beery is matched by his chemistry with the horse itself. Lady Q is present in nearly every scene, and there are several in which Mickey talks to the horse, using the narrative as a way for him to convey his thoughts aloud to the audience. The horse is majestic and beautiful, and her very presence anchors each scene. She responds nicely to the actor, and the scenes of Rooney and Lady Q are some of the strongest in the movie.

Once he leaves Doc, Mickey convinces some wealthy horse owners to allow him the fee to enter Lady Q in a big race. The wealthy horse owners agree after seeing Lady Q perform on the track. However, the horse exhibits some lameness just prior to the race, and Mickey tearfully believes the horse has to be pulled. Just in time, Doc enters the stable. Mickey frantically tells him to leave, revealing that the cops are after him. Doc realizes now that Mickey slapped him and started the argument earlier in order to save him from prison. They resume addressing each other as Pop and Son, as their relationship returns to its original status. Doc fixes Lady Q's hoof; it turned out to be a minor reaction to the recent operation. Mickey wants Doc to leave, but Doc insists on watching the race despite the danger he is in. He is spotted by the official, but asks that he be allowed to finish watching the race, and celebrates when Mickey and Lady Q win. Doc is also allowed to say goodbye to Mickey before he is taken away to prison.

Stablemates is essentially structured in the manner of a B movie with its rather perfunctory story, dollops of sentiment, and the comic highlights to offset the serious scenes. It achieves A-list status due to its stars. And its stars are also the reason the film comes off so effectively. The talent of the performers bolsters the material greatly. We see their relationship develop; we can perceive several layers to each character. Doc is bumbling, shuffling, and sloppy, and speaks with a slow drawl. But his skills as a veterinarian are brilliant, and he is able to exude enough charm to attract an angry five-time widow. Mickey has the experiences of a grownup and the heart of a child. He has been forced to survive alone in an unforgiving world, but he never loses his sense of enthusiasm or determination. His clinging to Doc, and the old vet's response, shows that both are emotionally needy and their connection fulfills that need.

The race scenes are nicely filmed, with some impressive close shots in the last race where Mickey (on Lady Q) must force his way through as a couple of jockeys attempt to block his way. With some good editing, the sequence builds in suspense and excitement, especially once Doc's fate becomes known to the viewer. The entire film builds up to this sequence. The sad conclusion culminates it.

B. R. Crisler's review in the *New York Times* stated that "*Stablemates* is Mickey's baptism of fire; anybody who can just break even before a camera with the invincible Beery is good, and Mickey, full of the fire of youth, even gets a shade the best of the encounter."[1] The film was another enormous hit at the box office as Mickey Rooney's stardom continued to rise. The *Motion Picture Herald* had a section for exhibitor comments titled "What the Picture Did for Me," and in its January 7, 1939, issue, one exhibitor raved,

> Plenty of thrills and throbs for the most rabid of movie fans. A swell show that should mean box office for all theaters. This pair cannot be beat for pulling them in the house.[2]

This was the last time Mickey Rooney would work in a movie with Wallace Beery, but the two did reprise their film roles on a sixty-minute *Lux Radio Theater* broadcast on March 31, 1941. Beery would remain a star at MGM until his death in 1949. When Mickey Rooney's father, the burlesque comedian Joe Yule, died a year later, he was buried next to Beery.

OUT WEST WITH THE HARDYS

(MGM, 1938)

Director: George B. Seitz
Screenplay: Kay Van Riper, Agnes Christine Johnston, William Ludwig. *Characters:* Aurania Rouverol
Producer: Lou Ostrow. *Cinematographer:* Lester White. *Editor:* Ben Lewis
Cast: Lewis Stone (Judge Hardy), Mickey Rooney (Andy Hardy), Fay Holden (Mrs. Hardy), Cecilia Parker (Marian Hardy), Ann Rutherford (Polly Benedict), Sara Haden (Aunt Milly), Don Castle (Dennis Hunt), Virginia Weidler ("Jake" Holt), Gordon Jones (Ray Holt), Ralph Morgan (Bill Northcote), Nana Bryant (Dora Northcote), Tom Neal (Aldrich Brown), Thurston Hall (H. R. Bruxton), Anthony Allen (Cliff Thomas), George Douglas (Carter), Eddy Waller (Doc), Joe Dominguez (Jose), Jesse Graves (Ambrose), Charles Grove (Al), Erville Alderson (Court Deputy), Mary Bovard (Girl at Party), Marilyn Stuart (Girl at Party)
Released: November 25, 1938
Specs: 84 minutes; black and white
Availability: DVD (Warner Archive Collection: *The Andy Hardy Film Collection: Volume 1*)

With the fifth film in the Hardy series, the screenwriters decided to relocate the family to a western setting. The judge was summoned by old friends to help them with a water rights issue, so the entire Hardy family traveled along. The judge's situation is relegated to a subplot, as the main portion of the film follows Andy's valiant attempts to settle into western life, including being thrown from a horse and learning to shoot a gun. His counterpart is a young ranch girl named Jake (Virginia Weidler), who is naturally a smooth hand at riding and shooting.

Trade ad for *Out West with the Hardys*

One of the more interesting aspects of *Out West with the Hardys* is how it examines gender roles in 1930s America. Andy is frequently spouting off about how the man runs things and a woman should hover in the background, which angers his girlfriend, Polly, in the earlier scenes set in Carvel. But once they head west, Andy is shown up by a little girl and must readjust his old-fashioned thinking. This is offset by Mrs. Hardy's naïveté, who, upon hearing they were visiting friends in the west, asks, "Do we still have that trouble with the Indians?"

Andy's sister, Marian, is once again at odds with a boyfriend at home and becomes interested in the ranch foreman, who is Jake's father. This allows for a dramatic conflict with Jake, who feels she is being replaced, especially when Marian starts doing their cooking and housework. This is another variation on gender roles, as Marian's domestic activities are suggested by Judge Hardy, who believes it will help her learn such chores for when she becomes a housewife and mother. Despite Polly's chagrin at Andy's chauvinism, and Jake's handily riding and shooting as well as any boy her age might, the underlying idea still reflects how American society felt in the late 1930s. Once World War Two began and women had to enter the workforce due to the shortage of men, it was the first step toward the equal rights that would take another two decades to happen.

Out West with the Hardys allows Rooney to work with horses again. However, unlike *Stablemates*, or other films in which the character he's playing has an understanding of horses, Andy Hardy is a city boy with no experience at all. When he defiantly attempts to ride a skittish horse despite warnings, it results in the horse's leg being broken. At first it appears the horse must be destroyed, but Andy summons a man who has invented a sling that keeps the horse off its leg until it heals.

Mickey Rooney had appeared with Virginia Weidler in *Love Is a Headache*, which had been released the previous January. Their chemistry in this film is as strong as in the earlier movie. As Rooney said, "Ginny stole this picture from me just like she did the other one!"[1] Virginia Weidler would appear again with Mickey Rooney in *Young Tom Edison* and *Babes on Broadway*. Her two best roles were in *The Great Man Votes* (RKO, 1939), starring John Barrymore, and *The Philadelphia Story* (MGM, 1940), in which she holds her own opposite the likes of James Stewart, Katharine Hepburn, and Cary Grant. However, her career did not survive awkward adolescence.

Mickey Rooney turned eighteen a few days into shooting *Out West with the Hardys*, meaning he no longer had to attend school on the lot and could work full days on the set like an adult. He enrolled in the University of Southern California in their new premed program, but left shortly afterward as his film career was too demanding.

The Andy Hardy series continued to be a low-budget moneymaker for MGM. *Out West with the Hardys* was made for approximately $310,000 and grossed nearly seven times that amount. In *Box Office* trade magazine, an exhibitor stated,

> The Hardy Family and their down-to-earth stories will thrill your audiences. They will laugh, cry, and enjoy to the utmost this picture. Rooney is tops. It's swell entertainment from start to finish. Guaranteed to have them rolling in the aisles one minute and using the good old weep rag the next. It's tops![2]

And the *Motion Picture Herald* had a section for exhibitor comments titled "What the Picture Did for Me," and in its January 28, 1939, issue, one exhibitor raved,

> I guess this is the best way to start the New Year off. All you have to do is let the people know they're playing. They'll take care of the rest. A real pleasure to greet your patrons after they've seen this. Mickey Rooney is undoubtedly the greatest box office attraction in the business. A knockout picture![3]

Mickey Rooney continued to be a solid movie star, and as 1938 closed he finished fourth among the top box office stars in American movies, placing higher than the likes of Spencer Tracy and Myrna Loy. *Boys Town* was the third-highest-grossing film of that year, *Out West with the Hardys* was the tenth highest, and *Stablemates* was eighteenth. To show his pleasure, Louis B. Mayer gave Rooney a $150,000 bonus on top of his salary. Meanwhile, his movies were making millions for the studio.

THE ADVENTURES OF HUCKLEBERRY FINN

(MGM, 1939)

Director: Richard Thorpe
Screenplay: Hugo Butler, based on the novel by Mark Twain
Producer: Joseph L. Mankiewicz. *Cinematographer:* John Seitz. *Editor:* Frank E. Hull
Cast: Mickey Rooney (Huckleberry Finn), Walter Connolly (The King), William Frawley (The Duke), Rex Ingram (Jim), Lynne Carver (Mary Jane Wilkes), Jo Ann Sayers (Susan Wilkes), Minor Watson (Capt. Brady), Elizabeth Risdon (Widow Douglass), Victor Kilian ("Pap" Finn), Clara Blandick (Miss Watson), Harlan Briggs (Mr. Rucker), Nora Cecil (Mrs. Shackleford), Roger Imhof (Judge Logan), Jesse Graves (Wilkes), Janice Chambers (Mary), Irving Bacon (Tad), Mickey Rentschler (Harry), Johnny Walsh (Sam), Billy Watson (Eliot), Delmar Watson (Joe), Harry Watson (Ben)
Released: February 10, 1939
Specs: 91 minutes; black and white
Availability: DVD (Warner Archive Collection)

The Adventures of Huckleberry Finn reworks the classic Twain novel into an MGM movie. While it was another box office success, it is one of the less interesting Mickey Rooney movies of this period. Despite his versatility as an actor, Rooney's approach to Huck Finn is as if Andy Hardy had lived in pre–Civil War Mississippi. It is only faithful to the literature in a most basic sense. It is mostly streamlined into a general entertainment within the studio's parameters. Tom Sawyer does not appear at all, while Rooney and Rex Ingram are central to the narrative as Huck and Jim. Choosing a literary source where a black actor is central to the film was a bold and commendable decision in

1939, but Huck Finn's speech about the futility of slavery is all MGM and not Twain. The movie maintains the raw essence of the book, where both Huck and Jim strive to be free of their own personal situations, but the limited connection to its source material is a problem.

Louis B. Mayer perceived the Andy Hardy character as the quintessential example of American youth, so presenting the literary character of Huck Finn with the qualities found in Andy Hardy seems to alter the original material more so than earlier versions of the film (one in 1920, and another in 1931). The *New York Times* was not impressed when it stated in its review,

> Pared down to its melodramatic essentials, or non-essentials, depending on how you look at it, Master Rooney's latest vehicle affords little, if any, insight into the realistic boyhood world of which old Mark wrote with such imperishable humor.[1]

Rooney offers his usual passionate performance and appears to be taking the material seriously. Rex Ingram's performance as Jim is committed and often quite moving. The scene in which Jim reveals that Huck's father died aboard ship is one of the stronger moments in the film, and is beautifully played by both actors. Meanwhile, Walter Connolly and William Frawley do a nice job of providing comic relief in their roles as the conniving brothers who plan to prey on an unsuspecting wealthy family.

The year 1939 is considered to be among the top years in twentieth-century American cinema. MGM scored with two films that would become iconic classics—*Gone with the Wind* and *The Wizard of Oz*. Other films this year included *Stagecoach*, *Wuthering Heights*, *Young Mr. Lincoln*, and *Mr. Smith Goes to Washington*. Among these timeless classics, *The Adventures of Huckleberry Finn* didn't register as much more than a run-of-the-mill feature that made money due to its star power and title recognition. Even Rooney admitted in his autobiography that the film was an uneventful experience.[2]

THE HARDYS RIDE HIGH

(MGM, 1939)

Director: George B. Seitz
Screenplay: Agnes Christine Johnston, William Ludwig, Kay Van Riper. *Characters:* Aurania Rouverol
Producer: Lou L. Ostrow. *Cinematographers:* Lester White, John F. Seitz. *Editor:* Ben Lewis
Cast: Mickey Rooney (Andrew "Andy" Hardy), Lewis Stone (Judge James K. Hardy), Fay Holden (Mrs. Emily Hardy), Cecilia Parker (Marian Hardy), Ann Rutherford (Polly Benedict), Sara Haden (Mildred "Aunt Milly" Forrest), Virginia Grey (Consuela MacNish), Minor Watson (Mr. Terry B. Archer), John King (Philip "Phil" Westcott), John T. Murray (Don Davis, the Druggist), George Irving (Mr. Jonas Bronell), Halliwell Hobbes (Dobbs, the Butler), Aileen Pringle (Miss Booth, Dress Saleslady), Marsha Hunt (Susan Bowen), Donald Briggs (Caleb Bowen), William Orr (Dick Bannersly), Truman Bradley (Clerk), Ann Morriss (Rosamund), Frances MacInerney (Sylvia), Erville Alderson (Bailiff), Alexander Pollard (Headwaiter), William Tannen (Desk Clerk), Phil Tead (Taxi Driver)
Released: April 21, 1939
Specs: 81 minutes; black and white
Availability: DVD (Warner Archive Collection: *The Andy Hardy Film Collection: Volume 2*)

In this Hardy family outing, Andy Hardy has the line "Why would I want to get married and make one woman miserable when I can stay single and make a lot of them happy?" This is somewhat telling in that Mickey Rooney's stardom, as well as how he represented the studio, was a bit at odds. Stardom, along with turning eighteen, led the young actor into newspaper headlines due to a bit of cavorting that was quite unlike the Andy Hardy image. Rooney recalled,

> Mr. Mayer called me into the office and basically told me I had to watch what I was doing. I told him that I worked very hard and made a lot of money for the studio, and so what I did in my private life was none of his business. He said that it wasn't private when it made the papers. I guess he had a point. So he got this guy named Les Peterson to follow me around, sort of like a bodyguard. We got to be pretty good friends.[1]

The screenwriters for the Hardy series wanted to continue exploring other avenues for the series. Having put the family out west in the previous outing, this time they investigate how the folksy Hardys would respond to being thrust into a world of wealth and privilege. Judge Hardy discovers that he has inherited $2 million from the estate of a long-deceased relative, so the family heads to Detroit and changes their status and tries to adjust to a world of servants, breakfast in bed, and other indulgences.

One of the more interesting things about *The Hardys Ride High* is the amount of screen time it gives Sara Haden, the venerable Aunt Milly, who has heretofore brought up the background. In this film, Milly's introspection about her own status comes out when she complains of being "an old maid schoolteacher" in an era when school teachers did not marry and had social parameters that were quite strict. Aunt Milly comes right out and admits, "I want to cut loose." So instead of Marian Hardy's romance, which is a tangent in the previous films, it is Aunt Milly who takes a shot at romance (with a handsome older man she meets on the plane to Detroit). And just as Marian's romances often come to naught, Aunt Milly fares no better. It turns out the man is a real estate agent wanting her to invest her savings. This leaves Milly tearfully humiliated.

The conflict in *The Hardys Ride High* involves disinherited heir Phil Westcott, the adopted son of the deceased relative who has to give up the mansion in which he is living in Detroit to the Hardys. Phil responds to them with an oily charm, but meanwhile is looking into the possibility of regaining what he's lost. It is revealed that Phil is a bit of a crook and this is why he was disinherited. But his ploy to find his way back into the wealth he'd been enjoying is to connect with Andy and take him to nightclubs, introduce him to chorus girls, and pretty much dazzle him with superficial indulgences.

Wanting desperately to put on airs, Andy doesn't want to reveal he is too young, but he doesn't want to drink liquor either. So he tells Phil that the judge is a drunk who beats his mother! Phil underhandedly sets up chorus girl Consuela to arrange a tête-à-tête with Andy. Rooney's scenes with Andy and the chorus girl are the most amusing moments in the film. Playing every bit the small-town bumpkin completely out of place in the posh room of a chorus girl, he panics as soon as she enters the room and runs away. He does not simply run from the room but is shown scurrying down the stairs, slipping onto the lobby floor, and bumping into others as he bursts out the front entrance.

Director George Seitz, who regularly helms the Hardy family movies, does a nice job of using mise-en-scène to show the vastness of the family's new digs. His establishing shots of the family in the mansion are wide enough to show them framed by their posh surroundings. The expanse of each shot calls attention to their having been displaced from smaller circumstances and placed rather abruptly into a bigger and wider environment that is not exactly conducive to the lifestyle with which they're familiar.

All of the scenes, both comical and for purposes of plot exposition, show that the Hardy family does not belong among the wealthy. They are best when settled in their comfortable middle-class environment in a small town. So, naturally, the plot reveals that, due to circumstances regarding the relationship of the heir and its lack of immediacy, the Hardys will not be inheriting any money. As Mrs. Hardy states, "We wouldn't ever be the Hardy family with two million dollars. We'd just be separate people living in the same house." But as another plot point that extends beyond those parameters, *The Hardys Ride High* is another typical, enjoyable series entry, as the films continued to enjoy box office success.

There is more emphasis on the family as a unit, especially with Aunt Milly getting the tangential scenes that usually went to the Marian character, so with the next Hardy film, the idea was to spotlight Andy almost completely. *Andy Hardy Gets Spring Fever* would be among the most popular entries in the entire series. At the same time, producer Arthur Freed began preparing a movie version of the musical *Babes in Arms*, the property having been secured with the intention of casting Mickey Rooney and Judy Garland in the leading roles. The year 1939 was already appearing to be even more promising for Rooney's career than the triumphant 1938 had been.

ANDY HARDY GETS SPRING FEVER

(MGM, 1939)

Director: W. S. Van Dyke II
Screenplay: Kay Van Riper. *Characters:* Aurania Rouverol
Producer: Lou L. Ostrow. *Cinematographer:* Lester White. *Editor:* Ben Lewis
Cast: Lewis Stone (Judge James K. "Jim" Hardy), Mickey Rooney (Andrew "Andy" Hardy), Cecilia Parker (Marian Hardy), Fay Holden (Mrs. Emily "Emmy" Hardy), Ann Rutherford (Polly Benedict), Sara Haden (Aunt Milly Forrest), Helen Gilbert (Miss Rose Meredith), Terry Kilburn (Harmon "Stickin' Plaster" Higgenbotham Jr.), John T. Murray (Don David), George Breakston ("Beezy" Anderson), Charles Peck (Tommy), Sidney Miller (Sidney Miller, Stage Manager), Addison Richards (Mr. George Benedict), Olaf Hytten (Mr. Harmon Higgenbotham Sr.), Erville Alderson (Henry, the Bailiff), Robert Kent (Lt. Charles Copley), Stanley Andrews (James Willet), Barbara Bedford (Miss Howard), James Bush (Bill Franklin), John Dilson (Mr. Davis), Byron Foulger (Mark Hansen), Harry Hayden (Mr. MacMahon), Ivan Miller (Mr. Miller), Ralph Remley (Mr. Anderson), William Bailey (Bank Employee), Mildred Coles (Doria), Mickey Lee (Mimi), Maxine Conrad (Usher)
Released: July 21, 1939
Specs: 85 minutes; black and white
Availability: DVD (Warner Archive Collection: *The Andy Hardy Film Collection: Volume* 2)

About this movie, Mickey Rooney said,

> I always thought *Andy Hardy Gets Spring Fever* was one of the best Hardy pictures we did. Andy starts to become a man, and the fact that they have him putting on a show sets up the pictures I was about to do with Judy Garland.[1]

Rooney was correct with his recollections many decades after appearing in this pivotal 1939 effort. By now, the seventh entry in the series, there were some constants that audiences simply expected.

The films invariably open with Judge Hardy sentencing a wayward young man in his court, retiring to his chambers, and being visited by a man, or men, who are instrumental in his portion of the narrative. Then we move to Andy's central part of the movie. First, he discovers girlfriend Polly is once again smitten with a handsome older man. In many of the films she seems to frequently give some level of attention to various college boys or service men who are family friends, but her interest is no more than a distant attraction. However, it always makes Andy feel more like a boy than a man, and he usually feels he has to respond in some manner.

Poster for *Andy Hardy Gets Spring Fever*

In this movie, Andy develops a crush on the young woman who takes over as drama teacher at his school. When a play he has written is chosen as the one the students will be performing for the school, he works closely with Miss Meredith and his infatuation deepens to the point where he wants to marry her. Rather than presenting this situation as comical or as merely a ploy to upset Polly, Andy is shown to be quite serious, to want to enter the workforce upon graduation rather than college and truly pursue this choice.

Less concentration is allowed Judge Hardy's subplot where the old aqueduct land he purchased in an earlier film is brought up again as being worth money. The judge discovers that this is a sham and finds himself amid the shady deal, which challenges not only his authority but also his reputation. As a respected member of the community, he inspired others to invest in the enterprise. The subplot involving the judge does result in his sitting down and having a serious talk with Mrs. Hardy, whom he usually shields from his troubles. In one of the more moving scenes in the dramatic portion of the film, the judge tells his wife, "I've been a fool," and rather than being naive and without understanding, as presented rather stereotypically in earlier efforts, she is very grounded, optimistic, and shows genuine loving support for her husband. Mrs. Hardy's belief in him gives the judge confidence. Of course, it all works out in the end.

The most fun occurs when Andy's play is performed for five hundred members of the audience. Young student "Stickin' Plaster," a stage hand in charge of the moon's appearance on stage, pulls a little too hard on the string attached to the prop, and it glides across the sky in the background (and then back again) as the audience laughs. This scene takes on a more serious tone when, between acts, Andy discovers that Miss Meredith's boyfriend has arrived and sees them just as he is to once again take the stage. This trauma first results in him barely able to say his lines, but then he recites the lines with greater gusto, as they deal with rejection in much the same manner as what he's actually experiencing. Director W. S. Van Dyke, who took over the helm from regular Hardy family director George Seitz (who was busy with another project), does a nice job of cutting to Miss Meredith backstage responding nonverbally to Andy's recitation of the dialogue that she realizes is meant for her.

Andy is forced to confront the sort of heartbreak that is at a somewhat higher level than previous sorrows. Maturity is now crowding adolescence. He is forced to take stock of himself, his situation, his immediate future, and his long-range plans. This situation was a real turning point for the character. And the fact that Andy has the responsibility of putting on his own show, in which he has the lead, offers another level of enforced maturity and leadership. It is also the portent to Rooney's next film as Andy, *Babes in Arms*, which is the first of his putting-on-a-show musicals opposite Judy Garland.

However, the film ends on a comical note, which lets the audience know that there is still plenty of adolescent vitality left in Andy Hardy. He shows up at Polly's post-play party after having a serious talk with Miss Meredith and straightening everything out. He shows up acting very detached and mature, taking any compliments in stride, and approaching young Stickin' Plaster with forgiveness. Polly, however, will have none of this and plants a big kiss on his mouth. In full Andy Hardy mode, he shouts, "Woo-woo," and embraces her as the picture fades.

Helen Gilbert does a nice job as Miss Meredith, exhibiting a mature contrast to Polly Benedict and the other girls in Andy's life. MGM hoped the attractive Gilbert would be a successful actress for their studio (the Hardy series continuing to be something of a training ground for possible future stars). She was a cellist in the MGM orchestra when executives noticed her beauty and tried her out as an actress. This is her first film and might be her most substantial role, as she ended up making only a handful of movies, and often in very small parts. If she is recalled today, it is more likely for her six failed marriages than her movie career.

As far as Van Dyke's direction of the film, he was known for filming only one take for each scene, which wasn't always conducive to every project. He had a good track record, having helmed *Tarzan the Ape Man* (1932) and *The Thin Man* (1934), but according to Ann Rutherford in Scott Eyman's book *Lion of Hollywood: The Life and Legend of Louis B. Mayer*:

> "Woody" Van Dyke would print the first take if you got half the words right. But he had never worked with a Hardy film, and when they saw the rushes, they called back George Seitz.[2]

Along with Van Dyke's more hurried approach, his vision is also darker in tone. Usually when Judge Hardy is confronted by problems, he quietly works them out. And while his reaching out to Mrs. Hardy results in an interesting scene, he appears to be far more unsettled by his circumstances than in other movies. He appears flustered, less in control. It is an interestingly different take on the character, but, as Rutherford also stated for Eyman, "It wasn't a Hardy picture."[3] Frank Nugent in his *New York Times* review noticed the change:

> Serious-minded Hardy fans, who value integrity of character more highly than variety of incident, may well protest against the psychological violation

> of old Judge Hardy. It was only last April, in *The Hardys Ride High*, that the old judge figured as a shrewd, unmaterialistic philosopher, above such petty hurts as the loss of a $2,000,000 inheritance. Now, though we can see plainly that he is still Lewis Stone, we must accept him as a person sufficiently greedy and credulous to fall for a confidence scheme which the average boardwalk sucker would see through. Of course, he gets out handily in the end, but the principle's the same.[4]

However, the film was still accepted as a successfully produced Hardy family outing by most critics. *Variety* stated,

> The Hardy series swings into its third year, gaining audience popularity with each succeeding release. *Andy Hardy Gets Spring Fever* maintains the homey atmosphere of the typical American family of the Midwest town, pacing the situations with verve and speed in most competent fashion.[5]

Despite its darker town and some pivotal changes in the characters, *Andy Hardy Gets Spring Fever* became one of the top box office attractions of the year, and one of the biggest hits of the Hardy family series. In fact, over at Columbia Pictures' short-subject department, veteran comedian Andy Clyde, now engaged in a series of two-reelers for the studio, did a parody of the film's title, calling one of his movies *Andy Clyde Gets Spring Chicken*.

BABES IN ARMS

(MGM, 1939)

Director: Busby Berkeley
Screenplay: Jack McGowan, Kay Van Riper, based on the play by Lorenz Hart and Richard Rodgers
Producer: Arthur Freed. *Cinematographer:* Ray June. *Editor:* Frank Sullivan
Cast: Mickey Rooney (Mickey Moran), Judy Garland (Patsy Barton), Charles Winninger (Joe Moran), Guy Kibbee (Judge Black), June Preisser (Rosalie Essex), Grace Hayes (Florrie Moran), Betty Jaynes (Molly), Henry Hull (Maddox), Douglas McPhail (Don Brice), Rand Brooks (Jeff Steele), Leni Lynn (Dody), Johnny Sheffield (Bobs[1]), Barnett Parker (William), Ann Shoemaker (Mrs. Barton), Margaret Hamilton (Martha Steele), Joseph Crehan (Essex), George McKay (Brice), Henry Roquemore (Shaw), Lelah Tyler (Mrs. Brice), Charles Brown (Larry), Frank Darien (Mr. Parks), James Donlan (Fred), Sidney Miller (Sid), Libby Taylor (Millicent), Mary Treen (Receptionist), Robert Emmet Keane (Agent), Cyril Ring (Vaudevillian), Ann Bupp (Girl), Lon McCallister (Boy)
Songs: "Babes in Arms" (music by Richard by Lorenz Hart; sung by Douglas McPhail, Mickey Rooney, Judy Garland, and chorus); "Where or When" (music by Richard Rodgers, lyrics by Lorenz Hart; sung by Douglas McPhail, Betty Jaynes, and Judy Garland); "Good Morning" (music by Nacio Herb Brown, lyrics by Arthur Freed; sung by Judy Garland and Mickey Rooney); "God's Country" (music by Harold Arlen, lyrics by E. Y. Harburg; sung and danced by Mickey Rooney, Douglas McPhail, Judy Garland, Betty Jaynes, and chorus); "You Are My Lucky Star" (music by Nacio Herb Brown, lyrics by Arthur Freed; sung by Betty Jaynes); "Broadway Rhythm" (music by Nacio Herb Brown, lyrics by Arthur Freed; sung by Judy Garland); "My Daddy Was a Minstrel Man" (music and lyrics by Roger Edens; sung by Judy Garland); "Gwine to Rune All

Night" ["De Camptown Races"] (music and lyrics by Stephen Foster; sung by chorus); "The Old Folks at Home [Swanee River]" (music and lyrics by Stephen Foster; sung by chorus); "Oh! Susanna" (music and lyrics by Stephen Foster; sung and danced by Judy Garland and Mickey Rooney); "Mr. Bones and Mr. Tambo" (music and lyrics by Roger Edens; performed by Douglas McPhail, Mickey Rooney, Judy Garland, and chorus); "Ida! Sweet as Apple Cider" (music by Eddie Munson, lyrics by Eddie Leonard; sung by Mickey Rooney); "Moonlight Bay" (music by Percy Wenrich, lyrics by Edward Madden; sung by chorus and danced by Mickey Rooney); "I'm Just Wild about Harry" (music by Eubie Blake, lyrics by Noble Sissle; sung and danced by Judy Garland, Mickey Rooney, and chorus); "My Day" (music and lyrics by unknown; performed by Mickey Rooney and Judy Garland imitating Franklin Delano and Eleanor Roosevelt[2])

Released: October 13, 1939

Specs: 94 minutes; black and white

Availability: DVD (Warner Home Video: *The Mickey Rooney and Judy Garland Collection*)

In his April 2014 obituary for Mickey Rooney in the *National Review*, writer Jack Fowler stated, "*Babes in Arms* has aged (a lot!), and can make *Leave It to Beaver* seem like *Mad Max*, but its watchability is overshadowed by its being the quintessential Rooney-Garland team-up."[3] While today *Babes in Arms* may indeed seem to be a relic from another age, that is very much a part of its charm.

Babes in Arms became the prototype for a short series of musicals about a group of ambitious teens putting on their own show. It launched Mickey Rooney and Judy Garland as the first teenage movie team. It started songwriter Arthur Freed's career as a top-level producer of movie musicals. And in a year where MGM offered such iconic films as *The Wizard of Oz* (which Garland had just completed when she started on this movie) and *Gone with the Wind*, *Babes in Arms* was one of the biggest box office hits of 1939 and garnered Mickey Rooney his first Oscar nomination.

Babes in Arms started life as a musical play by Richard Rodgers and Lorenz Hart. The two composers saw a group of children playing on a playground and became fascinated by the kids' behavior and talked about how effective youngsters might be if given adult responsibilities. They ended up writing a musical about teenagers putting on their own show. The songs they composed for this musical included many that later became standards, such as "Where or When" and "The Lady Is a Tramp."

Babes in Arms opened April 14, 1937, on Broadway at the Shubert Theatre. Three months later it transferred to the Majestic Theatre. It closed on December 18, 1937, after 289 performances. The cast included Dan Dailey, Mitzi Green, and the Nicholas Brothers.

Songwriter Arthur Freed was working in MGM's music department when he proposed to studio head Louis B. Mayer that the studio should do a movie version of *Babes in Arms*. He believed it would be a great vehicle for both Mickey Rooney and Judy Garland. Freed had also proposed that MGM do a film version of L. Frank Baum's children's book *The Wizard of Oz*, which was currently shooting. Mayer allowed Freed to produce a film version of *Babes in Arms* as an MGM movie. However, some changes were made immediately. Movie studios preferred their own songs be used in musicals, so only three written for the original show appear in the movie, and only two—the title tune and "Where or When"—are performed. The third, "The Lady Is a Tramp," is only heard as background music. The other songs were either old standards used in the show-within-a-show or composed specifically for the film version.

Mickey Moran (Rooney), his friend Patsy (Garland), and several other young people are the offspring of vaudeville stars. Outcasts in the community due to their nontraditional lifestyle, which includes frequent lapses in education due to traveling with their parents, the youngsters are at risk of being sent to boarding schools. Community leader Martha Steele's constant complaints to Judge Black about the welfare of these children are, however, usually ignored. The judge happens to like the show folk and appreciates that they work hard to entertain others.

The establishing scenes of *Babes in Arms* show a respect for authenticity on the part of the director, Busby Berkeley. Having helmed such Warner Brothers musical classics as *42nd Street* (1932) and *Footlight Parade* (1933), Berkeley knew how to tell a story while maintaining both the musical and humorous elements within the dramatic structure. The establishing shot, set in 1921, has the camera panning some photos of vaudeville legends like Will Rogers that are displayed in the lobby of the Palace Theatre in New York City. It then edits to an audience laughing happily at the antics of Joe Moran, Mickey's father, who finds out while on stage that he's become a father. Berkeley's authenticity not only includes the casting of actual vaudeville veteran Charles Winninger in the role, but there are also more subtle examples, such as there being no microphones on the stage while Joe Moran is performing. In 1921 vaudeville, one had to project without the help of any electronics. A montage of sequences showing how movies are slowly taking away the vaudeville audience follows this scene. When sound films come along, vaudeville is declared dead. As part of this montage, to show young Mickey becoming a part of his parents' act at a young age, Berkeley wisely edits in footage of young Mickey Rooney performing a dance act on stage from the 1933 movie *Broadway to Hollywood*, which is decidedly more authentic than simply hiring a youngster to play Mickey Moran as a child.

When the film then picks up with the modern era, things have become difficult for the struggling entertainers. Fortunately, a booking agent has decided to put together a revival show featuring all of these entertainers, believing the nostalgia might make for a successful tour. Meanwhile, Mickey has just received a hundred-dollar advance from a top musical publisher for a song he wrote. Chagrined that they are not to tour with the parents, Mickey and the other offspring decide to put on their own show.

Mickey Rooney's enthusiasm in this role is more emotionally uninhibited than any in his career to this point. He and Judy Garland were actually offspring of showbiz performers and really had been entertaining since they were infants. Rooney invests so much enthusiasm and confidence in the Mickey Moran role that it completely overrides some of the lapses in logic, such as the ability of someone so young to effectively put together a show of such magnitude, with a full orchestra and carefully choreographed musical numbers. Garland once again plays the plain Jane supportive friend who believes in Mickey completely but has her own abundant talent. Aware of her ability, but completely without ego or pretention, Patsy is excited to be the female lead in Mickey's ambitious production.

Busby Berkeley's penchant for big production numbers follows Mickey's announcement that the kids will put on their own show. Performing the title song, this large group of young people marches through town, singing how they are no longer "babes in arms," but individuals with their own talent who can deliver with greater success than their parents. Berkeley shoots this sequence mostly with medium shots, keeping most of the kids in the frame. The camera tracks them as they march through town, with leading singers like Douglas McPhail and Betty Jaynes out front with Rooney and Garland. Jaynes, a classically trained opera singer, is playing Mickey's younger sister. McPhail's operatic baritone, belting out the line "babes in arms" is perhaps the most forceful part of this musical number, as is his tall, imposing presence. McPhail and Jaynes would marry soon after this film, but their operatic style, popularized by Nelson Eddy and Jeanette MacDonald, was soon out of vogue. Their marriage failed; McPhail took to drinking and committed suicide in 1944. Jaynes would last be seen in a 1952 *I Love Lucy* episode, but she was still alive, in her nineties, well into the twenty-first century.

Berkeley spotlights Jaynes and McPhail again when the youngsters are shown rehearsing the "Where or When" musical number. In this scene, they are backed up by Carl Moldren's baby orchestra, a group of children who performed in an orchestra with specially made instruments. However, in this movie, the children are used as a visual only; the MGM orchestra is dubbing in the music. Berkeley uses this visual to exhibit how Mickey is incorporating the talents of all manner of showbiz children in the community, even if only for rehearsals. Berkeley offers a nice establishing shot, panning over the child orchestra as the camera tracks Mickey and Patsy walking toward singers Jaynes and McPhail.

The dramatic element of the story is essentially the difficulties of vaudeville has-beens trying to maintain any success in show business, while their children are ambitiously putting on a musical to appeal to more modern tastes. However, there is also a dramatic subplot specifically centering on Mickey and Patsy. In order to finance his expensive vision, Mickey agrees to cast a wealthy former child star in the lead. The former child star had once been Baby Rosalie in the movies, but now, as a teenager, has grown out of the role. Her success has made her wealthy, privileged, and not used to anything but a starring role. Taking a liking to the enthusiastic Mickey, Rosalie agrees to finance the show and star in it. This means Mickey must relegate Patsy to the role of understudy.

Mickey Rooney and Judy Garland

This plot development allows Garland's screen character to once again sadly realize her second-class status in her beloved Mickey's life despite her constant encouragement and support of his idea and his process. Patsy accepts her understudy status to the prettier and more popular girl—something that had already become a running thread in Garland's films opposite Rooney.

Along with the dramatic structure and musical sequences, *Babes in Arms* does not neglect comedy. Mickey's visit to Rosalie's palatial home begins with a stuffy butler saying she cannot see him because she is expecting a theater impresario. Mickey turns to leave, then does a comic double take and says, "Wait a minute, that's me!" More humor is garnered from his subsequent attempts to fit in with her as they have dinner, complete with his choking as he attempts to smoke an expensive cigar.

Impressions had been a part of Mickey Rooney's stage act for a while, but *Babes in Arms* is the first time they are showcased in a major film. Mickey Moran is directing a scene that is not going well, so he tells one actor to be more like Clark Gable and another to be more like Lionel Barrymore. To demonstrate, Mickey dons one actor's prop mustache and recites the dialogue as Gable, then hurries over and dons a white-haired wig to respond as Barrymore. Rooney said during an interview,

> We had been doing that scene in rehearsal, and word got back to both Gable and Barrymore, so when we filmed it they were on the set watching. Even though I knew and had worked with both of them by that time, it was still intimidating to be doing impressions of them while they watched. When we finished the scene, Barrymore said he liked it. But Gable came up to me and said, "Mickey, one of us stinks!"[4]

This delightful scene also further informs the conflict between Mickey and Patsy as Mickey ends the scene by kissing Rosalie, as it is part of the script. Patsy walks in just as that happens and runs away hurt. She leaves on the next train to catch up to her parents on the next vaudeville stop. Her mother, an old trouper, insists she never give up on a show. The valiant Patsy returns. Of course MGM movies always resolve things happily, so the night of the show Rosalie's father bursts into the backstage area as the actors are putting on their makeup. Having been out of town, he is furious to discover his child-star daughter has agreed to appear in a local production, believing she is too good for this level and stating, "I am working on a comeback for her!" Patsy, the understudy, goes on in her place. The fact that Rosalie was comfortable with appearing in the production despite her feelings of privilege and that the story gives her a stage father rather than the stereotypical stage mother are a couple of unusual and commendable elements of this part of the plot.

Political correctness has caused many to approach the scenes presenting Mickey's show with disdain, as it is all done in blackface with the youngsters performing old standards like "De Camptown Races" and "Swanee River," often with unsettling black vernacular. It can be somewhat defended by its context and the understanding that blackface was an ordinary part of vaudeville used even by some top-level African American performers like Bert Williams. However, decades after civil rights legislation, such scenes from films made during the first half of the twentieth century can be off-putting to some viewers.

Since the show is being performed outdoors it is at the mercy of the elements, so when a hurricane sweeps through, it is forced to end early. The parents' vaudeville revival tour is also cancelled due to a lack of ticket sales. Embittered, Joe Moran wants no more to do with show business. He and the other parents agree to send the students to boarding school, alleviating the financial burden but also allowing them to get an education and achieve a trade outside of show business.

Just in time, Mickey gets a letter from a top theatrical producer who saw his show and wants to produce it. Mickey convinces him to hire Joe as a technical adviser and all ends well. Once the story concludes, a new number from the show, "God's Country," is presented to close the film.

Babes in Arms began production just after producer Freed and Judy Garland had finished shooting *The Wizard of Oz*. Throughout the filming of *Babes in Arms*, Freed was battling to keep the song "Over the Rainbow" in *The Wizard of Oz* against the wishes of those who felt it slowed down the action. Fortunately, the producer got his way. Rooney recalled,

> I remember when we were recording the songs for the picture. Judy had to get in costume to do retakes on *Wizard of Oz*, and then hurried to the sound department to record a duet with me for *Babes in Arms*. So here I am singing a song with Judy in her Dorothy costume, including the pigtails.[5]

Filming on *Babes in Arms* went a few days over its scheduled production time, but the entire film, including rehearsals, setups, recording, filming, and postproduction, was completed in eleven weeks. Despite the efficiency of the production and the top-level performances and direction, it wasn't always easy. Judy Garland had a hard time connecting with director Busby Berkeley and lacked any time to rest after the grueling pace of *The Wizard of Oz*. Plus, as they finished filming *Babes in Arms*, Rooney and Garland were sent on a press junket to promote *The Wizard of Oz*, which had just been released. At one point on this tour, Garland collapsed backstage from exhaustion and Rooney had to ad-lib on his own until she recovered enough to join him. Some Garland bios claim that her pill consumption began around this time.

The premiere of *Babes in Arms* was a real triumph for all involved. Mickey Rooney recalled,

> We didn't realize then it would become such a big hit, or that it would be the first in a series of backyard musicals. After the premiere ended, Judy cried when she heard the applause. We were just two kids who worked hard and now we are being applauded by all of Hollywood.[6]

The film was an immediate box office smash once it was released to theaters, and it was applauded by critics as well. *Variety* stated,

> Despite the Rooney dominance throughout, there are several sterling performances by the younger talent. Judy Garland most effectively carries the adolescent romantic interest opposite him.[7]

The *New York Times* also liked the film and continued to be taken aback by Rooney's enthusiasm as well as his surviving what appeared to be overexposure:

> To us who have watched Mickey Rooney grow from a cloud no bigger than a man's hand on the horizon into a juvenile institution on whom Metro-Goldwyn-Mayer leans as the Ibsen drama used to lean on Mrs. Fiske, the screen version of "Babes In Arms" will come as no surprise. To those unprepared, on the other hand, he may burst as suddenly as did Noel Coward upon the circulation-library client who penciled in the margin of the master's autobiography the astonished query: "Who IS this man?" Not that Master Rooney does not personally justify himself: on the contrary, his adenoidal imitation of Clark Gable and his super-sibilant, explosive portrait of Lionel Barrymore may well be among the more cherished impersonations of the modern screen. Even his hair—which does seem a bit thick—might be acceptable, but the point is that even in musical comedy no one of his ostensibly tender years should be in the spotlight as often as Master Rooney is.[8]

As an indication of audience response, we have the section in *Box Office*, the trade magazine that offered a section where theater owners would report audience response to movies that were playing. For *Babes in Arms*, the comments included the following:

> "Pleased 100% and drew considerable extra business. This was Mickey's greatest opportunity and he didn't miss a step. Judy is mighty fine by herself too."
>
> "Enjoyed by all. Some saw it twice."

"This swell piece of entertainment really brought in the shekels for us. Rooney proved himself a real trouper. The Garland kid was right behind him all the way. She has more rooters with each picture."[9]

The budget for *Babes in Arms* was roughly $745,000 and grossed $3,335,000. Compare that to *The Wizard of Oz*, which had a budget of $2,777,000 and grossed $3,017,000.[10] *Babes in Arms* earned more at the box office than *The Wizard of Oz* when both were released in 1939. For his enthusiastic performance in *Babes in Arms*, Mickey Rooney received his first Oscar nomination for Best Actor. Rooney said,

> The competition I had for Best Actor included Jimmy Stewart for *Mr. Smith Goes to Washington* and Clark Gable for *Gone with the Wind*. And, of course, the actor who won, Robert Donat for *Goodbye, Mr. Chips*. What a year to be nominated! The greatest year in American movies! I didn't have a chance.[11]

On November 9, 1941, radio's *Screen Guild Theater* broadcast a thirty-minute adaptation of the movie with Mickey Rooney and Judy Garland reprising their film roles

Mickey Rooney was then placed in another Andy Hardy movie, which, by comparison, was a rather relaxing project after what he was expected to do in a big-budget musical and subsequent press junket. Even so, one has to marvel at the actor's energy during this period in his career.

21

JUDGE HARDY AND SON

(MGM, 1939)

Director: George B. Seitz
Screenplay: Carey Wilson
Producer: Lou L. Ostrow. *Cinematographer:* Lester White. *Editor:* Ben Lewis
Cast: Mickey Rooney ("Andy" Hardy), Lewis Stone (Judge James Hardy), Fay Holden (Mrs. Emily Hardy), Cecilia Parker (Marian Hardy), Ann Rutherford (Polly Benedict), Sara Haden (Aunt Milly), June Preisser (Euphrasia), Maria Ouspenskaya (Mrs. Volduzzi), Henry Hull (Dr. Jones), Martha O'Driscoll (Elvie), Leona Maricle (Mrs. Horton), Margaret Early (Clarabelle), George Breakston (Beezy), Eron Brecher (Mr. Volduzzi), Edna Holland (Nurse Trowbridge), Joe Yule (Munk, tire salesman), Cliff Clark (Officer O'Shea), James B. Carson (Mogilby), Marie Blake (Augusta)
Released: December 22, 1939
Specs: 90 minutes; black and white
Availability: DVD (Warner Archive Collection: *The Andy Hardy Film Collection: Volume 1*)

Judge Hardy and Son is an apt title for this eighth entry into the Hardy series as the conflict offered to Judge Hardy at the outset of the movie is solved with Andy's cooperation. Usually the judge deals with his own situation as a subplot while Andy's comical misfortunes take center stage. These are blended for *Judge Hardy and Son*, which fluctuates between heavy drama and light comedy at somewhat greater extremes than any other Hardy family movie.

As with most Hardy movies, *Judge Hardy and Son* opens in Judge Hardy's chambers. Mr. and Mrs. Volduzzi, an elderly couple, are with the judge. Mr. Volduzzi has been laid off from his job, and they are faced with foreclosure on their home. They deny having any children to help, insisting they once had a daughter, who is now dead. However, the way they say that makes Judge Hardy suspicious. Andy desperately needs some money to put new tires on his car. The judge tells Andy that if he can find the daughter of this couple, he will reward him with money for tires. Andy figures the daughter might have a daughter of her own whose middle name is the mother's maiden name (which was, in fact, fairly common at one time). Andy checks the school records for girls whose middle name starts with a V (for Volduzzi), and intends to visit each one to see if there might be a connection that can help his father and gain him the needed funds for his tires.

The comical plot involving Andy more specifically deals with a Fourth of July festival and an essay contest. The essay contest is on Alexander Hamilton, and there is a fifty-dollar prize, but only for girls (boys who enter can win a set of encyclopedias). The Fourth of July fireworks and dance is an event to which Andy plans to take Polly, and that means more money for the admission, flowers, and so on.

Nearly all of this is played for comedy. Andy wants to get a girl to enter the essay he has written, and then split the winnings with her. He gets nowhere with Clarabelle, a southern girl who insists the essay should be about Robert E. Lee despite the contest asking for a report on Alexander Hamilton. He tries to make a deal with giggly, airheaded Euphrasia, but she blackmails him into taking her to the fireworks and dance. Finally, there is Elvie, a girl who is angry at her family life despite material wealth and privilege. After a series of circumstances, Andy discovers that Elvie is really L.V., and her middle name is indeed Volduzzi. Her mother is the daughter Judge Hardy is seeking.

However, one lengthy tangential sequence completely throws this film off kilter. Mother Hardy falls ill with pleurisy that develops into pneumonia. She remains at home in her room, but with round-the-clock nurses and frequent home visits from a doctor. Until she passes her crisis, the family, led by Judge Hardy, audibly prays for her. It is a very dark sequence, rests heavily on the religious factor, and doesn't particularly fit the rest of the proceedings. But audiences liked this sort of thing, and its presence in the movie was successful at the time. The sequence mainly served to show that being confronted with a life-or-death situation perhaps helped Andy grow up a bit.

MGM studio head Louis B. Mayer continued to give special attention to the Hardy family series, especially to how Andy Hardy was presented. According to Bosley Crowther's book *The Lion's Share*, screenwriter Carey

Poster for *Judge Hardy and Son*

Wilson was working on the script when Mayer came into his office objecting to a scene where Andy prays for his mother's recovery. Mayer stated, "You see, you're now a Hollywood character. You've forgotten your simple, honest boyhood. You don't remember how a real boy would pray. This is how a boy would do it." Mayer got on his knees and said, "Dear God, please don't let my mom die, because she's the best mom in the world. Thank you, God."[1]

One delightful cameo in *Judge Hardy and Son* features Joe Yule, Mickey's real-life father, who had left the family when Mickey was very young. Continuing to tour in burlesque, he was playing in the Los Angeles area and Mickey went to see him backstage. They had not seen each other in many years. Rooney recalls in his autobiography that the two tearfully embraced and remained connected for the rest of Yule's life. Mayer, however, became quite angry when Joe Yule started billing himself as Mickey Rooney's father in his burlesque show. Risqué burlesque shows were hardly conducive to the Andy Hardy image Mayer had cultivated and continued to fiercely protect, so he asked Rooney to intervene and ask his father to stop billing himself that way. Rooney refused. Mayer then gave Yule a job doing small roles in MGM films for more money than he was getting in burlesque. Rooney supported this and was pleased to play a scene with his father in *Judge Hardy and Son*.

Frank Nugent stated in his *New York Times* review,

> Mom gets sick but pulls through all right, just in time to avoid spoiling Andy's Fourth of July; Andy piles up a load of amusing debts, but manages to liquidate them all by the exercise of kindness, unselfishness and honesty, and the old foreign couple who come to the judge for help don't get evicted from their home after all. But for a minute there, our hitherto exclusively comical friends Lewis Stone, Mickey Rooney, Cecilia Parker, Fay Holden and Ann Rutherford had us scared. Everybody, of course, gives a beautiful performance. With such veterans of the screen as Lewis Stone and Mickey Rooney what else could you expect?[2]

While filming *Judge Hardy and Son*, Mickey Rooney and Lewis Stone appeared in a short film titled *Andy Hardy's Dilemma*. Andy balks at the judge, refusing to give him money to buy a car when he has no problem writing a $200 check to charity. Judge Hardy takes Andy to an orphanage, an orthopedic hospital, and other places that show people in need who depend on charitable donations. The short film was a quintessential "message short" similar to what the studio would eventually start doing with the Our Gang series once they purchased it from the Hal Roach Studios in 1938.

Judge Hardy and Son was Mickey Rooney's final film release for the year 1939. This has been considered the greatest year for American movies, and it was also perhaps the greatest in Rooney's career. He ended the year as the number one box office star in the nation, his films being more popular and making more money than those featuring any of the stars then active, including Clark Gable, Bette Davis, Spencer Tracy, James Cagney, and other such heavyweights. Amazingly, he would continue to be the number one star in the nation for the next two years. His salary increased from $5,000 per film to $2,500 per week. This was a lot of money in 1939—but not when one considers that the studio was making many millions from each Mickey Rooney movie.

YOUNG TOM EDISON

(MGM, 1940)

Director: Norman Taurog
Screenplay: Bradbury Foote, Dore Schary, Hugo Butler, based on material by H. Alan Dunn
Producer: John W. Considine Jr. *Cinematographer:* Sidney Wagner. *Editor:* Elmo Veron
Cast: Mickey Rooney (Tom Edison), Fay Bainter (Mrs. Samuel Edison), George Bancroft (Samuel Edison), Virginia Weidler (Tannie Edison), Eugene Pallette (Mr. Nelson), Victor Kilian (Mr. Dingle), Bobby Jordan (Joe Dingle), J. M. Kerrigan (Mr. McCarney), Lloyd Corrigan (Dr. Pender), John Kellogg (Bill Edison), Clem Bevans (Mr. Waddell), Eily Malyon (School Teacher), Harry Shannon (Captain Brackett), Wade Boteler (Si Weaver), Eddy Chandler (Mr. Briggs), Fern Emmett (Mrs. McCartney), Mitchell Lewis (McGuire), Emory Parnell (Bob), Victor Potel (Tompkins), Mickey Rentschler (Johnny), Marvin Stephens (Frank Allen), Joe Whitehead (Hodge), Frank Whitbeck (Narrator)
Released: March 15, 1940
Specs: 86 minutes; black and white
Availability: DVD (Warner Archive)

After the success of *Boys Town*, MGM was at a loss as to how to once again team Spencer Tracy and Mickey Rooney in an effective vehicle. Producer John Considine wanted to do a film on the life of Thomas Edison, with Rooney playing him as a boy and Tracy portraying the inventor as a man. However, there were many details to each portion of the story, so the decision was made to produce two films. The Spencer Tracy feature *Edison the Man* was in production close to the same time as *Young Tom Edison* and would be released two months after this film. Considine secured the services of *Boys Town* director Norman Taurog, and one of the film's writers, Dore Schary, for *Young Tom Edison.*

Young Tom Edison is a delightfully entertaining Mickey Rooney movie, but it is not much for history. Even the opening written prologue indicates that this is about "a typical American boy" and "in all its essential facts it is a true story." Some of the facts about Edison's boyhood are accurate, but in order to paint a more exciting and heroic picture of the inventor, the film has him rescuing a train by sending a danger message in code with a steam whistle; jumping onto a young child playing on train tracks and covering him as a train rolls over them, its wheels on either side; and setting up lamps and a mirror reflector for brightness, allowing a surgeon to perform surgery on his mother. Some of the fabrications are done for amusement, such as a scene when Tom mixes chemicals on a train, ending up with dangerous nitroglycerin and putting all on board in danger. The comical reaction of the conductor and the passengers, plus the shot of rotund Eugene Pallette climbing across train cars to get to the engineer and ask him to stop the train, makes this scene more breezily amusing than tense. The tension comes when Tom has to carefully lower the bottle of nitroglycerin on a string into the rapids below. It explodes when safely away.

There is also some element of melodrama that is utilized for purposes of cinematic entertainment. When Tom goes from place to place attempting to find a job and gets laughed at by every potential employer, Rooney is shown, center frame, walking dejectedly, and angrily, in the rain, their laughter echoing in his head.

While Rooney had played noted literary character Huckleberry Finn with the usual Andy Hardy exuberance, his performance as Edison is quieter and subtler. As noted elsewhere in the text, Louis B. Mayer considered Andy Hardy the quintessential Hollywood depiction of a young male. Thus, all of Rooney's portrayals had some element of that character. This could be off-putting to reviewers, who sometimes had a more jaded reaction to superstardom than audiences. Rooney had his picture on the cover of *Time* magazine on March 18, 1940, just as this movie was going into general release. The piece, by James Agee, called Rooney "a rope-haired, kazoo-voiced kid with a comic-strip face, who until this week had never appeared in a picture without mugging or overacting it," but admitted that in it Rooney offered his "most sober and restrained performance to date." Agee wasn't impressed with the film itself, however, stating, "If this picture has any influence on the Edison legend, the inventor of electric light will be thought of in future years as an inspired masochist."[1]

The film succeeds as entertainment where it doesn't succeed as history, with a typically strong performance by Rooney and a supporting cast filled with veterans, including Virginia Weidler as Edison's younger sister, George Bancroft as his father, Fay Bainter as his mother, and Bobby Jordan of *The Dead End Kids* as his rival, Joe Dingle. Jordan's tenure as a Dead End Kid at Warner Brothers was just concluding, and he was about to do double duty as one of the East Side Kids at Monogram studios, and the Little Tough Guys at Universal. Rooney recalled,

> Even though we didn't work at the same studios, I knew the actors who played with the Dead End Kids well. A lot of the younger Hollywood actors went to the same parties, and we all got to know each other. Bobby Jordan was a friend of mine and I was happy that he got a part in a picture I was doing at MGM. Bobby Jordan was a very good actor A few years later when I was married to Ava Gardner and we found her a role in one of their pictures,[2] I called Leo Gorcey and asked him to watch out for her. He helped her through the picture. Gorcey was nothing like his tough guy movie character in real life. He was intelligent, friendly and funny.[3]

Critics generally enjoyed *Young Tom Edison*, acknowledging that the film is more MGM than history. Frank Nugent of the *New York Times* stated,

> Perhaps the safer course would be to forget Mr. Edison's early career completely and concentrate on the career of Mickey's young Tom, which seems to be amusing—especially in light of later developments—and splendidly backgrounded and reasonably human in its primary dramatics. The film covers the Port Huron years of the boy inventor; years when most of the townsfolk, his father among them, thought there was something "addled" about a lad who spent his pocket money on chemicals, almost blew up the school house with an experiment in the cloak room, became candy butcher and Civil War publisher on the Grand Trunk Railway, almost wrecked a train with a bottle of home-made nitroglycerine. But ultimately he showed them, of course, and at sixteen had come into man's estate and the stature of local boy making good. Mr. Rooney's portrait defers to its subject only to the extent of being a trifle less Rooneyish than his Andy Hardy, the implication being that, if young Tom Edison was not Mickey Rooneyish, the fault was with Edison, not M. Rooney.[4]

Young Tom Edison was another box office hit for Rooney, and for MGM. Exhibitors reporting in *Box Office* magazine raved,

> This picture should be a hit anywhere. Mickey Rooney, Virginia Weidler, as well as the rest of the cast, turn in top-notch performances. Your patrons will not be disappointed.[5]

At the conclusion of *Young Tom Edison*, a portrait of the actual inventor is shown, announcing the next film, *Edison the Man*, featuring Spencer Tracy. The camera pans back and shows Tracy looking up at the Edison portrait.

Upon completion of this film, Rooney was placed in another Andy Hardy movie, *Andy Hardy Meets a Debutante*. And Judy Garland was once again cast in the role of Betsy Booth she had played so effectively in *Love Finds Andy Hardy*.

ANDY HARDY MEETS A DEBUTANTE

(MGM, 1940)

Director: George B. Seitz
Screenplay: Aurania Rouverol, Thomas Seller, Annalee Whitmore
Producer: J. J. Cohn. *Cinematographers:* Charles Lawton Jr., Sidney Wagner. *Editor:* Harold F. Kress
Cast: Lewis Stone (Judge Hardy), Mickey Rooney (Andy Hardy), Cecilia Parker (Marian Hardy), Fay Holden (Mrs. Emily Hardy), Judy Garland (Betsy Booth), Ann Rutherford (Polly Benedict), Diana Lewis (Daphne Fowler), Addison Richards (George Benedict), Clyde Willson (Butch), Cy Kendall (Carrillo), George Lessey (Underwood), Claire Du Brey (Mrs. Hackett), Marjorie Gateson (Mrs. Fowler), John Merkyl (Prentiss), Charles Trowbridge (Davis), Herbert Evans (Betsy's butler), Edwin Stanley (Judge)
Songs: "Alone" (music by Nacio Herb Brown, lyrics by Arthur Freed; played on a record and sung by Judy Garland); "I'm Nobody's Baby" (music and lyrics by Benny Davis, Milton Ager, and Lester Santley; sung by Judy Garland at the party)
Released: July 5, 1940
Specs: 88 minutes; black and white
Availability: DVD (Warner Archive Collection: *The Andy Hardy Film Collection: Volume 1*)

Judy Garland returns in her second of three appearances as Betsy Booth in a Hardy family movie, giving *Andy Hardy Meets a Debutante* more appeal than the usual Hardy fare. Andy's problems are central here, and the judge's situation (taking a trip to New York in order to save a local orphanage) is peripheral. In fact, Rooney's scenes with Lewis Stone are somewhat less interesting and compelling in this film than in others, while his connection to Judy Garland remains the highlight. For some reason the judge comes off as more stern in this film than he does in the previous movies. His advice to Andy actually feels too preachy and over the top; their relationship in this movie isn't developed well at all.

This one features Andy being totally smitten by New York debutante Daphne Fowler, whom he has never met. He clips her pictures out of magazines and newspapers and keeps them in a scrapbook, which he pines over. He believes that his tastes may be too sophisticated for his usual homespun girlfriend, Polly Benedict, and prepares to break up with her, but she breaks up with him first, indicating she believes him to be too immature. Daunted by this reversal, Andy boasts that he is currently dating New York socialite Daphne. Polly, who along with Andy and Beezy is one of the editors of the school's newspaper, challenges Andy to prove his boast, but he dismisses her.

Judge Hardy then receives word that he and the family must travel to New York. Realizing they have Andy over a barrel, Polly and Beezy insist that Andy return with a photo of him and Daphne while they write a story about Andy's union with Daphne. The embarrassed Andy worries that he will get caught in his own lie, until he arrives in New York and discovers that Betsy Booth is good friends with Daphne, so arrangements are made. The judge wins his case, Andy ends up with Polly by the end of the movie, and all loose ends are tied up, as per the usual Hardy formula.

According to Rooney, it was around this point that the Hardy series was becoming less attractive:

> I had done *Boys Town*. Judy had done *The Wizard of Oz*. We both did *Babes in Arms*. All big pictures. I was nominated for an Oscar. Judy and I both had received special Oscars. So when we went into another Hardy picture, it was small budgets, the same type stories, and just another way for the studio to make a pile of money. But we did our jobs.[1]

The enthusiasm in both actors is certainly on display, as Rooney has opportunity to run the gamut of emotions.

First, in Andy's initial quest to meet Daphne, he attends an upscale restaurant that she sometimes frequents. Not wanting to seem like a small-town hick, Andy loftily orders "the specialty of the house" for his entrée and his dessert. Betsy attempts to warn him ahead of time about the prices, but he is dismissive, stating, "I have eight dollars on me." However, when he is offered a toy dog by one of the cigarette girls and is told it costs fifty dollars, he realizes how expensive his meal must be. He must tearfully ask for mercy from the manager of the restaurant, referring to his father's position as judge to get out of any reprimand. While the scene is played within the context of a comedy, Andy going from feeling lofty and important to suddenly realizing he is well beyond his area of comfort and understanding attempts to make a point. Andy continually dismisses Betsy Booth as a "child" who could not possibly comprehend his "grown-up" problems (they are roughly two years apart), but it is she who knows Daphne, it is she who understands New York society. When a despondent Andy reveals his plight to Betsy, she responds with a relieved, "Oh is that all?" and goes directly to the phone and makes a call. "Hello Daph? It's Betsy!" It is Ms. Booth's connections at a level higher than Andy can reach that save the day. Andy is forever the bumpkin. In fact, at one point, the judge goes so far as to say, "When a boy is stupid, he's just stupid and there isn't much one can do."

Andy triumphantly returns home, now having a picture of him and Daphne Fowler to go with the cover story that Polly and Beezy created. Their mea culpa is accepted, and Andy decides that the glamour girl type isn't for him. He is happily back with Polly as the movie concludes. He also realizes Betsy is not the child he believes her to be, and they even share their first kiss. It is a friendly kiss, as Andy will soon be returning to his life in Carvel. Judy Garland has two good songs to play, one of which, "I'm Nobody's Baby," would be her next chart hit for Decca Records. Two other songs were cut from the movie: "All I Do Is Dream of You" was removed before the film's release, and "Buds Won't Bud" was cut after the preview.

Despite Rooney's lessening interest in continuing with the series, *Andy Hardy Meets a Debutante* was another moneymaker. Shot for a mere $436,000, the film grossed $2,623,000. MGM had no plans to discontinue a film series that was netting profits at this level. In the *Motion Picture Herald*, the section for exhibitor comments offered praise for *Andy Hardy Meets a Debutante*:

> They can't make too many pictures with Mickey Rooney for me. Had the best business on this I've had in months. I saw customers that I thought had forgotten they made movies. This is just as good as any of the Hardy series. Please don't stop making them.[2]

Critics were also pleased. James Agee in *Time* stated,

> Mickey Rooney thrives on his ability and determination to steal anything up to a death scene from a colleague. Some of cinemactor Stone's heartiest chuckles may be explained by the fact that 17 year old Judy Garland, growing prettier by the picture and armed for this one with two good songs, "Alone" and "I'm Nobody's Baby," treats Mickey with a dose of his own medicine.[3]

Variety stated,

> With second appearance of Judy Garland in the series indicating that she might move in for regular assignment later, if the Rooney-Garland duo might

Judy Garland and Mickey Rooney

> be required to strengthen later issues. . . . Miss Garland is prominent and lovely as the adoring girl friend in the big city.[4]

Mickey Rooney and Judy Garland went from this low-budget Hardy family series movie into another big-budget lavish musical. *Strike Up the Band* would continue to solidify their relationship, promote their careers, and make big money for the studio.

STRIKE UP THE BAND

(MGM, 1940)

Director: Busby Berkeley
Screenplay: Fred F. Finklehoffe, John Monks Jr.
Producer: Arthur Freed. *Cinematographer:* Ray June. *Editor:* Ben Lewis. *Music:* Roger Edens, George Stoll
Cast: Mickey Rooney (Jimmy Connors), Judy Garland (Mary Holden), Paul Whiteman (Paul Whiteman), June Preisser (Barbara Frances Morgan), William Tracy (Phillip Turner), Larry Nunn (Willie Brewster), Margaret Early (Annie), Ann Shoemaker (Mrs. Connors), Francis Pierlot (Mr. Judd), Virginia Brissac (Mrs. May Holden), Harry McCrillis (Booper Martin), George Lessey (Mr. Morgan), Enid Bennett (Mrs. Morgan), Howard Hickman (Doctor), Sarah Edwards (Miss Hodges), Joe Yule (Ticket Seller), Virginia Sale (Music Teacher), Henry Roquemore (Mr. Mollison), Dick Paxton (Dick), Sherrie Overton (Romeo and Juliet Girl), Margaret Marquis (Antony and Cleopatra Girl), Vondell Darr (India Love Lyrics Student), Jack Albertson (Barker), Sidney Miller (Sid), Jack Mulhall (Man Phoning in Contest Winner). Note: Phil Silvers appeared as a pitchman during the carnival scene, but his footage was deleted before release.
Songs: "Strike up the Band" (music by George Gershwin, lyrics by Ira Gershwin; played during the opening credits; sung by Judy Garland, Mickey Rooney, and chorus in the finale); "Our Love Affair" (music by Roger Edens, lyrics by Arthur Freed; played during the opening and end credits; played on piano by Mickey Rooney and sung by Judy Garland and Mickey Rooney with orchestral accompaniment; reprised by the animated fruit orchestra; reprised by the band at rehearsal and at the dance; reprised by Judy Garland and Mickey Rooney in the finale; played as background music often); "Do the

La Conga" (music and lyrics by Roger Edens; performed by Judy Garland, Mickey Rooney, Sidney Miller, William Tracy, and chorus at the dance; reprised by the cast in the finale); "Nobody" (music and lyrics by Roger Edens; sung by Judy Garland); "Oh Where, Oh Where Has My Little Dog Gone?" (traditional; played as background music at the start of the fair sequence); "The Gay Nineties" (music and lyrics by Roger Edens; performed by Judy Garland, Mickey Rooney, William Tracy, Margaret Early, and chorus at the Elks Club show); "Nell of New Rochelle" (music and lyrics by Roger Edens; performed by Judy Garland, Mickey Rooney, and chorus in the Elks Club show); "Sidewalks of New York" (music by Charles Lawlor; a few notes played at the start of the "Nell of New Rochelle" sequence); "Walking Down Broadway" (traditional; music arranged by Roger Edens; sung by the chorus in the "Nell of New Rochelle" sequence); "A Man Was the Cause of It All" (music and lyrics by Roger Edens; sung by Judy Garland in the "Nell of New Rochelle" sequence); "After the Ball" (music by Charles Harris; played as dance music in the "Nell of New Rochelle" sequence); "Sobre las olas (Over the Waves)" (music by Juventino Rosas; played as background music in the "Nell of New Rochelle" sequence); "Heaven Will Protect the Working Girl" (music by A. Baldwin Sloane, lyrics by Edgar Smith; sung by Judy Garland, Mickey Rooney, and chorus in the "Nell of New Rochelle" sequence); "Home, Sweet Home" (music by H. R. Bishop, played as background music when Nell rocks the cradle); "Ta-ra-ra Boom-der-é" (music and lyrics by Henry J. Sayers; danced to and sung by June Preisser and sung by the chorus in the "Nell of New Rochelle" sequence; reprised in the finale of the "Nell of New Rochelle" sequence); "Come Home, Father" (music and lyrics by Henry Clay Work; sung by Larry Nunn and Judy Garland in the "Nell of New Rochelle" sequence); "The Light Cavalry Overture" (music by Franz von Suppé; played in the "Nell of New Rochelle" sequence several times); "Rock-a-Bye Baby" (music by Effie I. Canning; played as background music when Willie is told to go home); "Five Foot Two, Eyes of Blue (Has Anybody Seen My Girl)?" (music by Ray Henderson; played as background music when Jimmy and Barbara wait for her parents); "When Day Is Done" (music by Robert Katscher; opening number played by Paul Whiteman and Orchestra at Barbara's party); "Wonderful One" (music by Paul Whiteman and Ferde Grofé Sr.; played as dance music by Paul Whiteman and Orchestra at Barbara's party); "Drummer Boy" (music by Roger Edens, lyrics by Roger Edens and Arthur Freed; performed at Barbara's party by Judy Garland, Mickey Rooney—on drums and vibraphone—and other band members; reprised by the cast in the finale); "China Boy" (music and lyrics by Dick Winfree and Phil

Boutelje; played as background music during the travel and contest montage); "Hands across the Table" (music by Jean Delettre; played as background music during the travel and contest montage); "Limehouse Blues" (music by Philip Braham; played as background music during the travel and contest montage); "Tiger Rag" (music and lyrics by Edwin B. Edwards, Nick LaRocca, Tony Sbarbaro, Henry Ragas, and Larry "Shields"; played as background music during the travel and contest montage); "Columbia, the Gem of the Ocean" (music arranged by Thomas A. Beckett; played as background music when the flag is raised at the end)

Released: September 27, 1940

Specs: 120 minutes; black and white

Availability: DVD (Warner Home Video: *The Mickey Rooney and Judy Garland Collection*)

Strike Up the Band is another Mickey Rooney–Judy Garland pairing in an attempt to recapture the magic, and success, of *Babes in Arms*. The plot once again centers on young people putting together a big musical show in an attempt to show the town that their showbiz ambitions are not the simple dreams of starry-eyed adolescents but serious choices made for their future.

While *Strike Up the* Band is also the title of a Broadway show by George and Ira Gershwin, this film has nothing to do with that show, which was a political satire. Only the title song from that show was used, and it was decided it should also be the title of the movie by Louis B. Mayer because he felt it sounded patriotic. MGM had been considering Mickey and Judy for the musical *Good News*, but the patriotic title that attracted Mr. Mayer was another reason why they were switched over to this movie. *Good News* was finally made in 1947 with June Allyson and Peter Lawford.

Rooney stars as Jimmy Connors, an Andy Hardy–esque high schooler whose mother wants him to be a doctor like his late father, but he dreams of someday leading his own orchestra. Judy Garland is Mary Holden, once again longing for Rooney's character, while he is preoccupied with ambition and only responds to her as a buddy, completely oblivious to the feelings that everyone else notices. Jimmy convinces the principal to allow him to take over the school orchestra and turn it into a swing band. Their community success gives Jimmy even greater confidence and he wants to raise $200 to get his band to Chicago so they can audition for noted bandleader Paul Whiteman (who appears in the movie as himself).

Poster for *Strike Up the Band*

As the dynamic between Jimmy and Mary is introduced and initially develops, there is a truly imaginative scene in which Jimmy, at Mary's house, takes a bowl of fruit and starts placing it around the table, showing the formation of the orchestra as it appears in his imagination. The scene then evolves into one where the fruit comes to life and starts playing instruments—a clever bit of animation that is unusual for a movie such as this. This was the idea of a visitor to the set. Vincente Minnelli had just been hired by MGM as a director and was visiting the set of *Strike Up the Band* producer Arthur Freed during filming. Freed casually mentioned to Minnelli that they needed a big production number at this point in the movie and couldn't come up with anything. Minnelli suggested the idea using fruit; the producer liked it and asked animator George Pal to come up with something. It is one of the most unusual and amusing sequences in the film. Minnelli and Judy Garland would be married in another five years, their union resulting in their famous daughter Liza Minnelli.

Unlike *Babes in Arms*, which established the prototypical "let's put on a show" spirit that has since stereotyped the Rooney-Garland pairings, *Strike Up the Band* offers a different perspective. In the former film, Rooney, Garland, and company were showbiz kids whose parents were also entertainers. Here they are high schoolers with ambition, enthusiasm, and dreams separate from their parents. These are well-to-do kids who live in nice homes and enjoy privileges that appear somewhat beyond the middle class depicted in the earlier movie. Rooney's character, who comes from a single-parent household, appears to live in a home that is more middle class than the others, eating in a kitchen rather than a dining room, and without the high ceilings and vast space of the home in which Garland's character resides.

And while there are some good song numbers, including a rousing conga number and the Oscar-nominated "Our Love Affair," a film highlight, *Strike Up the Band* also allows comedy to be emphasized. This is especially evident in a well-staged parody of old-fashioned melodrama complete with florid gestures, overacting, and even a scene where Mary is tied to the railroad tracks and Jimmy must rescue her. In the context of the film, it is an attempt to generate money toward the needed $200 to get the band to Chicago. However, it also displays director Busby Berkeley's ability for fluid direction in something other than a musical number.

The romantic conflict comes along when a new girl moves in—blonde, giggly Barbara, to whom Jimmy must reluctantly give attention because she has talents that add to the shows and because she gives Jimmy and his band an invitation to her birthday party, at which her wealthy father has arranged for Paul Whiteman to appear. Acrobatic dancer June Preisser, who specialized in playing ditzy blondes, plays Barbara with her usual aplomb, similar to her amusing turn as Euphrasia in *Judge Hardy and Son*.

Dramatic tension develops separately when one of the group, the diminutive Willie,[1] who has a puppy dog longing for Mary, breaks his arm severely and Jimmy must give up the $200 he earned for the Chicago trip in order to pay for a doctor to care for him. Since $50 of the money was borrowed against the drums as collateral, Jimmy trades his entire future for his friend. His character's sacrifice allows Rooney to tap into his resources as a dramatic actor after having already exhibited his talent for comedy, singing, dancing, and drumming. *Strike Up the Band* was a tour de force for Rooney, who continued to maintain his status as the number one box office sensation in the country. This movie continues to prove how well the Rooney-Garland formula worked, but it is definitely more Rooney's movie. Garland's supporting role is pleasant, but she mostly only gets the chance to stand out during her musical numbers.

The film concludes with Barbara's wealthy father, a railroad magnate, arranging for a special train to get to Chicago in time to compete in Paul Whiteman's contest for high school bands. They win the first prize of $500.

With drama feeding into comedy, and disappointment ending with triumph, *Strike Up the Band* is the ultimate crowd-pleaser and it showed at the box office, making over a million dollars in profit. When Paul Whiteman delivers a line like, "Take that boy on the street. Teach him to blow a horn, and he'll never blow a safe," a 1940 crowd couldn't keep from cheering. Critics did a bit of cheering as well, the *New York Times* stating,

> Roll out the red carpet, folks, and stand by. That boy is here again, the Pied Piper of the box offices, the eighth or ninth wonder of the world, the kid himself—in short, Mickey Rooney. With a capable assist by Judy Garland, Mr. Rooney strutted into the Capitol on Saturday at the head of "Strike Up the Band," and it should surprise no one this morning to learn that the show is his from beginning to end. For a boy of his years he has accumulated quite a bag of tricks and he will show them off at the tap of a drummer's stick. He charges about like the short-handed cast of an old stock melodrama. Mr. Rooney is having himself a time in this one, and—being the frantic actor that he is—chances are that everyone else will too.[2]

And *Variety* stated,

> *Strike Up the Band* is Metro's successor to "Babes in Arms," with Mickey Rooney, assisted by major trouping on the part of Judy Garland. . . . Picture

> is overall smacko entertainment . . . and Mickey Rooney teamed with Judy Garland is a wealth of effective entertainment.[3]

Judy Garland turned eighteen during the filming of *Strike Up the Band*. She was still finishing up her stint in *Andy Hardy Meets a Debutante* when she began rehearsing for this movie, and she was already rehearsing for her next, *Little Nellie Kelly*, before completing her work here. Meanwhile, Mickey Rooney was placed in another Andy Hardy movie for his next project.

ANDY HARDY'S PRIVATE SECRETARY

(MGM, 1941)

Director: George B. Seitz
Screenplay: Jane Murfin, Harry Ruskin. *Story:* Katharine Brush. *Characters:* Aurania Rouverol
Cinematographer: Lester White. *Editor:* Elmo Veron
Cast: Lewis Stone (Judge James K. Hardy), Mickey Rooney (Andrew "Andy" Hardy), Fay Holden (Mrs. Emily Hardy), Ann Rutherford (Polly Benedict), Sara Haden (Aunt Milly Forrest), Ian Hunter (Steven V. Land), Kathryn Grayson (Kathryn Land), Gene Reynolds (Jimmy McMahon), George Breakston (Beezy), Todd Karns (Harry Land), Addison Richards (George Benedict), Margaret Early (Clarabelle Lee), Bertha Priestley (Susan Wiley), Joseph Crehan (Peter Dugan), Lee Phelps (Barnes), John Dilson (Mr. Davis, High School Principal), Erskine Sanford (Mr. Bosinny), Charles Smith (Bob), Frederick Burton, (Governor Spaulding), Donald Douglas (J. O. Harper), Betty Jane Graham (Student)
Songs: "The Voices of Spring [Voci di primavera]" (music and lyrics by Johann Strauss; sung by Kathryn Grayson); "The Mad Scene" aria from "Lucia di Lammermoor" (music by Gaetano Donizetti [as G. Donizetti], libretto by Salvatore Cammarano; sung by Kathryn Grayson at graduation); "I've Got My Eyes on You" (music and lyrics by Cole Porter; sung by Kathryn Grayson at graduation)
Released: February 21, 1941
Specs: 101 minutes; black and white
Availability: DVD (Warner Archive Collection: *The Andy Hardy Film Collection: Volume 1*)

While the Hardy series had settled into a formula that audiences still appreciated, by the time of *Andy Hardy's Private Secretary*, the tenth film in the series, the writers were attempting to investigate areas beyond usual narrative parameters. The film still opens in Judge Hardy's chambers and shows him offering homespun philosophy to a runaway (thus turning the boy's life around). But the next case is a portent to the plot as it involves Andy, who has bounced a check based on the school treasury funds.

It is discovered that one of the checks to the treasury is no good. The check has come from the Land family, who is poor, and as a result, the students in the family do not run with Andy's crowd. The judge discovers that Mr. Land speaks nine languages and had a good position in Europe but is struggling in America. The judge uses his connections to help out, getting Mr. Land a job with the State Department, while Andy hires young Kathryn Land as his private secretary due to her prowess in typing and shorthand. Meanwhile, Kathryn's brother strives to achieve at a more scholarly pursuits, hoping to graduate with the highest honors.

The Hardy series usually concentrated on the same middle- to upper-class citizens who inhabited the family's immediate world. Lower income classes might be represented with bit players but never as central characters. However in *Andy Hardy's Private Secretary*, Andy and the judge must confront the fact that some very good people simply don't have a lot of money. The Land family is struggling, with Kathryn and (especially) her brother, Harry, having an envious dislike of Andy and his social status, not only in town, but also in school. Andy tries to earnestly reach out by using Kathryn's skills, but Harry remains suspicious and tells his sister, "You'll do all the work and he'll get all the credit." Kathryn, however, is pleased to have the opportunity to contribute, and Andy does credit her assistance.

And while investigating lower income households and their struggle during this era, the film maintains consistent patriotism. More than once we are reminded via dialogue from those who have visited Europe that America is the best country in the world. Part of the way the film proves this is by having the struggling family receive an opportunity through Judge Hardy's benevolence.

For a film with an essentially serious point, *Andy Hardy's Private Secretary* is one of the funniest of the Hardy family series. Andy wants to surprise his secretary with a pair of stockings to wear to the graduation dance, as she can't afford any. His embarrassment at even walking through the ladies' lingerie area of a department store is very amusing, as Andy insists that someone from the men's department wait on him. In another funny scene,

Judge Hardy borrows Andy's car, a broken-down old convertible. He not only has to respond to its bouncing and jerking, but also a rainstorm that drenches him (there is no top to put over him). The car ends up in a mud puddle and cannot be salvaged. Andy can't go without a car, so the judge promises to buy him a new one as a graduation present.

There is a running gag where Andy's use of Kathryn as his secretary gets him in trouble with girlfriend Polly Benedict. Polly seems to run into Andy at all the wrong times—when he is innocently given a thank-you kiss on the cheek by Kathryn, as he is buying the stockings, and so on. Each time Polly storms off angrily, and Andy reacts comically but later admits, "Whenever Polly gets sore at me, when she later forgives me she likes me even more."

The strongest portion of the film occurs when Andy discovers that the many committees he is on at school (from class president to choosing the outfits the boys will wear at the senior dance) have caused him to neglect his studies. He fails English and is not going to graduate. In one of the film's very few dramatic moments, the judge admonishes Andy for wasting a year of his life, and Andy must also deal with his mother's tearful reaction. Because the judge has helped their family and Andy has proven he is supportive, Kathryn and Harry Land arrange with the principal to allow Andy to take the English final exam again. There is a statute in the student code book that if a failed exam is not representative of a student's usual work, he can be allowed to retake it. Andy had been an honor roll student in the subject up to the final. What follows is a fun scene where Andy is sitting droopy-eyed at a desk, surrounded by Kathryn, Harry, and Polly all firing questions at him to help him cram for the exam, which he does pass.

One of the more unusual things about *Andy Hardy's Private Secretary* is how little of it takes place in the Hardy home. There are a few fleeting scenes in the judge's home office and one scene at the dinner table, but nearly all of Judge Hardy's scenes are away from the house; most of what we see of Aunt Milly is at school (she is also Andy's English teacher), and Mother Hardy barely registers. Sister Marian Hardy does not appear in the movie at all (the mother mentions that she's traveling in New York). The real reason for Marian's absence is due to actress Cecilia Parker getting into trouble with the top brass at MGM, complaining about her misuse by the studio, and being loaned out to the low-budget Producer's Releasing Corporation (PRC) to appear in the movie *Gambling Daughters* (1941). She would be absent from the next Hardy movie as well.

Rooney recalled that the Hardy series was often a stepping-stone to introduce young up-and-coming starlets, and Kathryn Grayson is no exception. A singer with a beautiful classically trained voice, Grayson would go on to appear with Abbott and Costello in *Rio Rita* (1942) and would soon be starring in such top musicals as *Show Boat* (1951) and *Kiss Me, Kate* (1953). Kathryn Grayson gets to do here basically what Judy Garland did in *Love Finds Andy Hardy*. She sings a few nice songs to show off her voice, including Cole Porter's "I've Got My Eyes on You" (which is also a pretty funny scene as it cuts between Andy reacting to Kathryn overenthusiastically and Polly glaring at him). Grayson makes her debut in this movie. Also making his debut is Todd Karns, who plays Kathryn's brother, Harry Land. He remains best known for his role as Harry Bailey in the holiday classic *It's a Wonderful Life* (1946).

By the time of *Andy Hardy's Private Secretary*, the Hardy family unit was functioning beautifully, with the writers, director, actors, and crew all understanding exactly what was expected. But they were also smart enough to investigate ideas outside the strict parameters of the series and add more humor to this particular effort. The films remained low-budget productions; this one was produced for only $329,000. But it grossed over $2.5 million, making it the tenth most popular film of 1941.

Upon completion of *Andy Hardy's Private Secretary*, MGM decided to revisit the popular *Boys Town*, which continued to achieve box office success upon its occasional rereleases over the three years since it was produced. *Men of Boys Town* was no more than a rehash, but it was exactly what audiences, and MGM, wanted for Mickey Rooney.

MEN OF BOYS TOWN

(MGM, 1941)

Director: Norman Taurog
Screenplay: James Kevin McGuinness
Producer: John W. Considine Jr. *Cinematographer:* Harold Rosson. *Editor:* Fredrick Y. Smith, Ben Lewis
Cast: Spencer Tracy (Father Flanagan), Mickey Rooney (Whitey Marsh), Larry Nunn (Ted), Bobs Watson (Pee Wee), Darryl Hickman (Flip), Henry O'Neill (Mr. Maitland), Mary Nash (Mrs. Maitland), Lee J. Cobb (Dave Morris), Anne Revere (Mrs. Fenely), Sidney Miller (Mo), Addison Richards (Judge), Lloyd Corrigan (Gorton), George Lessey (Bradford Stone), Robert Emmett Keane (Burton), Arthur Hohl (Sadistic Reform School Guard), Ben Welden (Superintendent), Paul Stanton (Trem Fellows), Frank Coghlan Jr. (Frank), Vondell Darr (Agnes), William Haade (Jake), Edward Gargan (Detective), Paul Kruger (Guard), Aubrey Mather (Butler), Harry McKim (Murdock), Dick Paxton (Jack), Charles Smith (Slim), Edwin Stanley (Dr. Carlton), Master Stanworth (Tuba Player), Barbara Bedford (Nun)
Released: April 11, 1941
Specs: 106 minutes; black and white
Availability: DVD (Warner Home Video, as an extra on the *Boys Town* DVD)

Essentially a rehash of *Boys Town* (1938), operating from the same framework, *Men of Boys Town* is MGM's attempt to recapture the magic of one of their most profitable films. Spencer Tracy and Mickey Rooney return to the cast, as do Bobs Watson and Sidney Miller. However, in the original movie, Mickey Rooney's character of Whitey Marsh is a tough kid reformed

Trade ad for *Men of Boys Town*

by the institution, while in this film, he is a good kid helping others who finds himself back in a reform school, having to dig deep to find the former toughness that Father Flanagan's kindness had obliterated.

The story begins with Flanagan bringing Ted, a new student, to Boys Town, a young man convicted of murder whose back was broken during a beating at a reform school. The boy's anger and bitterness is impossible to penetrate until a couple of visiting donors give him their dog, which brightens his spirit and makes him more accepting of painful surgery that could restore his ability to walk. The donors are impressed with Whitey's exuberance and obvious leadership qualities and arrange to adopt him. This removes the Whitey character from Boys Town and into other environments that play for both comedy and drama.

Whitey's attempt to play golf and dance at a cotillion is played for laughs. Unlike the privileged Andy Hardy, Whitey's tough street background had him well versed in fighting and shooting pool, not dancing and golf. Mickey Rooney recalled,

> In *Men of Boys Town* there is a scene where I am dancing with a girl, and I am supposed to be unable to dance. I had been dancing since I was a kid on stage, so instead of learning to dance like most actors, I had to learn how not to dance. It's harder than you might think.[1]

There is a dark scene where Flip, a youngster, escapes from a reformatory where Whitey had been going to see a friend of Ted's. During Whitey's last visit, as he is again confronted by a difficult guard, Flip sneaks out of the reform school and hides in Whitey's car. Whitey tries to help him, but the boy steals Whitey's gun and holds up a gas station. This implicates Whitey, who is arrested when he attempts to return the money to the gas station. Flip is returned to the reformatory and Whitey is sent there with him. The scenes in the reformatory do not take up much footage, but they offer a brutality and darkness that separates them from the rest of the movie. The guard that Whitey had confronted at the gate indicates he was fined two weeks' pay due to Flip's escape. He punishes Whitey by treating him especially brutally. Father Flanagan soon comes to the reformatory and takes both Whitey and Flip with him.

Some of the elements of the original movie remain intact. Flanagan overspends in his updates and additions to Boys Town, having too much faith in the kindness of donations, and almost loses the entire enterprise to the state. A last-minute contribution from the couple who attempted to adopt Whitey saves the day. But this is after the rather mawkish sequence where Ted's dog runs into the street and is run over by a truck. Ted is heartbroken but insists on walking to where the other boys have dug a grave for his pet. Played straight and earnestly, it is a bit too much for even a sentimental drama such as this.

Actor Sidney Miller recalled for Arthur Marx in his book *The Nine Lives of Mickey Rooney* that he and Rooney used to write songs on the sets of movies they did together. At one point during the filming of *Men of Boys Town*, Rooney finished doing the scene where he is sobbing to Father Flanagan about having to leave Boys Town. Upon completing his work for the camera, he went to the piano to compose with Miller. Rooney was then informed that there was a microphone shadow on one of the actors, so he had to go back and redo the scene. Miller was impressed with Rooney's ability to leave the happy experience of playing piano and singing and jump right back into a heavy dramatic scene where he is sobbing. Rooney recalled,

> Yeah I did plenty of crying in those pictures, and I know how to cry on camera if I need to. But remember we had Bobs Watson on that picture playing Pee Wee. Bobs' specialty was crying. When he turned on the water works he flooded the whole set.[2]

Watson later left show business to pursue work as a Methodist minister. Three decades later he visited the set of Spencer Tracy's final film, *Guess Who's Coming to Dinner*, and after a warm reunion, told Tracy that it was his portrayal of Father Flanagan that inspired him to become a minister.

Although the character of Whitey Marsh helped solidify Mickey Rooney's superstardom, he wasn't enthused about playing the character again:

> I was playing Andy Hardy in a series of pictures, doing musicals with Judy, and then some roles that allowed me to stretch out a little. Well, this time there was no stretching out. I had to play a character I had done before. Mr. Tracy wasn't interested in doing the role again either. We both knew it wouldn't be as good as the first picture. But MGM knew it would make money, and it sure did.[3]

Rooney was correct. The film was made for $862,000 and grossed over $3 million. And while Rooney may be playing the same character in this movie, Whitey's personality is completed changed from the previous film.

The *New York Times* was generally unimpressed with this sequel, believing it was completely unnecessary. Bosley Crowther stated in his review,

> Father Flanagan's colony for homeless boys near Omaha, Neb., was served very well by Metro in its memorable *Boys Town*, but that service is in no way duplicated by the sequel that came yesterday to the Capitol. For *Men of Boys Town*, which matches its predecessor only in theme, is an obvious and maudlin

reassembly of clichés out of the cabinet marked Pathos, lacking completely the sincerity which did distinguish the first, and so frequently punctuated by close-ups of blubbering boys that one finally feels an embarrassed inclination to look away. A noble and worthy institution is certainly not enhanced by this firm. Mr. Tracy, as is his custom, gives a clean, sure and inspiring picture of a man devoted to a high ideal. But Mr. Rooney either bubbles with excess enthusiasm or falls into unconvincing moods, and his manifestations of deep emotion are the hardest of all to take. Bobs Watson, Larry Nunn and Darryl Hickman obviously do as Norman Taurog directed, which means swagger, brood and weep elaborately, and Lee J. Cobb bears himself with authority, at least, as a treasurer. But the lesson in *Men of Boys Town* is to stay away from sequels.[4]

Variety, however, was more enthusiastic about *Men of Boys Town*, stating in its review,

Like its predecessor *Boys Town*, this one carries socko entertainment for wide general appeal, including plenty of tear-jerking and sentimental episodes to blur the eyes of the most calloused, and spotlighting the life work of Father Edward J. Flanagan in his enterprise devoted to rehabilitation of wayward boys. Spencer Tracy again presents a sincere and human portrayal of the priest, while Mickey Rooney displays plenty of restraint in handling the assignment of the completely reformed boy who goes out briefly to practice the precepts of the school head. Lee J. Cobb, as the fund-raiser to keep the institution open, gives a fine performance. Story introduces Larry Nunn into the institution. Kid is bitter because of the crippled back sustained in a reform school beating, and Rooney heads a group of boys to try to make him laugh again. The kindly Father Flanagan and a dog do the trick. Picture hits a consistent gait, always pointing up the sentimental angles in its dramatic unfolding. Direction by Norman Taurog again demonstrates his unique talents in handling boys and their varied characteristics.[5]

Despite mixed reviews among the critics, MGM was pleased with the massive profit *Men of Boys Town* brought in, but no further sequels were planned. *Boys Town* would not lend itself as well to a series, although there was some discussion about doing more films with different characters. Furthermore, an actor with the stature of Spencer Tracy would not likely submit to a full series, just as Lionel Barrymore balked at continuing to play Judge Hardy after appearing in *A Family Affair*.

Rooney would next do yet another Andy Hardy movie. Boasting another appearance by Judy Garland, *Life Begins for Andy Hardy* would be not only the most unusual film in the series but also arguably the best.

LIFE BEGINS FOR ANDY HARDY

(MGM, 1941)

Director: George B. Seitz
Screenplay: Agnes Christine Johnston. *Characters:* Aurania Rouverol
Producer: George B. Seitz. *Cinematographer:* Lester White. *Editor:* Elmo Veron
Cast: Mickey Rooney (Andy Hardy), Judy Garland (Betsy Booth), Ray McDonald (Jimmy Frobisher), Lewis Stone (Judge James Hardy), Patricia Dane (Jennitt Hicks), Sara Haden (Aunt Milly), Fay Holden (Ma Hardy), George Breakston (Beezy), Joseph Crehan (Peter Dugan), John Eldredge (Paul McWilliams), Bess Flowers (Secretary), Nora Lane (Miss Howard), Tommy Kelly (Chuck), Hollis Jewell (Chuck), Sidney Miller (Man at Hotel), Pierre Watkin (Dr. Waggoner), Purnell Pratt (Dr. Storfen), Charlotte Wynters (Elizabeth Norton), Lester Matthews (Mr. Maddox), Mira McKinney (Miss Gomez), Leonard Sues (Kelly), George Ovey (Charlie), Byron Shores (Jackson). The following actors were in the movie, but their scenes were deleted: Ralph Byrd, Frank Ferguson, George M. Carleton, Manart Kippen, William Holmes, Gladden James, William Forrest Robert Winkler, Paul Newlan, Duke York.
Released: August 15, 1941
Specs: 101 minutes; black and white
Availability: DVD (Warner Archive Collection: *The Andy Hardy Film Collection: Volume 1*)

The best of the Hardy films, mostly because it is so courageous by challenging its own established formula, *Life Begins for Andy Hardy* has Andy, newly graduated from high school, choosing to spend the summer in New York City on his own. He sets out to find a job and learns what life is like outside the parameters of his small-town existence. Judy Garland returns as

Betsy Booth, a native New Yorker whose sophistication and understanding of the city could benefit Andy, but he stubbornly insists on forging ahead without her help. He learns very quickly about events and responsibilities he never had to confront in Carvel, from the pressures of maintaining a job and budgeting his money, to things like infidelity and even death. Similar to *Andy Hardy's Private Secretary*, this movie is barely concerned with the rest of the Hardy family at all. Marian is absent again, while Ma Hardy and Aunt Milly are barely present.

Andy checks into a male rooming house and sets out to find work. When the money with which he arrived is nearly depleted, he finds a job as an office boy making a sufficient but still limiting ten dollars per week. The young man from whom he took his room, Jimmy Frobisher, an aspiring dancer, is found sleeping on park benches, so Andy sneaks him up to his room. Upon returning home from work one night, Andy discovers the boy lying dead on the bathroom floor. He initially believes it to be a suicide, but then he discovers Jimmy had a heart condition and died of natural causes.

Still shaken, Andy pours his heart out to an understanding Betsy, but he is far more interested in the office's switchboard operator. Betsy's sophistication allows her to see through this woman's intentions (referring to her as a "wolfess") and discovers that she is only separated from but still married to her husband; she continues to charge expensive furs and other items to his account. Andy discovers this when, up in the woman's room about to embrace her, the husband comes to the door and confronts the woman about her charging to his account and their rocky marriage. When he leaves, he nods to Andy and says, "Good night, son." A stunned Andy leaves the woman's apartment and is soon back in Carvel, working at the local garage and planning to attend college in the fall.

The decision to take Andy out of his element is played for both comedy and drama. Enthusiastically wanting to make a good impression, a jittery Andy runs about the office performing his duties rapidly, from stuffing letters in envelopes to retrieving office supplies for the secretaries. Having not eaten all day and being unable to do so until he gets his first paycheck, he collapses with exhaustion and is taken to dinner by the switchboard operator, where he eats "for an hour and a half straight." It is an interesting scene within context of the Hardy series. At school in Carvel, Andy was the class president, fully in charge. When there was a play, he'd be directing. When there were student body decisions, he would be in charge of making them. But here in the big city, even the role of lowly office boy was an insurmountable task where he was at the mercy of the most common

Poster for *Life Begins for Andy Hardy*

responsibilities. His nervousness causes carelessness and he puts the letters in the wrong envelopes, causing confusion and problems for the firm.

Andy's discovery of Jimmy lying dead in the bathroom is filmed with dark shadows across Rooney's face and a close shot so we can see his expression. Rooney plays it perfectly, exhibiting shock, confusion, and sorrow all at once. His mouth closes, his jaw tightens, and his eyes widen. He pauses for several seconds before hurrying out of the room for help. It is far beyond anything the small-town boy has ever been forced to encounter. Always an idealized look at American life, the Hardy series decides now to confront reality. Andy does not seem so much out of place as he does naive.

There is another rather daring scene when Judge Hardy comes to visit Andy and takes him to lunch. As they leave, the judge notices the switchboard operator wink at Andy. He feels that lunchtime is the right opportunity to discuss fidelity with Andy, and, in so many words, explains that remaining virginal until marriage is showing fidelity with one's future wife. Andy doesn't quite know how to respond, so the judge states, "You're probably thinking what I was thinking when my father had this talk with me. Thanks anyway for listening."

It is somewhat important to the character that *Life Begins for Andy Hardy* takes him away from his comfort zone and places him in a more realistic world with more sophisticated situations. His decision to return to where he came from, where he truly belongs, is not so much an indictment of the big city as it is an understanding of his own limitations. He has his goals, his ambitions, but they are comfortable in more familiar surroundings. MGM was pleased with this production, and the trailer advertised it as "the best Hardy picture." They were right. But some audiences did not like being taken so far from Andy's usual reality, depending on the formulaic nature of the Hardy pictures as something comfortable and familiar. Critics, however, were duly impressed. Thomas Pryor of the *New York Times* stated,

> The boy grows older and a mite wiser in the ways of the world in *Life Begins for Andy Hardy* though Mickey Rooney plays him with the same boyish gusto he has exhibited in the past ten episodes of this popular series. Andy still is a long way from man's estate at the fadeout of the Capitol's new film, but Metro has at least got him safely through a romantic adventure, which, for a time, had Old Judge Hardy himself reeling on the ropes of uncertainty, and to the threshold of a college education. The producers apparently will make greater efforts to reach mature audiences with Andy's future escapades, for the dialogue in the current chapter is rather on the smart side for this type of film.[1]

Ray McDonald, as Jimmy, turns in a particularly impressive performance. Suffering on the inside, Jimmy is far more savvy than Andy, but his unsuccessful quest to enter the showbiz world makes the big city even more difficult for him to endure. The script originally had him committing suicide, but the censors insisted on changing it to a heart condition of long standing. It is actually rather unfortunate that the censors forced the cause of Jimmy's death to be changed from suicide. That was a missed opportunity to make a statement about the challenges confronting youth while also packing a huge punch for Andy, who probably had never thought much about suicide before.

Judy Garland makes her final appearance in an Andy Hardy film. The nineteen-year-old Garland was tired of playing juvenile roles and wanted to transition into more adult roles. Always a welcome presence, Ms. Garland turns in the best of her Hardy movie performances for this film. In the closing credits, she is billed among most of the Hardy family actors. Oddly, Garland recorded several songs for this movie, including Cole Porter's "Easy to Love," "America (My Country 'Tis of Thee)," "Abide with Me," and "The Rosary." Miss Garland's one musical moment is her singing "Happy Birthday to You." The movie's original poster advertised "Mickey woos! Judy sings!" but only one of those claims is true. Since two of Garland's numbers are religious ones, it is likely a funeral scene for Jimmy was planned but not used.

As the switchboard operator, Patricia Dane is a striking presence, and she plays her sophisticated big-city role perfectly to augment Rooney's innocent presentation of the Andy Hardy character he had honed over ten previous movies. Ms. Dane would later endure a rocky marriage to bandleader Tommy Dorsey.

Here Judge Hardy once again shows a quiet understanding of the big-city world despite his humble small-town position. The switchboard girl dismisses him as "one of those holier-than-thou types," and to some extent she is correct. But Andy reacts negatively: "I don't want to ever have any fun if it means I have to think like that."

While audiences may have balked at the change of perspective with *Life Begins for Andy Hardy*, it really is natural for the writers to move Andy out of high school and into more of an adult setting. But since audiences did not like him out of his element, the next film would return to a more formulaic approach. Still, Rooney was now twenty-one and a bit too old to be the "gee whiz, she kissed me" innocent adolescent for moviegoers of the era that rested between the Depression and World War Two. His next film had him teaming again with Judy Garland for another big-budget musical.

BABES ON BROADWAY

(MGM, 1941)

Director: Busby Berkeley
Screenplay: Fred Finklehoffe, Elaine Ryan. *Story:* Fred Finklehoffe
Producer: Arthur Freed. *Cinematographer:* Lester White. *Editor:* Fredrick Smyth. *Music:* Georgie Stoll, Burton Lane, Roger Edens, Harold Rome
Cast: Mickey Rooney (Tommy Williams), Judy Garland (Penny Morris), Fay Bainter (Miss Jones), Virginia Weidler (Barbara Jo), Ray McDonald (Ray Lambert), Richard Quine (Morton Hammond), Donald Meek (Mr. Stone), Alexander Woollcott (Woollcott), James Gleason (Thornton Reed), Donna Reed (Secretary), Joe Yule (Mason), Margaret O'Brien (Maxine), Luis Alberni (Nick), Emma Dunn (Mrs. Williams), Fredrick Burton (Mr. Morris), Cliff Clark (Moriarity), William Post Jr. (Announcer), Barbara Bedford (Mrs. Crainen), Lester Dorr (Reed's Writer), Bryant Washburn (Reed's Director), Sidney Miller (Tony), Anne Rooney (Jenny), Roger Steele (Robert Phillips), William A. Lee (Shorty), Joe Yule (Mason), Jean Porter (Chorus Girl), Jack "Tiny" Lipsom (Customer at Nick's), Six Hits and a Miss, the Debutantes, the Notables, the Peter Brothers, the Stafford Quartet, Stop Look and Listen Trio
Songs: "Babes on Broadway" (music by Burton Lane, lyrics by E. Y. Harburg; played and sung by a chorus during the opening credits; reprised as a production number with the principal cast near the end); "How about You?" (music by Burton Lane, lyrics by Ralph Freed; played during the opening credits; reprised by Judy Garland playing piano; sung and danced to by Mickey Rooney and Judy Garland; played as background music often and during the end credits); "Anything Can Happen in New York" (music by Burton Lane, lyrics by Ralph Freed; sung and

danced to by Mickey Rooney, Ray McDonald, and Richard Quine); "Hoe Down" (music by Roger Edens, lyrics by Ralph Freed; played at rehearsal and sung by Judy Garland; danced to by the principal cast); "Chin Up, Cheerio, Carry On" (music by Burton Lane, lyrics by E. Y. Harburg [contains portions of "Rule Britannia"—music by Thomas Augustine Arne, lyrics by James Thomson; sung by Judy Garland and the St. Luke Choristers); "Mary's a Grand Old Name" (music and lyrics by George M. Cohan; sung by Judy Garland imitating Fay Templeton); "She Is Ma Daisy" (music by Harry Lauder, lyrics by Harry Lauder and J. D. Harper; sung by Mickey Rooney imitating Harry Lauder); "I've Got Rings on My Fingers (Mumbo Jumbo Jijjiboo J. O'Shea)" (music by Maurice Scott, lyrics by Fred J. Barnes and R. P. Weston; sung by Judy Garland imitating Blanche Ring); "The Yankee Doodle Boy" (music and lyrics by George M. Cohan; sung by Mickey Rooney imitating George M. Cohan); "Bombshell from Brazil" (music and lyrics by Roger Edens; sung by Judy Garland, Ray McDonald, Richard Quine, and others); "Mamãe Eu Quero" (music and lyrics by Jararaca and Vicente Paiva; sung by Mickey Rooney imitating Carmen Miranda); "By the Light of the Silvery Moon" (music by Gus Edwards, lyrics by Edward Madden; danced to by Ray McDonald and sung by a chorus); "Franklin D. Roosevelt Jones" (music and lyrics by Harold Rome; sung by Judy Garland in the "Babes on Broadway" number); "Waiting for the Robert E. Lee" (music by Lewis F. Muir, lyrics by L. Wolfe Gilbert; sung by the principal cast in the "Babes on Broadway" number; danced to by the chorus)

Released: December 31, 1941

Specs: 118 minutes; black and white

Availability: DVD (Warner Home Video: *The Mickey Rooney and Judy Garland Collection*)

Babes on Broadway was another hit musical for Mickey Rooney and Judy Garland and once again dealt with spirited teens putting on a show. The film was in the same tradition as *Babes in Arms* and *Strike Up the Band*, but in direct opposition to the innocent fun being performed in the film, both Rooney and Garland became involved in very grown-up situations during filming.

The story has Rooney's and Garland's characters, along with some other talented young people, putting on a Broadway show to benefit an orphanage. They put on a block party to raise funds to rent the theater, but just as they are about to give their show, the theater is condemned. Further, Rooney's character is revealed as only using the orphanage benefit for his own opportunity to get on Broadway. So the plot goes through the myriad

Poster for *Babes on Broadway*

of highs and lows among the characters, especially Rooney and Garland, who are once again pals who become a couple, have their conflict, and make up in the end. Their musicals were following a formula as much as the Andy Hardy films had. Using the Rooney character to exhibit some level of self-centered cynicism is the only break from the usual fresh-faced exuberance.

Once again, Busby Berkeley stages enormous musical numbers that are rousing and uplifting, and it is these that carry the movie, not the threadbare plot upon which they hang. The hoe down number, with the cast in bib overalls and aproned skirts, the minstrel number paying homage to past songs, and the big closing number are shot from several angles, mostly medium and long shots. Berkeley's penchant for shooting from above and panning the camera back, allowing the rhythmic movement on the screen to take center frame, is most effective in the bigger musical numbers. During the block party dancing, this choice of camera placement allowed the scene of dancers to be in the center, framed by surrounding buildings, in an effective and impressive shot.

Along with both Rooney and Garland, other members of the cast are allowed the spotlight. Ray McDonald, who had played Rooney's ill-fated roommate in *Life Begins for Andy Hardy*, has an impressive solo during the hoe down number. Virginia Weidler, who appeared in a few other movies with Rooney, plays a role that was originally intended for Shirley Temple. Temple had just left her longtime studio of 20th Century Fox and was hired by MGM. However, when her first film, *Kathleen* (1941), was a flop, MGM dropped her contract. Weidler was no longer the cute tomboy but an awkward adolescent, taller than Rooney and gangly in appearance. MGM was not interested in her type despite a good performance in this movie. She left MGM in 1943 and the movie industry not long afterward. Weidler married, raised a family, and never spoke of her movie career or watched her old films on television. By the time she died in 1971, she had been forgotten by the industry and received almost no attention in the press. *Babes on Broadway* also featured appearances by a very young Margaret O'Brien in her film debut, and Donna Reed, who would figure more prominently in Rooney's next film.

A lengthy minstrel sequence, complete with blackface makeup and broad dialect, is unsettling to see in the twenty-first century, but it has some level of historical/cultural significance in that the filmmakers and performers had no interest in being derogatory or insulting. Perhaps this can be considered ignorance, and it is an issue that should have more discussion than space will allow in a chapter such as this. But such acts were indeed a part of show business at one time, and that they are captured on film gives us a sociocultural checkpoint to inspire further study. This is not to defend or excuse its presentation, of course, but to defend our right to see it and respond to it during these more enlightened times.

Judy Garland turned nineteen during the filming of this movie and secretly flew to Vegas to marry musician David Rose. She asked for time off to have a honeymoon, but Louis B. Mayer ordered her back on the set the next day. He was angry that she eloped rather than allowing the studio the publicity of a lavish wedding. Rooney became smitten with a visitor to the set, a very pretty young lady named Ava Gardner. Despite the fact that Rooney was dressed up as female Mexican personality Carmen Miranda for a musical number, his pursuit of Gardner was successful and she became the first of Mickey Rooney's many wives.

Babes on Broadway was an expensive production for its time with a budget of $955,000, but it grossed nearly $4 million. The *New York Times* review stated,

> When Metro spreads itself on a production number, it invariably does a handsome job. And, it has done right nicely by the finale of *Babes on Broadway*, providing a mammoth eye-filling setting for the minstrel show which is the only racy and really entertaining episode in this otherwise dull and overly-long potpourri of comedy, drama, third-rate jokes and music. The humor department reached its zenith with the remark, "I'm going out to get some air, I feel rather flat," which Mickey Rooney tosses off rather sheepishly. As the title of the Music Hall's new offering implies, it is basically a story about the youngsters who hang out in the Times Square theatrical precincts, hoping for that one break which will open the gates to the pearly highway of the show world. You can observe, any day in the week, dozens of youngsters like those portrayed by Mickey Rooney and Judy Garland, congregating on the corners of Forty-fourth and Forty-fifth Streets and swapping tales of their experiences in trying to see this producer or that one. It's a sight familiar to most New Yorkers, and out of it some enterprising showman may yet evolve an entertaining musical edition of *Stage Door*. But Metro, with Mr. Rooney on its hands, just couldn't follow a simple straightforward story line. So, except for an occasional and pleasant musical interruption by Miss Garland, the plot is thickened with some trite nonsense about Mickey and Judy staging a settlement house show to raise funds to send some underprivileged children to the country. As usual, Mickey Rooney does not confine himself to a single characterization, but gives also his impersonations of Sir Harry Lauder (very bad), George M. Cohan (fair), a hillbilly idiot (exaggerated but amusing) and a black-faced end man (lively and in the best Elks Club tradition). Though Mickey doesn't leave much room for anybody else, Judy Garland manages to

> stand out in the musical interludes, as does the graceful and nimble-footed Ray McDonald in a brief tap dance.[1]

Movie theaters were pleased with the turnout for this musical, reporting to the trade magazine *Box Office* that "Mickey Rooney can do anything, including bring the people to the theater."[2]

Babes on Broadway is entertaining as it follows the same trajectory as the other Rooney-Garland musicals, but because it leans so heavily on an already established method of storytelling, it comes off as decidedly less interesting than either *Babes in Arms* or *Strike Up the Band*. While the music was outstanding and the singing and dancing were spectacular, the story was a bit too much of the same thing. Both Rooney and Garland were outgrowing their roles and would soon have to adapt their screen personae.

Babes on Broadway was also Mickey Rooney's final release of 1941, premiering in the big cities on New Year's Eve and beginning its regular run in January of 1942. Rooney would once again, for the third time, emerge as the number one box office star in the country. However, his huge career and massive stardom would now have to compete with challenges in his personal life, and Rooney, now in his twenties, was getting a bit too old to play the roles with which he had been identified. His next film would turn out to be perhaps the weakest effort in the Andy Hardy series.

THE COURTSHIP OF ANDY HARDY

(MGM, 1942)

Director: George B. Seitz
Screenplay: Agnes Christine Johnston, Aurania Rouverol
Producer: Carey Wilson. *Cinematographer:* Lester White. *Editor:* Elmo Veron
Cast: Lewis Stone (Judge James K. Hardy), Mickey Rooney (Andrew "Andy" Hardy), Cecilia Parker (Marian Hardy), Fay Holden (Mrs. Emily Hardy), Ann Rutherford (Polly Benedict), Sara Haden (Aunt Milly Forrest), Donna Reed (Melodie Eunice Nesbit), William Lundigan (Jefferson "Jeff" Willis), Steve Cornell (Stewart), Frieda Inescort (Olivia), Harvey Stephens (Roderick), Betty Wells (Susie), Joseph Crehan (Peter Dugan), George P. Breakston (Beezy), Todd Karns (Harry Land), Frank Coghlan Jr. (Red), Dick Paxton (Kirk), Charles Peck (Tommy), Jay Ward (Byron), Lois Collier (Cynthia), Betty Jean Hainey (Dolly), Barbara Bedford (Elsa the Maid), Ken Christy (Jenkins), Tim Ryan (Farrell), Floyd Shackeford (Joe), John Butler (Postman), Erville Anderson (Bailiff)
Released: March 29, 1942
Specs: 95 minutes; black and white
Availability: DVD (Warner Archive Collection: *The Andy Hardy Film Collection: Volume 2*)

In one of the weakest Hardy family efforts, *The Courtship of Andy Hardy* was also a difficult film for Mickey Rooney to make. He wanted to arrange a plum part for his new bride, Ava Gardner, and having just been voted the number one box office star for the third year in a row, he felt he had the clout to guarantee such a thing. MGM, however, felt Gardner, newly arrived in Hollywood from the south and having only had one small speaking role in a movie, wasn't ready for such a promotion. The Hardy series was a stepping-stone for actresses who had proven some potential to go farther: Lana Turner, Kathryn Grayson, and, in this movie, Donna Reed. Although disappointed, Rooney would later admit that Donna Reed was perhaps the best up-and-coming actress he worked with in the Hardy films. However, his wife would often chastise him for being unable to secure her the role, and there was a great deal of tension at home. It affected his appearance as well as his performance. One executive, after seeing the day's rushes in the projection room, complained that Rooney was looking older than his father.

The Courtship of Andy Hardy also marks the return of Cecilia Parker, who had been exiled to poverty row for the movie *Gambling Daughters* (1941) and then was off screen to give birth to her child. She returns here, and would for the next Hardy family film, and would then, at the end of 1942, leave movies altogether, choosing instead to raise her family. In this film, she once again has rather serious trouble with a beau, and both Andy and the judge coming to her rescue.

The central plot of *The Courtship of Andy Hardy* is a couple's impending divorce and how it is affecting their daughter, played by Donna Reed. Andy is asked by the judge to help the young lady meet people and make some friends, as her social skills are severely lacking. The gregarious Andy has no problem doing this, but of course this causes a problem with his vacationing girlfriend, Polly Benedict, once she returns home. This was also Ms. Rutherford's penultimate Hardy film appearance.

The Courtship of Andy Hardy offers something of a holding pattern for the series. Andy has now graduated and plans to attend college, having attempted the big-city working world in the previous movie. However, this film finds him spending the summer in Carvel, working at the garage, and helping out his father by escorting the young lady around while the judge helps to settle the conflict her parents are having.

Marian's tangential subplot deals with her returning to small-town Carvel from New York (a reference casually made in the last two movies to explain her absence). It is odd as far as continuity's sake, as one would assume Andy and Marian would have had at least some contact when Andy was in the Big Apple in the previous film. However, the writers instead have Marian taken by big-city living, believing herself too sophisticated for her quaint home town. She hooks up with a young man who has a bit of a reputation, he gets drunk when they go out, and there is a car accident. Nobody is hurt, and everything works out comfortably, with Marian realizing her small town is much more grounded and comfortable than she realized.

The trade ad for *The Courtship of Andy Hardy* highlighted Rooney's twenty years in show business.

The Courtship of Andy Hardy did not impress Bosley Crowther of the *New York Times*, who stated in his review,

> As usual, Mickey Rooney plays Andy with the bounce of a rubber ball, and the rest of the tribe falls in around him without a single defection in the ranks. Donna Reed, who plays the new girl, is a welcome addition, however, for she has looks and grace and a most appealing charm. Andy should keep in touch with her; he could go far and do a lot worse. Otherwise, this is one of the less distinguished Hardy films. Some comedy, some homely words of wisdom, some heart-to-hearts—and there's the sum of it.[1]

Audiences, however, were perfectly satisfied with this standard entry that did not progress Andy's story. It was made for a modest budget of $338,000 and grossed over $2 million more than that.

Mickey Rooney's marital troubles continued and, as he admitted in his autobiography, he dealt with these problems by completely throwing himself into his work. His next film allowed him to utilize several elements of his previous screen characters, from Whitey Marsh to Andy Hardy.

A YANK AT ETON

(MGM, 1942)

Director: Norman Taurog
Screenplay: George Oppenheimer, Lionel Houser, Thomas Phipps
Producer: John W. Considine Jr. *Cinematographers:* Karl Freund, Charles Lawton Jr. *Editor:* Albert Akst
Cast: Mickey Rooney (Timothy Dennis); Edmund Gwenn (Headmaster Justin); Ian Hunter (Roger Carlton); Freddie Bartholomew (Peter Carlton); Marta Linden (Winifred Dennis Carlton); Juanita Quigley (Jane "The Runt" Dennis); Peter Lawford (Ronnie Kenvil); Raymond Severn (Inky); Dennis Chaldecott (Whitson); Valerie Cole (Imogen); Terry Kilburn (Hilspeth); Aubrey Mather (Widgeon); Paul Matthews (Graham); Tina Thayer (Flossie); Cyril Thornton (Judson); Byron Shores (Rocky Brown); Jerry Rush (Darrence); Charles Irwin (Gelson); Wally Albright, Bill Cartledge, Roger McGee, Billy Smith, Charles Stroud (Boys in Locker Room); Herbert Clifton (Chauffeur); Harry Cording (Bartender); Bobby Hale (Gardener); Harry Duff, Wayne Kerrush, Richard Clucas, Ricardo Lord Cezon, Jack Lynn, Robert Lynn, Schuyler Standish (Students)
Released: September 25, 1942
Specs: 88 minutes; black and white
Availability: DVD (Warner Archive)

In the 1938 MGM film *A Yank at Oxford*, Robert Taylor stars as a cocky American who accepts a scholarship at Oxford and must learn humility and acceptance. The film was a hit, doubling its production cost at the box office. Now, at the height of Mickey Rooney's career, the studio revisits this premise with Rooney as a young American athlete whose mother marries an Englishman and who must now cope with a very different atmosphere

Poster for *A Yank at Eton*

at Eton school in England. Most of the film deals with misunderstandings within the differing cultures, the studio's intent being that our two countries could coexist comfortably if shallow differences were overlooked. American troops were entering the United Kingdom to join World War Two at the time. The Rooney film was even more popular than the Robert Taylor movie, its box office returns more than tripling its production costs.

Rooney plays Timothy, an American boy who excels at football as his late father once had, and plans to follow in dad's footsteps by playing for Notre Dame. However, just before the school's big game, Timothy is told by his sister Jane that their mother, who has been traveling in Europe, has met and married a man in England and they are to move there immediately. This completely disrupts Timothy's entire future.

The film could explore the very real situation of adults conducting their lives in a manner that directly affects the children, but with no regard to how it affects them. Completely upending Timothy's plans is never discussed. He is expected to simply comply with the situation. The film instead concentrates on Timothy's attempts to cope with the social situation at Eton where upper classmen have the power to boss around lower classmen. In one of the comic highlights, Timothy and a young friend whom he calls "Inky" are assigned to bake a cake for a birthday party of upper classmen. They replace a layer of frosting with some harmless "stick-jaw" and when the cake is consumed, everyone's jaw gets stuck as Timothy and Inky laugh uproariously. The scene cuts to Timothy being disciplined with a paddling, still laughing over the experience.

This comical spirit is maintained throughout the film, even in transition scenes such as Timothy walking across the street with the upperclassmen's laundry, several top hats on his head, several jackets draped over his arms, as he narrowly dodges passing cars. He sets the clothes down near a fountain, walks away, and of course the fountain comes on, drenching the material. His punishment is psychological. All of the lower classmen are physically disciplined except him.

Peter Lawford, just beginning his long career, is quite good as the snobby upperclassman who takes an immediate dislike to Timothy. Late in the film, when Lawler's character gets drunk and is injured in an accident with the headmaster's car, Timothy is blamed. A fight they have early in the movie, where Timothy asserts himself, is broken up by Carlton, who is Timothy's new stepbrother by marriage. Carlton is played by Freddie Bartholomew, who appears for the first time with Rooney since *Lord Jeff* (1938). Bartholomew has grown and matured considerably, now a full head taller than Rooney, while Mickey himself has changed little since their first screen teaming in *The Devil Is a Sissy* (1936). The rest of the cast is rounded out with welcome veterans like Ian Hunter (who played Bartholomew's father in *The Devil Is a Sissy*, in which the delicate English child has to adapt to his rougher American peers) and Edmund Gwenn, who is typically grounded and impressive as Eton's headmaster. The only romance in *A Yank at Eton* is also comical, made especially so by Marta Linden's affected performance as Winifred.

Child actress Juanita Quigley, appearing here at the age of eleven, was already seven-year veteran of movies, even having a brief stint with Our Gang (the Little Rascals) in a couple of their MGM short subjects in 1940. She would appear again with Rooney in *National Velvet* (1944).

It seems Timothy can only do wrong. After his constant troubles at Eton, he returns home and attempts to impress Winifred by letting his stepfather's prize horse out of its stable. The horse runs away and ends up breaking its leg. In the context of an otherwise comical movie, this unsettling dramatic scene slows down the pace of the film and changes its direction. It does remind us what a fine actor Rooney is, able to switch from comedy to drama within the same movie, riding the unevenness of its structure with a consistently strong performance. This scene serves as the catalyst for Timothy's wanting to pay his stepfather back by responding better to an Eton education, and he proves himself during the next term as a successful scholar and athlete, adapting to England's way of doing things. The film concludes with the family's returning to America, where Timothy will get to attend Notre Dame.

During the filming of this movie, Mickey Rooney continued to have serious marital difficulties with new bride Ava Gardner. They separated, and she filed for divorce. Louis B. Mayer, sympathetic to the actor's plight, moved up *A Yank at Eton* on the production schedule as some of it was shot on location in Connecticut, far from Hollywood and Rooney's marital troubles.

As America entered World War Two, Rooney became eligible for the draft. MGM naturally wanted to avoid having one of their biggest stars go into the army. When Rooney reported for his physical, he was designated 4F due to high blood pressure. Rooney indicated in his autobiography that it was likely his marital troubles with Ava Gardner that caused his blood pressure to rise.[1]

A Yank at Eton was yet another successful Mickey Rooney picture, and MGM was pleased with its profits. However, Rooney, now a married-and-separated twenty-one-year-old man, was getting a bit too old to continue to play Andy Hardy. Despite the series coming to a close, Rooney's next movie was yet another saga in the continuing adventures of the Hardy family.

31

ANDY HARDY'S DOUBLE LIFE

(MGM, 1942)

Director: George B. Seitz
Screenplay: Agnes Christine Johnston
Cinematographers: George J. Folsey, John J. Mescall. *Editor:* Gene Ruggiero
Cast: Mickey Rooney (Andy Hardy), Lewis Stone (Judge Hardy), Cecilia Parker (Marian Hardy), Fay Holden (Mrs. Emily Hardy), Ann Rutherford (Polly Benedict), Esther Williams (Sheila Brooks), William Lundigan (Jeff Willis), Robert Pittard (Botsy), Robert Blake (Tooky), Susan Peters (Sue), Addison Richards (George Benedict), Mantan Moreland (Prentiss), Mary Currier (Mr. Steadman), Micky Martin (Bud), Charles Peck (Jack), Johnny Walsh (Harry), Jay Ward (Byron), George Watts (Binks), Arthur Space (Attorney), Edward Gargan (Motorcycle Cop)
Alternate Title: Andy Hardy Steps Out
Released: December 17, 1942
Specs: 92 minutes; black and white
Availability: DVD (Warner Archive Collection: *The Andy Hardy Film Collection: Volume 2*)

The structure of *Andy Hardy's Double Life*, especially its conclusion, makes it seem as if the film is the last in the Hardy family series. In fact, Bosley Crowther in the *New York Times* wrote a veritable eulogy in the newspaper's February 21, 1943, issue when reviewing this film.[1] Crowther opined that since Andy leaving for college would remove him completely from his family and experiences back in small-town Carvel, forcing the character into a sharper reality, the series would have to end. In fact, however, there would be three more Hardy family movies, although this would be the final one for Ann Rutherford and Polly Benedict.

While sticking to the basic formula of Judge Hardy having to cope with a serious court case, Andy having girl and money trouble, and Marian dealing with a tumultuous romance, *Andy Hardy's Double Life* does center on Andy leaving for college, wrapping up his affairs at home, and transitioning away from the naive, enthusiastic youngster he'd been thus far. Of course, Andy's personality traits are so inherent to his character that his decision to evolve toward adulthood turns out to be just that.

Judge Hardy wavers between pondering a case where a young boy is injured after having been hit by a truck while playing on his wagon. The judge must determine just who was at fault, taking into consideration that his mother is a widow struggling to support her child. Marian is still dating Jeff Willis, whose drunk driving caused a serious accident in the previous Hardy family entry, *The Courtship of Andy Hardy*. Andy, meanwhile, wants to transition away from longtime girlfriend Polly, but just enough so that she still writes him letters while he is in college, which he believes will enhance his reputation at the all-male Wainright College he is attending. Andy is smitten by Polly's houseguest, a college girl who helps her friend teach the youngest Hardy a lesson by tricking him into being engaged to marry both. Naturally, the gullible Andy falls for their ruse completely.

There are many humorous moments in *Andy Hardy's Double Life*, as well as a very serious scene in which Andy must tell the judge that he does not want to be escorted around college for the first two weeks of his freshman year despite his father eagerly looking forward to doing so. Andy essentially reveals that he must now be on his own to face higher education without the judge's influence as a distinguished alumnus with connections to most of the faculty. The film ends on an amusing note with Andy running into another Wainright student on the train, shocked to discover she is a girl and that Wainright is, as of that very year, coeducational.

Swimmer Esther Williams makes her film debut in *Andy Hardy's Double Life* as Polly's houseguest. Along with the obligatory swimming scene, Williams comes off well as she uses her wiles to dupe Andy into falling for her, while he also tries to maintain his connection to Polly. Williams would go on to star in her own series of colorful musicals that centered on her swimming prowess, including *Neptune's Daughter* (1949) and *Dangerous When Wet* (1953).

While one would imagine it would be time to bring the Hardy family series to a close with this film, audiences were pleased when *Andy Hardy's Double Life* hit their theaters. One theater owner in Iowa told *Box Office*,

> Don't let them tell you Mickey Rooney is slipping. He can slip a long way and be ahead of most stars. If they have any laughs in them they'll laugh at this one.[2]

Costing less than $370,000 to produce, *Andy Hardy's Double Life* grossed nearly $3 million at the box office.

Only weeks after Bosley Crowther's eulogistic review appeared in the *New York Times*, MGM was given a special award at the March 4, 1943, Academy Awards ceremony "for its achievement in representing the American Way of Life in the production of the 'Andy Hardy' series of films." The year 1943 was also the first one since 1937 where a Hardy family movie was not released. They would not return until *Andy Hardy's Blonde Trouble* in 1944.

THE HUMAN COMEDY

(MGM, 1943)

Director: Clarence Brown
Screenplay: Howard Estabrook. *Story:* William Saroyan
Producer: Clarence Brown. *Cinematographer:* Harry Strandling Sr. *Editor:* Conrad A. Nervig
Cast: Mickey Rooney (Homer Maccauley); Frank Morgan (Willie Grogan); James Craig (Tom Spangler); Marsha Hunt (Diana Steed); Fay Bainter (Mrs. Macauley); Ray Collins (Mr. Macauley); Van Johnson (Marcus Macauley); Donna Reed (Bess Macauley); Jackie "Butch" Jenkins (Ulysses Macauley); Dorothy Morris (Mary Arena); John Craven (Tobey George); Ann Ayars (Mrs. Sandoval); Mary Nash (Miss Hicks); Rita Quigley (Helen); David Holt (Hubert Ackley III); Henry O'Neill (Charles Steed); Katharine Alexander (Mrs. Steed); Alan Baxter (Brad Stickman); Darryl Hickman (Lionel); Clem Bevans (Henderson); Adeliene DeWalt Reynolds (Librarian); Carl "Alfalfa" Switzer (Auggie); Barry Nelson (Fat); Robert Mitchum (Horse); Don DeFore (Texas); Frank Jenks (Larry); Howard Freeman (Reverend Holly); Morris Ankrum (Mr. Beaufrere); Lynne Carver (Beaufrere daughter); Mary Servoss (Mrs. Beaufrere); Wallis Clark (Principal); Byron Foulger (Track Coach); Irving Lee (Joe); Jay Ward (Felix); Anthony Mazzola (Hajohn Ara); Howard J. Stevenson (Mr. Mechano); Ernest Whitman (Black Man Waving from Train); Emory Parnell (Cop); Payne Johnson (Boy Stealing Peaches); Ernie Alexander, Don Taylor, James Warren (Soldiers); Clancy Cooper (Mess Sergeant); Jane Farrar, Jean Fenwick, John Shay, Leigh Sterling, James Carven, Jane Drummond (People at Steed Party); Bertram Marburgh (Steed Butler), Dora Baker (Steed Cook). *Note:* Cast members in the existing studio records but who

were not seen in the final film include S. Z. Sakall, Jessie Arnold, Connie Gilchrist, Margaret Armstrong, Sara Paden, Leila McIntyre, and Joseph E. Bernard.
Released: March 2, 1943
Specs: 117 minutes; black and white
Availability: DVD (Warner Archive Collection)

The Human Comedy is not only a quintessential wartime MGM feature, but it is said to have been one of Louis B. Mayer's favorite films. Rather than shoot yet another war movie, the idea was to examine what was happening on the home front, concentrating on sentiment and avoiding cynicism.

Writer William Saroyan was hired to pen a sentimental story about a typical American family exhibiting strong, wholesome values while living

Mickey Rooney in *The Human Comedy*

through, and responding to, the world war that was currently going on. Saroyan, however, also wanted to direct the film despite having no experience as a filmmaker. Mayer was certainly not about to let a beginner direct a major studio feature, but Saroyan argued that he had a particular vision when writing and another perspective would not provide that. Mayer also felt Saroyan's story was far too long for a feature film. Mayer hired Clarence Brown, one of the studio's top directors, to helm the movie, and studio writer Howard Estabrook to turn Saroyan's story into a screenplay. Saroyan was displeased and decided to publish his original story as a novel. The book came out right around the time of the movie, so each helped the other become quite a big hit. Saroyan would later win the Pulitzer Prize for this novel. He also is given a larger screen credit than Estabrook.

Set in the small town of Ithaca, California, *The Human Comedy* is the quintessential sentimental drama, offering folksy situations, religious platitudes, and homespun charm. This is evident with its opening scene. The story is introduced by the spirit of the deceased Mr. Maccauley (Ray Collins), who remains as narrator. The first scene shows the youngest Maccauley child, Ulysses (Butch Jenkins), responding to his environment from the perspective of a little boy. The child's response to a passing train and a freshly laid egg in the chicken coop is one of wonder, innocence, and discovery. The film asks its viewers to maintain the same sort of naïveté. We are asked to separate ourselves from any level of jaded skepticism that comes from experience, and respond to the world created by this movie with our hearts instead of our minds.

Mickey Rooney plays Homer Maccauley, the second oldest boy and man of the house now that his father is dead and his older brother Marcus (Van Johnson) is off fighting in the war. Unlike the exuberant mugging Rooney employed for his Andy Hardy character or the musicals he had been doing with Judy Garland, Homer is a quieter character and played with real restraint. Marcus is also quiet but has more of a pensive, brooding nature. Part of this might be due to his having to sort out his being in the service and having trouble detaching himself from the home life he misses so much: Mom (Fay Bainter), siblings, girlfriend, and the small-town life that symbolically represents what the soldiers were fighting for. Back home, Mother plays the harp as sister Bess (Donna Reed) accompanies her on the piano along with girlfriend Mary (Dorothy Morris). When approaching *The Human Comedy* in that manner, it comes off as a fascinating look at how moviegoers wished it could be, and how Louis B. Mayer imagined it was.

James Craig plays Tom Spangler, a former track star who now runs the telegraph office where Homer works.[1] Homer is currently on the track team, so he connects with Spangler. However, Willie Grogan (Frank Morgan) may be the most interesting character who is peripheral to the central figure Rooney plays. Grogan describes himself this way: "I'm an old time telegrapher, one of the last in the world. I'm also wire chief in this office. I am also a man with memories of many wondrous worlds gone by."

Grogan also asks that Homer douse his face with water and provide him with coffee when he overimbibes. In the idyllic small-town setting, Grogan is the one example that offers some level of skeptic realism. He is old, his life has passed him by; Spangler keeps him on pretty much as charity, as he drinks and wallows in melancholy. Grogan states, "They've been wanting to retire me for ten years. I don't know what I would do without this job. I supposed I'd be dead in a week. I was the fastest telegrapher in the business."

In a 2001 interview, Rooney recalled,

> Gable was away in the service so they were grooming James Craig to take his place. He had the same look, the same manner, even a voice that sounded like Gable. He never made it that far, especially after Gable returned when the war ended. Nice guy. I liked Jim. And I wish I had worked more often with Frank Morgan. He really became his character. If you look at me in our scenes together, you see a look of awe on my face. Only part of that is for the picture. Some of it is because I really was in awe of this guy. He'd be so good delivering his lines, and I'd be so busy watching him, I would forget mine![2]

Part of Homer's life is typical adolescent conflict. He runs track at school and has a rival on the track team as well as for the attentions of a girl with whom he is smitten. This innocence is thwarted by his job, where he must deliver tragic news to people. At one point he reveals to his mother how his life is changing with the added responsibility of being man of the house: "Ever since I started working everything seems to have changed. When a fella starts learning about people, almost everything you find out is sad. This job is good, but it sure makes school seem silly." Homer is so fraught with sadness upon having to deliver unhappy telegrams that he becomes even more revealing to Grogan when he states, "If my brother is killed in this war I'll spit at the world. I won't be good I'll be bad. I'll be the worst there is." Grogan understands.

Along with the responsibilities of being man of the house and realizing more fully the danger his brother is in, Homer must also deal with Grogan's alcoholism. When word comes through that Marcus has indeed been killed, Grogan dies at the telegraph before finishing the transcription. Homer understands.

While Homer's story at the center of *The Human Comedy* offers the most interest, there are tangential plots involving the other characters. Spangler's romance with society girl Diana Steed (Marsha Hunt) is a study in two separate classes (he being the consummate working man) that must reach a compromise. Ulysses is befriended by a myopic, buck-toothed outcast (Darryl Hickman), who, although he can't read, likes to walk around the library and stare at the shelves of books, fascinated by the amount of knowledge contained in one finite structure and readily accessible to the masses. Bess and Mary take in a movie with three soldiers passing through town (Barry Nelson, Dom DeFore, Robert Mitchum). The innocence of this meeting, with no sense of danger at all, is at once far-fetched and also acceptable in how it so comfortably fits in the proceedings.

Marcus is perhaps the least developed character. He is just a soldier who accepts his having been called by his country and misses the folks back home. He tells of his background to a fellow soldier, Tobey (John Craven), who had been raised in an orphanage. Tobey has spent his life longing for a family like the Maccauleys. On the day Homer gets the telegram about his brother's death, Tobey shows up in Ithaca.

During the preparation for the making of this movie, several actors were considered for roles. Gene Kelly was announced in the trades as being signed to play a part (probably Spangler, although no article makes that connection), and Lionel Barrymore was originally tapped to play Grogan. Spring Byington was originally cast as Diana Steed's mother (the part went to Katharine Alexander). Others who were announced as cast members during the early stages include Richard Quine, Margaret Wycherly, Kathleen Howard, Marjorie "Babe" Kane, and Horace McNally (a.k.a. Stephen McNally).

When looking at the novel version that Saroyan had published at the time of the film's release (causing the book to become a best seller in less than a week), we see that Saroyan's original vision differs from the film. The book has far less sentiment, the Ulysses character is more developed, and Saroyan offers some harsh social criticism. This would not do for an MGM feature. Screenwriter Howard Estabrook and director Clarence Brown reshaped Saroyan's 240-page script to fit not only the parameters of a two-hour feature film but also the vision of MGM, which embraced a more sentimental approach.

Clarence Brown's direction lends a great deal of atmosphere to the production. This is especially evident in an earlier scene where Grogan types up the first telegram of bereavement that Homer must deliver. Brown cuts from a close-up of the telegram being transcribed, to the look on Homer's face as he realizes the news he must deliver. When he does arrive at the woman's house at night, they are surrounded by darkness and quiet. The woman is so shocked that she comforts the stammering Homer for being so nervous. The news then sinks in and she breaks down. Homer stands there, powerless to help her. This moving scene is beautifully shot and offers a heartbreaking example of what was happening all too often in small towns across the nation during the war.

In his *New York Times* review, Bosley Crowther recognized not only the sentimentality but also the showmanship:

> *The Human Comedy*, in its two-hours-plus screen version which came to the Astor yesterday, can't help but attract wide attention on its incidental build-up alone. It is due for extensive popularity with Mickey Rooney in its title role. And it also gives ample promise of being the most hotly debated picture of the year. For here, cheek by jowl and overlapping, are set some most charming bits of fine motion-picture expression and some most maudlin gobs of cinematic goo. Here, in an almost formless tribute to the goodness and sweetness of man's soul, are spliced some quick, penetrating glimpses with long stretches of sheer banality. Here, in a picture which endeavors to speak such truths about Americans as should be spoken, pop up such artificialities as make one squirm with rank embarrassment.[3]

Just as the *New York Times* review wavered between praise for the talent and some misgivings with the sentiment, moviegoers during this period appeared to respond in much the same manner. In *Box Office*, where there is a section for theater owners to indicate how well or poorly a film played for them, one exhibitor in Iowa stated that *The Human Comedy* did "extra business" but "some thought it was too heavy."[4] A theater owner in South Dakota said that it was "a picture that holds an audience like it should" and "several left weeping."[5] So, even in 1943 when the movie was first released, its sentimental scenes evoked tears from some moviegoers, and were dismissed as "too heavy" by others.

When films played theaters during this period, they were often accompanied by a short comedy, cartoon, newsreel, or other such preliminary entertainment. Usually these additions were chosen by the exhibitor based on what might be available at the time and what usually pleased his audience. In the case of *The Human Comedy*, MGM specifically paired it with one of their own Tom and Jerry cartoons, the Technicolor *Sufferin' Cats*, which played with this feature at nearly all of its bookings.

The Human Comedy made nearly $3 million at the box office, resulting in a profit of over a million. Saroyan won an Oscar for Best Story, and Mickey Rooney received his second Academy Award nomination, this time losing to Paul Lukas for *Watch on the Rhine*. The film was also nominated for Best Picture, and Clarence Brown for Best Director, but this was the year of *Casablanca*. That film won Best Picture, and its director, Michael Curtiz, also took home the Oscar.

GIRL CRAZY

(MGM, 1943)

Directors: Norman Taurog, Busby Berkeley
Screenplay: Fred F. Finklehoffe, Dorothy Kingsley, William Ludwig, Sid Silvers, from the play by Guy Bolton and Jack McGowan
Producer: Arthur Freed. *Cinematographers:* William H. Daniels, Robert H. Planck. *Editor:* Albert Akst. *Original Music:* George and Ira Gershwin. *Choreographer:* Busby Berkeley
Cast: Mickey Rooney (Danny Churchill Jr.); Judy Garland (Ginger Gray); Gil Stratton (Bud Livermore); Robert E. Strickland (Henry Lathrop); Rags Ragland (Rags); June Allyson (Specialty Solo); Nancy Walker (Polly Williams); Tommy Dorsey (Himself); Guy Kibbee (Dean Phineas Armour); Frances Rafferty (Marjorie); Henry O'Neill (Mr. Churchill); Howard Freeman (Governor); Irving Bacon (John); William Beaudine Jr. (Tom); Jess Lee Brooks (Buckets); Dick Haymes (Vocalist); Peter Lawford (Student); Jo Stafford, Christine Stafford, Clark Yocum, Six Hits and a Miss, Merry Maids, Pied Pipers, Tommy Dorsey and His Orchestra (themselves) Karin Booth, Hazel Brooks, Georgia Carroll, Inez Cooper, Linda Deane, Natalie Draper, Mary Jane French, Carole Gallagher, Karen Gaylord, Aileen Hailey, Virginia Hunter, Lois James, Aileen Morris, Noreen Nash (Showgirls). Cast members in studio records/casting call lists but who did not appear or were not identifiable in the movie include Alphonse Martell, Barbara Bedford, Sarah Edwards, Harry C. Bradley, Spec O'Donnell, Sidney Miller, Helen Dickson, Melissa Ten Eyck, Vangie Beilby, Julia Griffith, Lillian West, Sandra Morgan, Peggy Leon, and Bess Flowers.
Songs: "I Got Rhythm" (music by George Gershwin, lyrics by Ira Gershwin; played during the opening credits; performed in the finale by Judy

Garland, Mickey Rooney, Six Hits and a Miss, the Music Maids, Tommy Dorsey and His Orchestra and chorus); "Treat Me Rough" (music by George Gershwin, lyrics by Ira Gershwin; performed by June Allyson, Mickey Rooney, the Music Maids, the Stafford Sisters, and Tommy Dorsey and His Orchestra); "Could You Use Me?" (music by George Gershwin, lyrics by Ira Gershwin; performed by Judy Garland and Mickey Rooney); "Bidin' My Time" (music by George Gershwin, lyrics by Ira Gershwin; performed by Judy Garland, the King's Men, and chorus); "Embraceable You" (music by George Gershwin, lyrics by Ira Gershwin; played during the opening credits; performed by Judy Garland and chorus; danced by Judy Garland and Charles Walters; played as dance music at the rodeo dance and as background music); "But Not for Me" (music by George Gershwin, lyrics by Ira Gershwin; performed by Judy Garland; played also as background music); "Fascinating Rhythm" (music by George Gershwin, lyrics by Ira Gershwin; performed by Tommy Dorsey and His Orchestra, with Tommy Dorsey on trombone and Mickey Rooney on piano [dubbed by Arthur Schutt]; from the stage musical "Lady, Be Good!"); "Sam and Delilah" (music by George Gershwin, lyrics by Ira Gershwin; performed by Tommy Dorsey and His Orchestra); "Happy Birthday to You" (music by Mildred J. Hill, lyrics by Patty S. Hill; performed by Rags Ragland and chorus); "Barbary Coast" (music by George Gershwin, lyrics by Ira Gershwin; performed by Tommy Dorsey and His Orchestra); "Boy! What Love Has Done to Me!" (music by George Gershwin, lyrics by Ira Gershwin; performed by Tommy Dorsey and His Orchestra)

Released: November 26, 1943

Specs: 99 minutes; black and white

Availability: DVD (Warner Home Video: *The Mickey Rooney and Judy Garland Collection*)

Girl Crazy was the last of the Mickey Rooney–Judy Garland musicals (although they would appear together again in the all-star *Words and Music* five years later). Some of the best music of any musical is contained in this film version of George and Ira Gershwin's hit 1930 Broadway show. *Girl Crazy* had been filmed at RKO studios in 1932 with the comedy team of Bert Wheeler and Bob Woolsey, emphasizing the humor more than the music. This one concentrates more on the music and the personalities of its leading stars.

Rooney plays Danny Churchill, a pampered playboy who comes from wealth and shirks his responsibility. His father arranges for him to attend a rustic all-male college out west, where he becomes smitten with pretty Ginger, the dean's granddaughter, who helps out by delivering the mail. The film concentrates on Danny's wavering between attempts to fit in, rebellion at the idea of fitting in, and his consistent attraction to Ginger. Unlike other films in which Rooney and Garland appear, it is Rooney's character of Danny who longs for the more aloof Ginger. Danny is about to leave the school and return to New York, but when he hears the school is about to be closed due to a lack of student enrollment, he decides to stay and help Ginger obtain the necessary 125 new freshmen to keep the school open. Of course this means putting on a show.

Danny Churchill is not like Andy Hardy, a small-town boy who becomes confused and out of place in the big city. And he is not Whitey Marsh, whose street-savvy limits him to the seedier areas of the bigger cities. He is a brash, confident, pampered rich boy, the sort that was especially unpopular during wartime when fighting men and a common purpose overrode the social structure. His attraction to Ginger, which is eventually reciprocated, causes him to become more understanding and altruistic.

Henry O'Neill, Mickey Rooney, Judy Garland, and Guy Kibbee

Girl Crazy is a bit more adult than the previous Rooney-Garland musicals. They are no longer teens putting on a show, as they had been in the other movies, but young adults connected to a college and investigating areas of their natural talent. The film also responds to the popularity of big band music of this period, prominently featuring Tommy Dorsey and His Orchestra. Everything blends effectively, including the areas of the story that seemed formulaic, as that is what audiences wanted. Some consider *Girl Crazy* to be the best Rooney-Garland pairing, making it a fitting culmination.

Along with the many great musical numbers, there are some fun comic highlights strewn throughout *Girl Crazy*. In their initial meeting, Danny helps Ginger start her car in the desert, and then she drives off, leaving him behind, and holds up a sign that states "No Riders." And, as can be predicted, there is a scene where the city-bred Danny first tries to ride a horse, causing it to gallop and buck while he holds on and yells frantically. One of the screenwriters, Fred Finklehoffe, was something of a comedy specialist, having penned the *Brother Rat* comedies at Warner Bros., and would later write what Jerry Lewis believes is his best film with Dean Martin, *The Stooge* (1952).

During many of the comical scenes featuring Rooney, Ginger is shown laughing derisively at Danny, being tickled by the fact that a swinging playboy from a life of privilege would be so inept in this environment. Judy Garland's contagious laugh has been discussed by many of her costars in their various autobiographies and in later interviews. It is evident more than once in *Girl Crazy*.

Arthur Freed once again produced, as he had the previous Rooney-Garland musicals, but Busby Berkeley left the directorial chores to Norman Taurog shortly after filming the finale (which was shot first). This was due to a combination of Berkeley's clashes with the arranger and with Garland herself, who felt his direction was too demanding. Rooney recalled,

> Judy was exhausted, and was already taking pills to stay awake, to go to sleep, when she was told she was too fat or too thin. She did it secretly. And Buzz was pushing us past our limits. So Judy had him taken off the picture and they brought in Norman Taurog, who was a friend of both of ours.[1]

Taurog's approach integrated the musical numbers with the story, whereas Berkeley presented them as separate scenes. This approach works effectively in *Girl Crazy* and is one of the film's strengths.

The supporting cast is uniformly good, as usual, with burlesque comic Rags Ragland balancing the humor in an affable role that bolstered many

MGM films during this period. Nancy Walker, who became quite popular in TV commercials and on shows like *The Mary Tyler Moore Show* and *Golden Girls* when she was older, gets to have some fun in a wisecracking role. And June Allyson appears early in her film career doing the specialty number "Treat Me Rough" early in the movie.

Filming was sometimes difficult. The temperature was quite hot, and a sandstorm ruined some of the equipment, delaying production while replacements were obtained. But Garland's exhaustion, the difficult conditions, and the delays are not at all evident in the final production. Everything flows nicely, and Garland's performance is spot-on as usual.

Girl Crazy originally had a different ending, which was shot but jettisoned. Originally Rooney, Garland, and others in the cast were going to go into a reprise of "Embraceable You" after Danny proposes to Ginger. Instead, it concludes with dozens of applicants for new students, but they are all girls. The school will remain open and also co-educational. The closing "I Got Rhythm" number was originally to be earlier in the movie.

Critics were generally pleased with *Girl Crazy*, with the reviewer for *Time* stating,

> As sung by actress Judy Garland, "Embraceable You" and "Bidin' My Time" become hits all over again and the new "But Not for Me" sounds like another. Her presence is open, cheerful, warming. If she were not so profitably good at her own game, she could obviously be a dramatic cinema actress with profit to all.[2]

Variety also praised Garland, stating,

> Miss Garland is a nifty saleswoman of the numbers, right down to the over-produced "Rhythm" finale which was Busby Berkeley's special chore. Her "Embraceable You" delivery is a standout; ditto "Bidin' My Time" and "But Not for Me." She's also got two nice dancing sessions.[3]

However, Theodore Strauss was more measured in his review for the *New York Times*, stating,

> The immortal Mickey . . . is an entertainer to his fingertips. And with Judy, who sings and acts like an earthbound angel, to temper his brashness, well, they can do almost anything they wish, and we'll like it even in spite of ourselves.[4]

Girl Crazy was also a box office success, with a budget of less than $1.5 million and netting a profit of nearly $4 million. However, the film's place in Mickey Rooney's career shows it coming at the end of his tenure as an MGM superstar. Rooney enjoyed number one box office status for three years—1939, 1940, and 1941. He remained in the top ten for 1942 and 1943, *Girl Crazy* being his final film of '43. But Rooney, despite his success, had some concerns. He was getting too old to play Andy Hardy, especially since the public was aware that he was now in his twenties and had been married and divorced. However, with his short stature and youthful appearance, it didn't appear that he was going to grow into character roles any time soon. The movie business was fickle, and Rooney realized it. In fact, 1943 would be Mickey Rooney's final appearance among the top ten box office stars in movies.

ANDY HARDY'S BLONDE TROUBLE

(MGM, 1944)

Director: George B. Seitz
Screenplay: Aurania Rouverol, Harry Ruskin, William Ludwig, Agnes Christine Johnston
Producer: Carey Wilson. *Cinematographer:* Lester White. *Editor:* George White. *Art Director:* Cedric Gibbons. *Music:* David Snell
Cast: Mickey Rooney (Andy Hardy), Lewis Stone (Judge Hardy), Fay Holden (Mrs. Emily Hardy), Sara Haden (Aunt Milly Forrest), Herbert Marshall (Dr. M. J. Standish), Bonita Granville (Kay Wilson), Jean Porter (Katy Anderson), Keye Luke (Dr. Lee), Lee Wilde (Lee Walker), Lyn Wilde (Lyn Walker), Marta Linden (Mrs. Townsend), Jackie Moran (Spud), Cliff Clark (Officer Shay), Tommy Dix (Mark), Connie Gilchrist (Mrs. Gordon), Barbara Bedford (Dean's Secretary)
Song: "Easy to Love"[1] (music and lyrics by Cole Porter; sung by Lee Wilde and danced by Lee and Lyn Wilde)
Released: May 4, 1944
Specs: 107 minutes; black and white
Availability: DVD (Warner Archive Collection: *The Andy Hardy Film Collection: Volume 2*)

The Hardy series continued to evolve with *Andy Hardy's Blonde Trouble*, which continues where the previous movie left off with Andy headed to Wainright College. But despite taking Andy Hardy out of his small-town element and offering another dynamic to his character and situations, the film remains as pleasant and amusing as the other entries in the series. Polly Benedict is missing, as is Andy's sister, Marian (actress Cecilia Parker left movies to raise her family). The Hardy parents and Aunt Milly appear in occasional cutaways to what is going on in the household with Andy gone.

The film does not simply refer back to the previous movie; it begins exactly where *Andy Hardy's Double Life* ended. This film repeats the previous one's closing scene, where Andy discovers a young lady on the train headed for Wainright College, which is now co-educational. However, the actress in the closing scene of *Andy Hardy's Double Life*, Susan Peters, does not appear in the role here. She is replaced by Bonita Granville as Kay, who seems to be attracted to a middle-aged Dr. Standish, which raises Andy's jealous chagrin. Meanwhile, a pair of attractive blonde twin girls traveling together on the train, one flirty the other not, keep confusing Andy, who sees them separately—one appears to like him, the other clearly doesn't.

In the Hardy home, Judge Hardy is suffering from tonsillitis and he is cared for by Dr. Lee, played by Keye Luke. Both the judge and Mrs. Hardy are taken aback by the doctor's appearance (the film is made during wartime), so he has to clarify that he is American born and of Chinese descent. The judge's having to have his tonsils removed is the family crisis but it is played for laughs.

The twin girls have been told by their father to travel separately because he read a doctor's report that such a thing is healthy for twins. The girls cannot bear to do so and plan to go to Wainright together—the serious one attending college and the flirty one getting a job singing in a nightclub. Their dad starts to be suspicious of the ruse from afar, saying so in a letter, and Andy helps them out once he discovers there are, indeed, two of them.

The scene where Andy realizes they are twins is one of the funniest scenes in the movie. He bumps his head just beforehand, which causes his eyes to cross for a few seconds. When he sees both girls, he reacts in fear as if the bump on the head has seriously impacted his vision. Rooney shows his innate comic prowess often in his films, but this scene, done without dialogue, just with a series of facial expressions, is brilliantly executed. Andy does try to continue a relationship with Kay, but his attempt to assist the twins distracts this situation and causes misunderstanding and jealousy. Meanwhile, Kay continues her attraction for Dr. Standish, who turns out to be Wainright's dean. In a rather mature moment for the wholesome series, the dean very nearly succumbs to her charm (this being the first year coeds are in attendance, including all the temptations).

Another especially funny scene is separate from the principals of the Hardy series. Jean Porter plays the sister of Andy's old friend Beezy and has purchased Andy's car for eight dollars. She leaves it with the judge, who reimburses her money, and Dr. Lee buys it. The doctor professes to "know as much about cars as I do medicine" and fixes it up so that it runs beautifully. Beezy's sister sees it parked in front of the Hardy house and decides to take it for a spin. As soon as she starts down the street, a burglar alarm the doctor has rigged goes off loudly, and a sign pops out of the trunk indicating, "POLICE! STOLEN CAR!" Ms. Porter, a young actress with a flair for comedy, has a reaction that helps this tangential scene to be among the film's highlights.

Andy Hardy's Blonde Trouble is pleasant and diverting, but critics were particularly harsh, believing the series continued only because of the special Oscar it received at the 1943 ceremonies. In fact, acknowledgment of the film being part of a Special Academy Award Series is noted during the opening credits. However, audiences never seemed to tire of the films. A theater owner in Washington told *Box Office*,

> This brought out the strangers and the regulars. It also brought out many smiles. Andy Hardy sure does the trick here. I hope they never stop making them.[2]

The draft board continued to beckon Mickey Rooney to enter the draft despite his 4F examination results. MGM kept asking for deferments so he could complete his assigned work for the studio. However, during the filming of his next movie, *National Velvet*, the military indicated it would wait no more. Designated 1A with a new physical exam, Mickey Rooney was about to enter the armed forces.

NATIONAL VELVET

(MGM, 1944)

Director: Clarence Brown
Screenplay: Helen Deutsch, Theodore Reeves, from the novel by Enid Bagnold
Producer: Pandro S. Berman. *Cinematographer:* Leonard Smith. *Editor:* Robert J. Kern
Cast: Mickey Rooney (Mi Taylor), Donald Crisp (Mr. Brown), Elizabeth Taylor (Velvet Brown), Anne Revere (Mrs. Brown), Angela Lansbury (Edwina Brown), Jackie "Butch" Jenkins (Donald Brown), Juanita Quigley (Malvolia Brown), Reginald Owen (Farmer Ede), Norma Varden (Miss Sims), Terry Kilburn (Ted), Arthur Shields (Mr. Hallam), Alec Craig (Tim), Eugene Loring (Taski), Arthur Treacher (Race Patron), Billy Bevan (Constable), Wally Cassell (Jockey), Mona Freeman (Student), Richard Haydel (Student), Jane Isbell (Jane), Fredrick Worlock (Stewart)
Released: December 14, 1944
Specs: 123 minutes; color
Availability: DVD (Warner Home Video)

National Velvet is known more as the film that catapulted young Elizabeth Taylor to stardom than as the final MGM film Mickey Rooney would make as a top-level star. Rooney was drafted into the military, passed his physical exam, and was scheduled to report for active duty. Director Clarence Brown was told to shoot all of Rooney's scenes ahead of time so he could meet his appointment, filming the scenes without him afterward. The director begrudgingly complied. Shot in Technicolor, it was Mickey Rooney's first color movie.

Elizabeth Taylor, a young English actress who had made only a few movies, was cast in the lead role of Velvet Brown, a twelve-year-old girl whose

Mickey Rooney, Elizabeth Taylor, and Jackie "Butch" Jenkins

love for a difficult horse is central to the story's development. Rooney, who is top billed, has essentially a supporting role as a young drifter who befriends Velvet and helps her nurture and train the horse. And while Rooney's performance is outstanding, it is the newcomer Taylor who is the real star of *National Velvet*. Mickey Rooney recalled,

> When I met Elizabeth Taylor I was struck by her beauty. I had been in pictures a long time by then and had seen a lot of beautiful girls and women. But

> there was something about Elizabeth's eyes that were striking. They were like violet pools of light. And her personality was so intelligent and confident, but not aloof or conceited. She was very warm, honest, and so naturally talented. Donald Crisp said to me during a break, "That little lass is going to steal this picture from all of us, boy." He wasn't kidding, because she sure did. We had a scene where she was supposed to cry. So I tried to help out by saying stuff that used to work on me—somebody dying, people who were very poor, that sort of thing. Well she bursts out laughing! A lot of good I did! She ended up doing the scene just fine.[1]

National Velvet is the story of Velvet Brown, who proves herself able to connect with a wild horse when she steps in front of the animal as it is running wild, and it responds favorably. The horse is put up for raffle, and she wins him with the intention of entering him in the Grand National steeplechase. Being told the horse is a pirate, Velvet names him Pie. Mickey Rooney plays the drifter Mi, who ends up at the home of Velvet's mother after finding her address in his deceased father's effects. Nevertheless, she convinces her husband (Donald Crisp) to hire Mi over his better judgment, and Mi is brought into the home as a hired hand. Mi is a former jockey who quit racing after being involved in a collision that killed another rider. Mi overcomes his misgivings and plans to ride Pie in the steeplechase. However, Velvet puts on a suit and insists on riding the horse herself. They win, and Velvet faints from the excitement. The race doctor revives her but discovers she is a girl, and they are disqualified from the race. Velvet doesn't care about the prize money; only that Pie has proven himself with a victory. Becoming a media star as a result, Velvet is offered a lot of money to tour with the horse and be filmed in Hollywood. Velvet turns the offer down, stating, "Pie would not like being looked at."

Both Paramount and RKO studios as far back as 1935 originally sought Enid Bagnold's novel; MGM acquired them in 1937. Various announcements were offered to the press attaching Shirley Temple and Spencer Tracy to a planned project, but nothing materialized. It was revived in 1941, but nothing happened until 1943, when director Clarence Brown became attached to the project, which had been considered for Mervyn LeRoy.

King Charles, whose grandfather was Man o' War, was the horse chosen to play Pie. Elizabeth Taylor sought the role of Velvet, pointing out her British background and experience working with horses. MGM executives thought she was too young and small to play the role. Fortunately, by the time filming was ready to commence on the project, Taylor had grown three inches. Gene Tierney and Susanna Foster were among the actresses considered for the role.

National Velvet was nominated for Academy Awards for Best Director, Best Art Direction (Color), and Best Cinematography (Color). Anne Revere won the Oscar as Best Supporting Actress, while Robert J. Kern won for Best Film Editing. In June 1945, *National Velvet* became one of the first films to be selected by the Library of Congress for their motion picture collection.

On February 3, 1947, Taylor and Rooney reprised their roles from *National Velvet* for a Lux Radio Theatre broadcast, and on October 6, 1949, the Hallmark Playhouse broadcast a version starring Roddy McDowell. Bryan Forbes directed Tatum O'Neal, Nanette Newman, Christopher Plummer, and Anthony Hopkins in a 1978 sequel to *National Velvet* called *International Velvet*. In the British-made sequel, O'Neal plays the grown Velvet's (Newman's) niece, who dreams of racing her horse in the Olympics. A television series based on *National Velvet*, also titled *National Velvet*, aired on the NBC network from September 18, 1960, to September 10, 1962. Lori Martin played Velvet in the series, and Arthur Space played her father.

While Mickey Rooney is very much a part of *National Velvet*, his role is clear support and could have been essayed by any capable actor. Various offscreen distractions, coupled with having to shoot his scenes ahead of time, made Rooney no less effective in the role. But it truly is Elizabeth Taylor's film, and she comfortably overshadows all of her supporting players.

Upon completing his scenes, Mickey Rooney was called to report to the armed forces for induction. He would be leaving behind his motion picture career for a two-year stint in the army. Clark Gable had enlisted after his wife, actress Carole Lombard, was killed in a plane crash while on a USO tour in January 1942. James Stewart had also enlisted. MGM was not pleased with losing yet another of its top stars to the military, but Rooney understood his duty to his country and willingly accepted the appointment, planning to make the best of it. Just prior to leaving, he reconciled with ex-wife Ava Gardner, who promised to wait for Rooney while he was away serving his country.

While in the army, Mickey Rooney had no real connection to the other soldiers. He had been in show business all of his life, so he could not relate to the rather ordinary lives they could converse about, outside of an unhappiness with the drudgery of army life. Some would jealously chide him for his star status. Rather than allow it to get to him, Rooney responded with a wink and a smile, and soon became well liked in his unit, especially when the others saw he neither received nor requested any special treatment.

Rooney made it through basic training and engaged in active duty but soon was called by his superiors to spend most of his time doing camp shows, the military using Rooney's star power and ability to entertain to get the talents of a top performer for no money. Rooney was happy to contribute in this manner and worked hard, on little sleep, to keep the soldiers entertained.

Not long after Rooney was in the service he received a phone call from Ava Gardner asking him to stop writing to her. He pleaded for her to reconsider, but she hung up on him. While in the service, he eventually met a pretty southern woman named Betty Jane Rase, and the two fell in love and got married over the course of two weekend furloughs. After a third one, Betty Jane discovered she was pregnant. She gave birth to Joe Yule III (who went by the name of Mickey Rooney Jr.) while her husband remained in the army. Rooney was delighted. As his stretch in the army continued, he was eager to return home to a new wife and a new baby, and resume his career as one of MGM's top box office stars.

LOVE LAUGHS AT ANDY HARDY

(MGM, 1946)

Director: Willis Goldbeck
Screenplay: William Ludwig, Harry Ruskin, story by Howard Dimsdale. *Characters:* Aurania Rouverol
Producer: Robert Sisk. *Cinematographer:* Robert Planck. *Editor:* Irvine Warburton
Cast: Mickey Rooney (Andrew "Andy" Hardy), Lewis Stone (Judge James K. Hardy), Sara Haden (Aunt Milly Forrest), Bonita Granville (Kay Wilson), Lina Romay (Miss Isobel Gonzales), Fay Holden (Mrs. Emily Hardy), Dorothy Ford (Coffy Smith), Hal Hackett (Duke Johnson), Dick Simmons (Dane Kittridge), Clinton Sundberg (Haberdashery Clerk), Geraldine Wall (Miss Hattie Geeves), Addison Richards (Mr. George Benedict), Holmes Herbert (Dr. White), Lucien Littlefield (Telegraph Clerk), Charles Peck (Tommy), Eddie Dunn (Police Sergeant), Si Jenks (Driver)
Released: December 25, 1946
Specs: 95 minutes; black and white
Availability: DVD (Warner Archive Collection: *The Andy Hardy Film Collection: Volume 2*)

Mickey Rooney returned from the army to a young wife, a new baby, and his career at MGM. At first, it would seem things could not be better. Sam Stiefel, a business manager whom he'd hired just prior to entering the service, had negotiated with MGM to continue paying Rooney a $6,250-per-month salary while he was stationed overseas. This was unprecedented. Actors were always off the payroll while in the military. But Stiefel did not stop there. He also renegotiated Rooney's contract with the studio, with the actor receiving $7,500 per week with a forty-week guarantee, or $300,000 per year. Rooney also was allowed, by contract, to have his own radio show. Radio was in direct competition with movies and disliked by the studio, but Stiefel felt it could provide extra income and opportunity. Stiefel also felt that Rooney should have some say in the projects in which he would appear, and not be at the whim of the studio moguls. While this sort of situation would be the norm for top movie stars years later, at this time it was revolutionary. Stiefel set up Rooney, Inc., renting a plush suite of offices on Sunset Boulevard, where he would conduct business. Rooney had an office there too, but did little more than sign his name to the contracts Stiefel thrust in front of him.

However, all was not blissful on the home front. Once Rooney returned to civilian life and settled down with his new bride, he found that their hasty marriage was a bit too hasty. She and he had nothing in common. He enjoyed his time with the new baby, but his relationship with Betty Jane was little more than a series of quarrels. Plus, he also discovered that he owed Stiefel $100,000. Before his contract was negotiated, when Rooney was not on salary, Stiefel, as his business manager, was giving money to Rooney's mother, allowing her to maintain the lifestyle to which she'd now grown accustomed. Despite being back on his MGM contract, Rooney did not have $100,000 immediately available. So, it was arranged that Stiefel would accept half of Rooney's earnings until the amount was paid up.

Rooney could escape his tumultuous home life and business troubles by filming his first postwar movie. That would be *Summer Holiday*, a remake of Rooney's earlier success *Ah, Wilderness!*, based on the Eugene O'Neill play. This time, of course, Rooney played an adult role rather than the juvenile. *Summer Holiday* was filmed from June through October 1946, but it was withheld from release until 1948. It was instead decided that Mickey Rooney would return for one last Andy Hardy film, after which the series would finally conclude. But, while Rooney was a top box office superstar when he went into the army in 1944, there was no new Mickey Rooney movie released to theaters in all of 1945—the first time in twenty years. A year was a long time in Hollywood during the 1940s. MGM and Rooney were confident that he could easily pick up where he left off, especially when returning for some real closure on the always bankable Hardy series.

Love Laughs at Andy Hardy follows the usual formula. Both sister Marian Hardy and old flame Polly Benedict are referred to but do not appear. The judge, Andy's mom, and Aunt Milly do appear. They provide essentially the same household Andy had left, and his welcome home is comfortable and familiar. But Andy has other ideas. He remained smitten with Kay, whom he met at college (actress Bonita Granville repeating the role she'd played in the previous Hardy film), and reveals that he is interested in marrying her. Of course his parents want to meet her, so they plan to attend the homecoming celebrations, since the judge is an alumnus. However, when Kay is not available to attend the homecoming dance, Andy settles for a blind date in her absence. The date turns out to be Coffy Smith, a very pretty girl who, unfortunately, towers over him in height (played by actress Dorothy Ford, who stood a full foot over Rooney).

The biggest comic highlight in *Love Laughs at Andy Hardy* is when Andy shows up at the dance with Coffy. His parents conclude that this is his intended. The others chortle at the difference in height. Undaunted, Andy determinedly tells his date that they will prove themselves on the dance floor. This sets up a delightfully funny sequence where five-foot, two-inch Mickey Rooney and six-foot, two-inch Dorothy Ford dance together. The visual contrast is striking, but their rhythm is tight. Rooney is barely up to Ford's chest in the clinches, and when he wants to spin her, she must

The poster for *Love Laughs at Andy Hardy* welcomed Mickey Rooney back from the service.

duck and he must jump in the air. It is all very amusing and beautifully performed. Rooney recalled in an interview,

> That dance bit is one of my favorite scenes in all the Hardy pictures. Dorothy and I worked out a lot of the business ourselves, trying to make it funnier. She wore high heels, making her taller yet. She was beautiful and a great sport.[1]

Of course it is all explained to the Hardy parents that it is Kay, not Coffy, who is Andy's intended.

Another, perhaps more mechanical, comic highlight in *Love Laughs at Andy Hardy* is a scene where Andy, home alone, is about to take a bath, but he must go outside and turn the water back on, as it had been turned off for maintenance. He throws on the first garment he sees, which turns out to be his mother's robe, but the wind shuts the door behind him and he is locked out. Naturally the family returns, with Mr. Benedict and a pretty young visitor to the Benedict home, finding Andy bundled up outside in his mother's robe, with mud all over his bare feet, trying to get back in through a window.

The film eventually goes from amusing to heartbreaking when Kay reveals she plans to wed another and they want Andy to be the best man. Andy never gets the opportunity to even propose. He gamely performs best man duties, and then plans to leave college and go off to South America to forget her. Circumstances result in Andy changing his mind before the end of the movie (of course he quickly becomes smitten with the Benedict houseguest) and his plans to finish college and go to law school remain intact as the film ends, neatly capping the series.

The moviegoing public had not forgotten Mickey Rooney and, after the troubles of wartime, seemed happy to relax with the familiar situations of the Hardys once again. The movie was budgeted at around a million dollars and profited more than twice that amount. However, critic Bosley Crowther of the *New York Times* stated,

> For those who had come to love the Hardys, including Fay Holden and Lewis Stone (who are back playing mama and papa deferentially, as usual), this return of Andy to juvenile pre-eminence may be a most gratifying thing. It is plainly to them that Mr. Rooney—and MGM—have directed this jape. But for those who are moderately hopeful of progress in the educational field—and in the education of veterans, in particular—it will be a letdown of major magnitude.[2]

Mickey Rooney agreeably fulfilled the request to give the Hardy family series some closure and was now eager to play more grown-up roles. His next film, the prizefight drama *Killer McCoy*, was a remake of an old Robert Taylor drama from 1939, *The Crowd Roars*.[3] This film was to begin Mickey Rooney's transition into adult roles.

KILLER MCCOY

(MGM, 1947)

Director: Roy Rowland
Screenplay: Frederick Hazlitt Brennan, George Bruce, Thomas Lennon. *Story:* George Oppenheimer
Producer: Sam Zimbalist. *Cinematographer:* Joseph Ruttenberg. *Editor:* Ralph E. Winters
Cast: Mickey Rooney (Tommy McCoy/Killer McCoy), Brian Donlevy (Jim Caighn), Ann Blyth (Sheila Carrson), James Dunn (Brian McCoy), Tom Tully (Cecil Y. Walsh), Sam Levene (Happy), Walter Sande (Bill Thorne), Mickey Knox (Johnny Martin), James Bell (Father Patrick Ryan), Gloria Holden (Mrs. Laura McCoy), Eve March (Mrs. Martin), June Storey (Arlene, Waitress), Douglas Croft (Danny Burns, Newsboy), Bob Steele (Sailor Graves), David Clarke (Pete Mariola), Larry Cisneros (Patsy), Joseph Crehan (George), Vincent Graeff (Jacky), Jane Green (Miss DeHaven), Marie Harmon (Gewn Brady), Johnny Indrisano (Rocky), Lew Jenkins (Sailor), David Gorcey (Joe), Dick Wessel (Danny Burns's Father), Rudy Wissler (Pete), Allen Wood (Harry), Chet Brandenburg (Corner Man), Wally Cassell (Louie), George Chandler (Photographer), Joe Devlin (Fight Fan), Sig Frohlich (Attendant), Jimmy Lennon (Announcer), Frank McClure (Clerk), Cy Schindell (Henchman), Milburn Stone (Henchman), Shelley Winters (Waitress)
Released: December 18, 1947
Specs: 104 minutes; black and white
Availability: DVD (Warner Archive Collection)

MGM still had *Summer Holiday* in the can but continued to withhold it from release, making *Killer McCoy* the first film release in which Mickey Rooney has a truly adult role. *Killer McCoy* is a pretty standard prizefight drama with many of the usual conflicts found in films of this subgenre.

Rooney is Tommy McCoy, a disgruntled young man with a drunken showbiz has-been as a father and a patient, long-suffering mother. Tommy and his father perform a song-and-dance act at a town benefit that also includes a few boxing matches. Tommy recognizes one of the fighters as a young man with whom he had a conflict earlier, and challenges him to a bout. Despite having no pugilistic skills, Tommy's ability to hit hard nets him a win in his first fight.

The way Tommy's first fight is presented is especially impressive. Naturally the boy he is fighting has some level of ring prowess, so he is able to bob and weave while Tommy flails wildly. However, the current champion is in attendance as is his trainer, and the two of them offer Tommy some between-rounds instructions. A quick study, Tommy refines his approach enough to find an opening, and knocks out his opponent. This allows the fighter and trainer to see his potential and convince him to enter pugilism. While he's training for his first fight, he and his father will open for the champion's bouts with their music act. A musical comedy act opening for prizefighting might seem incongruous to a modern audience, but it was not terribly unusual at one time. Often audiences enjoyed song and dance entertainment or comedy between matches at a boxing show.

Director Roy Rowland uses montages to show the passage of time, including the champion losing his title and leaving the fight game. His trainer then starts working with Tommy, who wins his first several bouts. However, when the champion returns to the ring several months later, in need of money, he is put in a match against Tommy. Out of shape and in poor health, the ex-champ has a difficult time in the ring against the now-experienced Tommy, who carries the bout by dancing away and pulling his punches. Encouraged to deliver a blow to simply end the match, Tommy lands a hit that's hard enough to kill his opponent and friend. Hereafter, he is known as Killer McCoy.

In Rooney's earlier films, especially his comedies, he is a boy sometimes forced to deal with grown-up problems. In *Killer McCoy* he is an adult, in an adult world, and has to confront something as emotionally stirring as killing a friend in the ring. Oddly, other than the name change and a scene where Tommy goes to his friend's widow, this aspect is not part of the character of the story. Tommy is not continually haunted by the image of his friend, and does not refer to it. The basis of the film continues with the conflict between Tommy and his father.

Tommy has been sending money to his mother, but his father has been using it to drink and gamble. When a letter arrives from the family minister that the woman has died, the minister indicates that she had not heard from either Tommy or his father in months, but spoke of them with understanding and forgiveness. Tommy realizes what his father has done. When gambling results in the father being severely in debt to gangsters, the head gambler takes over Tommy's contract to settle the debt. When Tommy falls for the gambler's daughter, a refined girl who had been sent away to school, his conflict extends to the gambler, who wants something better than a fighter for his daughter.

The situation between Tommy and the girl especially shows how Rooney has been allowed to play a more mature role. While Tommy is not really a lot older than Andy Hardy had been when we last visited the Hardy family, he is far more adult in his dealings and his approach to people and events. Andy would be all "gee whiz" and "woo-woo" over the gambler's daughter. Tommy McCoy approaches the situation as an adult. His confidence is borne of maturity and experience. He takes things slowly, pragmatically. He cares for the girl but understands her father's reach.

When rival gamblers want to score big in a championship bout, they kidnap the girl and Tommy's father, holding them for ransom until Tommy takes a dive in the eighth round. The father manages to fake out the criminals by playing sick, grabs one of their guns so the girl can escape, and shoots it out with the gangsters. All three men die. The girl gets to the arena before the eighth round and Tommy wins the bout.

The cast and performances in *Killer McCoy* are excellent. Aside from Rooney's exhibiting a greater maturity in his screen character, Ann Blyth, as the girl, wavers between pompous breeding and savvy understanding. It is a difficult balance, and she plays it effectively. Having made a significant impact a couple of years earlier in the MGM drama *Mildred Pierce* (1945), Blyth is well cast as Mickey Rooney's first grown-up screen romance. James Dunn, as the father, is recalling his Oscar-winning role in *A Tree Grows in Brooklyn* (1945), and does so splendidly. Brian Donlevy, as the gangster, exhibits a wily stoicism that adds tension to each of his scenes.

Roy Rowland's direction of the fight scene is every bit as impressive as the performances. Editing from several angles, using close-ups, medium shots, and long shots, and using the spectators as a supportive foreground, Rowland makes each fight scene an exciting highlight. This allows the rhythm of the film to maintain a steadier pace, and overshadows some of the predictability in the writing.

MGM was pleased to find that audiences were quite happy to welcome Mickey Rooney to grown-up roles. *Killer McCoy* cost over $1.4 million to produce and grossed over $3 million. Mickey Rooney had apparently become a consistently bankable commodity after the war, and the studio hoped he could reclaim his top spot among box office stars. His home life had also improved. Attempting to save his marriage to Betty Jane, they had another child, Tim Rooney, and Mickey delighted in watching his children interact. It seemed all was on track and heading in a good direction.

WORDS AND MUSIC

(MGM, 1948)

Director: Norman Taurog
Screenplay: Guy Bolton, Ben Feiner Jr., Fred F. Finklehoffe, Jean Holloway
Cinematographers: Charles Rosher, Harry Stradling Sr. *Editors:* Albert Akst, Ferris Webster
Cast: Mickey Rooney (Lorenz Hart); Perry Como (Eddie Lorrison Anders); Tom Drake (Richard Rodgers); Ann Sothern (Joyce Harmon); Cyd Charisse (Margo Grant); Betty Garrett (Peggy Lorgan McNeil); Janet Leigh (Dorothy Feiner Rodgers); Marshall Thompson (Herbert Fields); Mel Tormé (Himself); Vera-Ellen (Herself); Lena Horne (Herself); Jeanette Nolan (Mrs. Hart); Richard Quine (Ben Feiner Jr.); Dee Turnell (Himself); Edward Earle (James Kelly); Harry Antrim (Dr. Rodgers); Ilka Grüning (Mrs. Rodgers); Emory Parnell (Mr. Feiner); Dick Haymes (Himself); the Blackburn Twins (Themselves); Irving Bacon (Realtor); Gino Corrado (Waiter); Gower Champion (Dancer); Marietta Canty (Mary); June Hedin (Mary, age 12); Lora Lee Michel (Mary, age 5); Mary Stack (Mary, age 2); Damian O'Flynn (Producer); George Meeker (Producer); Allyn Ann McLerie (Singer); Eilene Jensen (Linda, age 8); Sherry Hall (Tommy); Bob Graham (Eddie); George Carleton (George); Stanley Blystone (Brakeman); Dorothy Abbott, Sue Casey, Jeanne Coyne, Mary Ellen Gleason, Martha Montgomery, Rita Rend, Sandra Spence, Candy Toxton (Showgirls)
Music: Richard Rodgers
Songs: "The Lady Is a Tramp" (music by Richard Rodgers, lyrics by Lorenz Hart; performed by Lena Horne); "Manhattan" (music by Richard Rodgers, lyrics by Lorenz Hart; performed by Mickey Rooney, Tom Drake [dubbed by Bill Lee] and Marshall Thompson); "Where or

When" (music by Richard Rodgers, lyrics by Lorenz Hart; performed by Lena Horne); "I Wish I Were in Love Again" (music by Richard Rodgers, lyrics by Lorenz Hart; performed by Judy Garland and Mickey Rooney); "Johnny One Note" (music by Richard Rodgers, lyrics by Lorenz Hart; performed by Judy Garland); "Spring Is Here" (music by Richard Rodgers, lyrics by Lorenz Hart); "Where's That Rainbow?" (music by Richard Rodgers, lyrics by Lorenz Hart; sung and danced by Ann Sothern, with Ramon Blackburn and Royce Blackburn); "This Can't Be Love" (music by Richard Rodgers, lyrics by Lorenz Hart; Danced by Cyd Charisse and Dee Turnell with ballerinas); "On Your Toes" (music by Richard Rodgers, lyrics by Lorenz Hart; sung by Cyd Charisse [dubbed by Eileen Wilson] and Dee Turnell [dubbed]; "Thou Swell" (music by Richard Rodgers, lyrics by Lorenz Hart; performed by June Allyson, Ramon Blackburn, and Royce Blackburn [dubbed by Pete Roberts and Eugene Cox]); "Way Out West" (music by Richard Rodgers, lyrics by Lorenz Hart; sung by Betty Garrett); "Mountain Greenery" (music by Richard Rodgers, lyrics by Lorenz Hart; sung by Perry Como; "Blue Room" (music by Richard Rodgers, lyrics by Lorenz Hart; sung by Perry Como, danced by Cyd Charisse; "Blue Moon" (music by Richard Rodgers, lyrics by Lorenz Hart; sung by Mel Tormé; "Slaughter on Tenth Avenue" (music by Richard Rodgers; danced by Gene Kelly, Vera-Ellen, and uncredited dancers; performed by the MGM Symphony Orchestra conducted by Lennie Hayton); "There's a Small Hotel" (music by Richard Rodgers, lyrics by Lorenz Hart; sung by Betty Garrett; "With a Song In My Heart" (music by Richard Rodgers, lyrics by Lorenz Hart); "With a Song in My Heart (Reprise)" (music by Richard Rodgers, lyrics by Lorenz Hart; sung by Perry Como)

Released: December 31, 1948
Specs: 120 minutes; Technicolor
Availability: DVD (Warner Home Video)

Before the release of *Words and Music*, which was the musical biography of songwriters Richard Rodgers and Lorenz Hart, MGM finally released *Summer Holiday*, which Rooney had filmed in 1946. Studio executives were not pleased with the finished film, despite interesting direction from Rouben Mamoulian and a cast that included Rooney, Walter Huston, Frank Morgan, Marilyn Maxwell, and Butch Jenkins. They were correct. *Summer Holiday* came out in April of 1948 and was an enormous flop. With a budget of over $2 million, *Summer Holiday* lost over $1 million.

Despite the modest success of *Love Laughs at Andy Hardy* and the impressive success of *Killer McCoy*, the failure of *Summer Holiday* forced

Rooney to have to prove himself with his next project. Saddled with a flop movie and a home life that was again becoming difficult (Mickey loved his sons but still had a hard time loving the woman he hastily married), Rooney entered *Words and Music* sans his usual enthusiasm and determination. Even he had misgivings about this lavish project's slim plotline. Sadly, this musical biography is a mess. Filled with great music performed by a top cast, the story of these great songwriters is so disjointed, and so inaccurate, it continues to maintain the reputation as a nearly complete misfire.

The threadbare plot attempts to follow the trajectory of Richard Rodgers and Lorenz Hart's partnership, with Richard writing the music and Lorenz (Larry) providing the lyrics. It follows their rising success putting on Broadway musicals and composing songs that have become timeless classics. Tom Drake is dull and complacent as Richard Rodgers. Rooney is alternately jumpy and melancholy as Larry Hart. And while the weak plot is just an excuse for a series of musical numbers, its inaccuracies are so unnerving that Rodgers himself denounced the finished film.

In real life Lorenz Hart was a brilliant lyricist but given to depression over his diminutive height as well as his troubling closeted homosexuality. In the movie, his height is depicted as a problem that bothers him, but, of course, his gayness could not be discussed in a film from this era. So, Rooney plays Hart with jittery enthusiasm that suddenly lapses into staggering unhappiness after he is rejected by a woman (played by Betty Garrett) with whom he had been smitten. When she turns down his proposal, and his ring, he lapses into a depression and blames his height.

Along with this ridiculous reworking of who Larry Hart was, the film is filled with even more blatant inaccuracies. Rodgers is shown attending a silent movie, being shown with orchestra accompaniment, after being rejected by Joyce Harmon, an actress in his latest show. This is set in 1927. The movie he attends is *Camille* featuring Greta Garbo and Robert Taylor, a 1936 talkie. Hart is reunited with twenty-six-year-old Judy Garland, playing herself, in a scene set in 1930. In 1930, Garland was eight years old. Hart collapses back stage after a performance of *On Your Toes* and is sent to the hospital, where, in a drugged state, he puts on his clothes, wanders out into the rain, and dies once he gets to the theater. In actuality, Hart died seven years after *On Your Toes* was on Broadway. The fact that he and Rodgers split beforehand (when Rodgers started working with Oscar Hammerstein II) is not discussed. The film shows the two of them together until Hart's death.

Rooney was so unenthusiastic about this project that he started calling in sick every Monday. Judy Garland did two numbers in the film for $100,000.

But at the time she owed the studio that much for medical bills they'd paid, so she ended up with no money for her performance. *Words and Music* is partly saved by the song numbers, including Gene Kelly and Vera-Ellen's brilliant "Slaughter on Tenth Avenue," and Rooney and Garland performing "I Wish I Were in Love Again," a song that had been edited out of their movie *Babes in Arms*.

Another highlight is Lena Horne doing "The Lady Is a Tramp," which was carefully placed in the film so it could be easily edited out when the movie was shown in southern U.S. cities, a repugnant practice that occurred all too frequently with black performers in movies during this time. Janet Leigh, who plays Rodgers's wife, recalled Lena Horne's performance in her autobiography *There Really Was a Hollywood*:

> Those eyes were so on fire they needed an extinguisher, that mouth passionately caressed each word, each syllable. She was dynamite. It wasn't in the script but the "audience" spontaneously responded with a standing ovations.[1]

Domestically, *Words and Music* lost money. But after a worldwide release it made a marginal profit. Critics, however, were dissatisfied with the story's inaccuracies, but all praised the music. Mickey Rooney took most of the criticism for his uneven portrayal of Lorenz Hart, which was also poorly written and inaccurate. Pleased with *Killer McCoy*, MGM was not satisfied with Rooney's failure at the two other grown-up roles he'd essayed. Thus, while he remained in a solid contract with MGM, there were no projects immediately lined up for him. Rooney could not afford that with his debts, so he and Sam Stiefel decided to take his option to do a radio show. They decided an Andy Hardy radio show could be a success. Rooney might have been too old to play Andy on screen, but his voice sounded the same, so playing the character on radio would work just fine.

Stiefel and Rooney made an appointment to see Louis B. Mayer and made the request for the rights to do a show on an MGM property. Although it had been announced that there would be no more Hardy family movies, Mayer did not want a Hardy radio series to compete with any possible plans to resurrect the series or rerelease earlier efforts. Rooney angrily balked at that decision, and Mayer responded by saying, "Do you know what I have done for you?" Rooney replied, "I know what I've done for you, I made you millions!"[2] He then turned and walked out of Mayer's office, slamming the door. Rooney was put on suspension by the studio.

Rooney's friends and stepfather told him to cool off, let Mayer cool off, and make amends. But Stiefel told him to take this opportunity to get out of MGM and make movies for his own company, where he'd enjoy creative control. With a combination of anger and pride, Rooney asked Stiefel to get him out of his contract. Rooney still owed MGM another five years. Things were worked out as follows: Rooney had to forgo his guaranteed forty-week salary and accept $2,500 for twenty weeks. Mickey would also have to put up a $500,000 bond to be reduced by $100,000 for each movie he made under the new contract. He would receive $125,000 for each movie, but $100,000 of that would go toward paying off the bond, leaving Rooney with $25,000 per movie. When taking away the half he had to give Stiefel and 10 percent to the William Morris agency, that left the actor with a paltry $10,000, which would not support his lifestyle, especially now that Rooney had finally moved out on Betty Jane and divorce proceedings were under way.

Stiefel began investigating for independent movie productions in which Mickey Rooney could appear, finding backers to put up enough money to produce some films for Rooney's own company. In the meantime, Rooney was not making any money, so he took a few personal appearance gigs that paid him enough to get by while waiting for a movie deal to come through. While performing out of town, Rooney spent a lot of time thinking about the situation he was in, and how hiring Stiefel was netting him less money rather than more. When he returned from the live shows, he spoke to Stiefel about dissolving their partnership. However, Stiefel had set up independent movies for Rooney to appear in, and refusing to do so could get him sued for breach of contract. So, Mickey Rooney made a movie away from MGM for the first time since *Hoosier Schoolboy* a dozen years earlier.

THE BIG WHEEL

(United Artists, 1949)

Director: Edward Ludwig
Screenplay: Robert Smith
Producers: Mort Briskin, Samuel H. Stiefel. *Cinematographer:* Ernest Laszlo. *Editor:* Walter Thompson
Cast: Mickey Rooney (Billy Coy), Thomas Mitchell (Arthur "Red" Stanley), Mary Hatcher (Louise Riley), Michael O'Shea (Vic Sullivan), Spring Byington (Mary Coy), Hattie McDaniel (Minnie), Steve Brodie (Happy Lee), Lina Romay (Dolores Raymond), Allen Jenkins (George), Dick Lane (Reno Riley), Monte Blue (Deacon Jones), Denver Pyle (Intern), Kippee Valez (Carla), Joe Gray and George Lynch (Drivers), Jack Colin and George Fisher (Announcers), Franklyn Farnum, Jack Perry and Mike Donavan (Race Spectators), Eddie Kane (Waiter)
Reissued as: Thundering Wheels
Released: November 4, 1949
Specs: 92 minutes; black and white
Availability: DVD (Goodtimes Home Video)

Mickey Rooney's first film after leaving his longtime studio home, MGM, and entering independent production, *The Big Wheel* is reasonably entertaining but hardly a triumph at any level. Rooney begrudgingly fulfilled the duties necessary based on projects business manager Sam Stiefel had arranged before the actor realized he was making less money and therefore asked to dissolve their relationship. He does not falter on his screen performance, however, and he is surrounded by a few familiar character players with whom he'd worked at MGM, which was likely comforting. The director is top notch, as is the cinematographer. But that does not make *The Big Wheel* more than an average action drama.

Mickey Rooney plays Billy Coy, an auto mechanic who wants to be a race-car driver like his father, who was killed on the track. He gets hired by his father's old mechanic, Red, who is now courting Billy's mother, Mary. After becoming friends with young tomboy Louise, whose father owns a racetrack, Billy gets a chance to prove himself as a driver. His arrogance does not endear him to the other drivers, and he eventually ends up crashing into another car on the track when that car's rear wheel comes off. This crash causes the driver to be killed, so Billy leaves California. He starts over as a race-car driver and remains in touch with Louise, who comes to see him when he participates in the Indianapolis 500. Red and Mary, now a married couple, come with Louise. Billy wins the race despite his car catching fire during the final laps. It explodes into flames shortly after he leaves it upon concluding the race victorious.

Financing for *The Big Wheel* came from a variety of sources, including former heavyweight boxing champion Jack Dempsey. Funds were enough to secure the good cast and director Edward Ludwig as well as cinematographer Ernest Laszlo. Ludwig nicely combines actual race footage with film he shot on location at a speedway in Gardena, California. Some of the actual footage comes from the forty-fourth Indianapolis 500 from May of 1949, so *The Big Wheel* has always been popular with auto-racing fans. The story is pretty standard, and Rooney can play a character like this with little real effort. What is significant about the character is that it is another adult role for Rooney. Now that he was away from MGM, one of the things Rooney concentrated on was distancing himself from the juvenile roles he'd done well past his twenty-first birthday. He was beginning to do that at MGM after the war and continued to essay more mature roles.

Mickey Rooney was also newly involved with his third marriage, this time to actress Martha Vickers. Vickers had made quite a hit in the film noir *The Big Sleep* (1946). She appeared in three feature films during 1949, but left the screen to raise a family after her marriage to Rooney. Their son Teddy was born in 1950.

The Big Wheel was one of the few films for singer Mary Hatcher, who does an earnest job playing the tomboy Louise. Hatcher was also a successful Broadway actress until her retirement in the early 1950s. She has a particularly good scene in *The Big Wheel* where Billy asks Louise to meet him at the garage that evening. She thinks it is for a date and dresses up accordingly. When she arrives, Louise discovers that Billy only wanted her help working on a carburetor. While the exchange is presented as comic relief to augment some of the heavier dramatics, it emerges as one of the better scenes in the movie.

This was the final film appearance for Hattie McDaniel, an impressive actress who usually played domestics, most notably in *Gone with the Wind* (1939), which also featured Thomas Mitchell, who plays Red in *The Big Wheel*. And Spring Byington, who plays Mary Coy, had played Andy Hardy's mom in *A Family Affair* (1937), the hit film that spawned the Hardy family series, after which Fay Holden took over the role.

The Big Wheel, on the strength of Rooney's name, was picked up for distribution by United Artists and received wide release at the end of 1949 and into the beginning of 1950. It made its money back and enjoyed some level of profit, but it did nothing to enhance Mickey Rooney's career. Rooney was disgruntled about where he had landed since coming home from the war. MGM did not appear to have plans for him, but he owed them several movies upon breaking his contract. He owed a lot of money to his business partner, who was more of a hindrance than a help to his career. The attraction of creative freedom upon entering independent production resulted in a lackluster B movie that was not bad, but certainly not near the level of what Rooney had accomplished earlier in his career. Mickey Rooney left for the service as one of the biggest stars in the world. Now he was low on money and trapped by responsibilities in his career.

QUICKSAND

(United Artists, 1950)

Director: Irving Pichel
Screenplay: Robert Smith
Producers: Mort Briskin, Samuel H. Stiefel. *Cinematographer:* Lionel Lindon. *Editor:* Walter Thompson
Cast: Mickey Rooney (Daniel Brady), Jeanne Cagney (Vera Novak), Barbara Bates (Helen), Peter Lorre (Nick Dramoshaq), Taylor Holmes (Harvey), Art Smith (Oren Mackey), Wally Cassell (Chuck), Richard Lane (Lt. Nelson), Patsy O'Connor (Millie), John Galludet (Moriarty), Minerva Urecal (Landlady), Sidney Marion (Shorty), Jimmie Dodd (Buzz), Lester Dorr (Baldy), Kitty O'Neil (Madame Zaronga), Alvin Hammer (Auditor), Ray Teal, Tom Monroe (Motorcycle Cops), Jack Elam (Man at Bar), Jimmy Cross (Sailor in Arcade), David McMahon (Smitty)
Released: March 24, 1950
Specs: 79 minutes; black and white
Availability: DVD (Image Entertainment)

Mickey Rooney was always dismissive of this film despite it being one of his finest performances and most challenging characters. In his autobiography, Rooney said, "The film was aptly titled. We sank in it."[1] In an interview, he said, "I made some good pictures and some bad ones. This was a bad one."[2] Perhaps it was because *Quicksand* was made during Rooney's uncomfortable association with Sam Stiefel. Maybe his misgivings are because it was filmed during a bad period in his personal life. His dismissive attitude could be because he and costar Peter Lorre were planning to start their own production company with Rooney producing, Lorre directing, and both of them acting, but the deal fell through, causing Lorre to declare bankruptcy and leave American films for Europe. Finally, it might be a combination of all of these factors. *Quicksand* is, in fact, a quintessential film noir that has all of the necessary ingredients to offer a taut, suspenseful structure that builds effectively to a satisfying conclusion.

Mickey Rooney plays Daniel Brady, a garage mechanic who meets Vera, a woman who works in a diner, and falls for her quickly and completely. She likes money, and Dan is limited to working-class funds, so he starts lifting bills from the cash register at work with the idea that he will replace the money before the bookkeeper does inventory. The bookkeeper arrives early, so Dan charges a hundred-dollar watch, hocks it for twenty dollars at a pawnshop next door, and quietly replaces the money for the bookkeeper. He then robs someone on the pier at night at a noisy carnival in order to get the money to pay for the watch he charged. Dan's past is revealed as being sordid and difficult (he ran away from home as a young boy due to an abusive father) and probably involved some level of petty crime, so when he becomes smitten with Vera, it is not difficult for him to lapse into theft. But when he meets Vera's former boyfriend Nick, who runs an arcade, the relationship becomes complicated and includes blackmail and deeper levels of crime. Nick realizes Dan stole the money and blackmails him into stealing and delivering a new car to him from where Dan works. Dan's boss finds out Dan stole the car and wants either the vehicle returned or the money for it. Dan and Vera steal $3,600 from Nick to pay for the car, but Vera spends half of it on a mink for herself. When Dan's boss is dissatisfied with only $1,800, a stressed Dan strangles him and leaves him for dead.

When Dan believes himself to be in trouble for attempted murder, Vera has no interest in fleeing with him. The story allows for a tangential character named Helen (Barbara Bates), who cares about Dan and is willing to help him when he sinks so heavily into the "quicksand." One small crime leads to a series of escalating ones as Dan Brady attempts to be resourceful, but his limited understanding of society's underbelly puts him at a disadvantage.

Perhaps it is a bit convenient for the fleeing Dan to carjack a sedan being driven by a sympathetic lawyer who convinces the frightened young man to accept his help. The man Dan believes he killed is not actually dead, so his crime is not as serious as murder. The lawyer does help, but Dan must still spend time behind bars for his crimes. When Dan goes to jail, Helen agrees to wait for him. Vera, meanwhile, is taken away by the police for her part in the robbing of $3,600 from Nick ($1,800 of which she spent on a fur, which is found in her apartment by detectives).

Jeanne Cagney and Mickey Rooney

Peter Lorre, as Nick, is quiet and pensive. Jeanne Cagney (sister of James), as Vera, is wily and controlling. Rooney's Dan Brady is a man who attempts to be in control but is jittery and prone to outburst. The film plays most of its scenes in the shadows, with occasional voice-overs by the Rooney character. Director Irving Pichel, who is perhaps best known for helming *The Most Dangerous Game* (1932), keeps the pace steady and builds the film effectively by responding to Robert Smith's screenplay.

The sets for this film include a small diner, a lakefront pier at night, a seedy arcade, small apartments, and a few backrooms. And while it is the first of several noir films Rooney would make, it is the darkest in both content and style. All of the central characters who immediately surround Dan Brady offer tension and danger. Tangential figures like his buddies from work and Helen present him with an escape, but his naïveté doesn't allow him to realize it. His passion for Vera blinds him to the point where he sees his escalating actions as a logical progression that can be stopped, and fixed, handily. When Dan finally realizes the depth of his situation, he chooses to run away. When Vera refuses to accompany him and Helen agrees to go along, Dan realizes how his focused devotion was the catalyst for his escalating trouble.

Stylistically, this movie works as a film noir. The use of shadows is well done, and it is a lot darker than previous Rooney movies. It's not as dark as most traditional film noirs of the 1940s, however. Fortunately, Dan Brady is a pretty likable character—he's a good guy who gets caught up in the wrong crowd and can't work his way out of it—so seeing him have a not entirely unhappy ending is fairly satisfying. It's still a good noir movie, but it does seem to mark a transition in the genre leaving the 1940s and heading into the '50s.

In all of the films Rooney made since returning from the army, even those that attempted to give him adult roles and move him away from his juvenile past, there is always that whiff of Andy Hardy innocence, or the put-on-a-show enthusiasm of the musicals with Judy Garland. There was a gee-whiz kid lurking beneath the surface of Tommy McCoy, or even Lorenz Hart, as Rooney played them. *Quicksand* leaves all that behind. Rooney would only display those traits again when the role called for it (usually in lightweight comedy). In subsequent dramas, Rooney would continue to play mature roles that separated him from his MGM past.

Unfortunately, this separation was also from the superstardom he had enjoyed before the war. Rooney was no longer at the top of the box office. He was now doing independent deals that were being met with little success. He and Lorre lost money financing *Quicksand*, and Rooney left the project with unhappy feelings about it for the rest of his life. As indicated at the top of this chapter, other factors may also have clouded his negative feelings toward the movie. *Quicksand* remains a very strong film noir and includes one of Mickey Rooney's finest performances.

Due perhaps to the shaky financing on this project, *Quicksand* fell into the public domain and is not under copyright. Thus, the greater accessibility of the movie has caused it to become something of a cult classic that is championed by movie buffs interested in film noir.

THE FIREBALL

(20th Century Fox, 1950)

Director: Tay Garnett
Screenplay: Horace McCoy. *Story:* McCoy and Tay Garnett
Producer: Bert E. Friedlob. *Cinematographer:* Lester White. *Editor:* Frank Sullivan
Cast: Mickey Rooney (Johnny Caesar), Pat O'Brien (Father O'Hara), Beverly Tyler (Mary Reeves), James Brown (Allen), Ralph Dumke (Bruno), Milburn Stone (Jeff), Bert Begley (Shilling), Marilyn Monroe (Polly), Sam Flint (Dr. Barton), Glenn Corbett (Mack), John Hedlone (Ullman), Al Hill (Cop)
Released: November 9, 1950
Specs: 84 minutes; black and white
Availability: DVD (Warner Archive Collection)

After a film as interesting as *Quicksand*, a movie like *The Fireball* seems like a throwaway. Removing himself from his stern, forceful performance in his previous film, Rooney offers unbridled enthusiasm as Johnny Caesar, a young boy running away from an orphanage and making a name for himself as a roller derby champion. After achieving success, Johnny becomes cocky and condescending, until he is sidelined with polio and confined to a wheelchair. The therapy he undergoes is not only physical but also emotional. The whole movie is such a cliché from beginning to end, it's hard to even care when tragedy strikes because you can see it coming a mile away. It is also a bit bemusing that Johnny goes so quickly from barely being able to roller skate to being a roller derby champion.

Bosley Crowther stated in the *New York Times*,

> Never let it be said that Mickey Rooney doesn't try. *The Fireball* finds him at it on skates. Those who cherish Mr. Rooney as a shining symbol of the youthful

> All-American underdog should enjoy watching their idol puff his way from rags to riches as a professional roller champion. He has never been flashier. However, those who take Mr. Rooney's histrionics with a grain of salt had better make it a handful this time. For he is the whole show, seems completely aware of the fact and does everything but swallow the camera to prove it. He completely eludes director Tay Garnett, mugging, swaggering and churning away like a showboat paddle wheel.[1]

And it is precisely this level of enthusiasm that makes the entertaining film a bit of a weak effort in the realm of Mickey Rooney's career. Breaking away from youthful roles and wanting to be appreciated as an adult actor, twenty-nine-year-old Rooney is here playing a juvenile breaking out of an orphanage. And while his skills are commendable and his performance as a cocky upstart effective, the film is really little more than a series of clichés that are carried by the actor's exuberance.

Pat O'Brien's bravura performance as a priest in the 1938 Warner Bros. classic *Angels with Dirty Faces*, opposite James Cagney, had already reached some level of iconic status a dozen years later by the time *The Fireball* was being filmed. O'Brien offers the reserved alternative to Rooney's overacting and the balance is effective. They play well opposite each other and manage to bolster the rather thin material with their performances.

It is good to see O'Brien and Rooney on screen together, but it's like they're just playing clichés of themselves, O'Brien as the good-hearted priest and Rooney as the enthusiastic kid. It's really a step backward for Rooney, after tackling some darker roles. The only significant claim *The Fireball* has is its featuring a very early appearance by Marilyn Monroe in a small role. In a short time, Ms. Monroe would become one of the biggest stars in films and continue to represent the decade of the 1950s long after her 1962 passing. However, at the time *The Fireball* was made, she was still taking small roles and hoping her beauty and charisma would effectively register. It would be another two years before Monroe's stardom would be solidified by such films as *Don't Bother to Knock* (1952) and *Monkey Business* (1952). By the time she made *Niagara*, *Gentlemen Prefer Blondes*, and *How to Marry a Millionaire* (all 1953), Monroe would be one of Hollywood's most glamorous (and troubled) superstars.

Mickey Rooney would soon return to downbeat film noir, as well as his old studio, MGM. He still owed them some movies on his old contract. But first, he had a film to do at Columbia where he would have the opportunity to do comedy again for the first time since *Love Laughs at Andy Hardy* four years earlier.

HE'S A COCKEYED WONDER

(Columbia, 1950)

Director: Peter Godfrey
Screenplay: Jack Henley
Producer: Rudolph C. Flothow. *Cinematographer:* Lester White. *Editor:* Richard Fantl
Cast: Mickey Rooney (Freddie Frisby), Terry Moore (Judy Sears), William Demarest (Bob Sears), Charles Arnt (J. B. Caldwell), Ross Ford (Ralph Caldwell), Ned Glass (Sam), Mike Mazurki (Lunk), Douglas Fowley (Crabs), Bill Phillips (Pick), Eddy Waller (Pops), Ruth Warren (Mrs. Morrison, the Landlady), Lola Albright (Actress in Drive-In Movie), Richard Quine (Actor in Drive-In Movie), Dick Wessel (Delivery Driver), Frank Ferguson (Sheriff), Tom Daly (Boy), Alyn Lockwood (Girl), Olin Howland (Hotel Clerk)
Released: December 2, 1950
Specs: 76 minutes; black and white

Mickey Rooney returned to comedy with *He's a Cockeyed Wonder*, a silly farce about Freddie Frisby, a small-town working-class guy who inherits his magician uncle's estate and decides to become a magician himself. He wants to make good in order to have enough money to marry Judy Sears, despite the angry misgivings of her father, Bob Sears, and the interest of Ralph, an up-and-coming salesman where Bob works as a factory foreman. Freddie gets mixed up with gangsters robbing a payroll and manages to use magic to foil them, earn Bob's respect, and win Judy's hand. It is all done quickly, painlessly, and pleasantly, and while this movie is by no means great cinema, it has some significance to Rooney's career. Rooney returned to comedy, and despite his brilliance as a dramatic actor, he had a light, affable manner that lent itself well to the sort of lightweight humor that this film provides.

Screenwriter Jack Henley, who penned many entries in the Blondie film series as well as several short comedies, had a knack for silly comedy that was bright and upbeat. And despite the film being unremarkable as cinema, within its own parameters it is pleasant and disarming. Rooney adds a great deal of amusing nuance to his character, from a stuttering sputter when he talks while excited to rather artful double-takes and other comic reactions that help enhance the humor in each scene. *He's a Cockeyed Wonder* is filled with welcome veterans in supporting roles, including attractive costar Terry Moore, who keeps up with the pace and the humor. William Demarest is delightfully gruff as Judy's father, Mike Mazurki offers his specialty as a bumbling gangster, and Ned Glass is at his boisterous best as Freddie's fast-talking agent. Rooney has good chemistry with Terry Moore despite their age difference.

Mickey Rooney had frequently exhibited his natural talent for comedy as early as his silent Mickey McGuire shorts. Thus, it was easy for him to settle into a silly comic farce like this and add comic nuance to his character. Everyone seems comfortable with their roles, and each actor offers a discernible enthusiasm for the material. It plays like a B movie, but Rooney still had enough star power to headline in what would be considered A-level pictures.

Mickey Rooney, Mike Mazurki, and Terry Moore

Bosley Crowther's scathing review in the *New York Times* seems a bit uncalled for, but it gives one a good idea of where Rooney stood with critics by 1950:

> In *He's a Cockeyed Wonder*, Mickey Rooney misses on all counts. His eyes, registering a sort of painful bewilderment, are perfectly normal and he's far from being a wonder. The witless farce dealing with an ineffectual sputterer who wins his lady love, Terry Moore, after inheriting his uncle's magician's tricks and capturing a gang of inept thieves, tries hard to be sprightly and only succeeds in being limp. The sole cockeyed note in the proceedings is the off-screen narrator who describes the California town where all this uninspired business takes place as being "an average place populated by average people."[1]

He's a Cockeyed Wonder is the first film Rooney made once his deal with Sam Stiefel had been fulfilled. Rooney was set to make three films for Stiefel, but he only made two—*The Big Wheel* and *Quicksand*—because the option for a proposed third picture, *Francis, the Talking Mule*, was dropped. *Francis* was soon picked up by Universal Studios, Donald O'Connor was hired to star, and the result was a hugely popular series of films for the next several years. Mickey Rooney was once again a victim of bad judgment. And while *He's a Cockeyed Wonder* holds up nicely as a pleasant diversion with a talented cast, it did not help to advance Rooney's career at the time.

The top box office star in the world when he entered the service during World War Two, Rooney was now looked upon as a relic from the wartime era who was struggling to keep his head above water in vehicles that did nothing to help him regain the sort of clout he'd once had in the industry. Along with his career, Rooney's personal life became increasingly more difficult. First, his father, Joe Yule, died in 1950. Although there were past issues and estrangement, Rooney still took his death hard. Things seemed to be looking up when Rooney was invited to be a presenter at the Academy Awards ceremonies. However, at the last minute, as he and Martha Vickers were ready to leave the house, he was phoned and told he had been replaced. The Academy had changed its mind. Unsuccessful movies, the recent death of his father, and now removed from the Oscar telecast—Rooney sat dejectedly at his kitchen table, clad in his tuxedo, and wept. Rooney recalled in his autobiography,

> From the beginning, I had been programmed to live by applause. If I got that applause, I was truly alive. If and when I didn't, I was dead. Martha never felt the same way about me again, and I didn't feel worthy of her. Soon we were living apart.[2]

THE STRIP

(MGM, 1951)

Director: László Kardos (as Leslie Kardos)
Screenplay: Allen Rivkin
Producer: Joe Pasternak. *Cinematographer:* Robert Surtees. *Editor:* Albert Akst
Cast: Mickey Rooney (Stanley Maxton), Sally Forrest (Jane Tafford), William Demarest (Fluff), James Craig (Delwyn "Sonny" Johnson), Kay Brown (Edna), Tommy Rettig (Artie), Tom Powers (Detective Bonnabel), Louis Armstrong (Himself), Jonathan Cott (Behr), Tommy Farrell (Boynton), Myrna Dell (Paulette), Jacqueline Fontaine (Frieda), Vic Damone (Himself), Monica Lewis (Herself), Don Haggerty (Detective), Earl "Fatha" Hines (Himself), Joyce Jameson (Girl), Art Lewis (Sam), Samuel London (Fred), Jeff Richards (Patient), Jack Teagarden (Himself)
Songs: "A Kiss to Build a Dream On" (music and lyrics by Bert Kalmar, Harry Ruby, Oscar Hammerstein II; performed by Louis Armstrong); "Shadrack" (music and lyrics by Robert MacGimsey); "La Bota" (music and lyrics by Charles Wolcott, Haven Gillespie); "Basin Street Blues" (music and lyrics by Spencer Williams); "Don't Blame Me" (music and lyrics by Jimmy McHugh, Dorothy Fields); "Hines' Retreat" (music and lyrics by Earl "Fatha" Hines); "Fatha's Time" (music and lyrics by Earl "Fatha" Hines); "J.T. Jive" (music and lyrics by Louis Armstrong); "Ole Miss Blues" (music and lyrics by W. C. Handy); "That's-a-Plenty" (music and lyrics by Lew Pollack)
Released: August 13, 1951
Specs: 85 minutes; black and white

In another adult role that shows no trace of his Andy Hardy past, Rooney is solid and effective as a jazz drummer in small clubs who gets mixed up in a murder. As with *Quicksand*, it is one of the actor's finest performances during his continued transition into adult roles. Unfortunately, also like *Quicksand*, the film's aesthetic success did not translate to box office success and did nothing to advance Mickey Rooney's continually dwindling career. Rooney was making good movies but not enjoying the success he deserved. And his status as the number one box office star seemed like a lifetime ago.

The film is told in flashback by Rooney's character, Stan Maxton, who is accused of killing a racketeer. Stan recalls when he was new to Los Angeles and got a job drumming in the house band at a Sunset Strip club called Fluff's. Fluff is played by William Demarest with his usual sincere gruffness, but he takes a liking to Stan just as Stan takes a liking to Fluff's daughter, Jane. Stan tries to help Jane, a singer and dancer, catch a break by introducing her to Sonny, one of his racketeer pals. Sally Forrest does nicely in the role of Jane, while James Craig seems to be channeling Robert Taylor from MGM's *Johnny Eager* (1941).

Rooney is once again quite effective as he plays a subdued noir-type Everyman who stumbles into a series of circumstances that get him deeper into danger. Stan is tricked by detectives into confessing to Sonny's murder when he believes Jane did it. However, further investigation indicates to the detectives that Jane did kill Sonny, but it was in self-defense. Sadly, after Stan is allowed to read Jane's confession, he is told that she died shortly after writing it. Stan returns to Fluff's and takes his sorrow out on the drums, his music being the catharsis to remove him from the tragic situation.

The film does a nice job of presenting the jazz club subculture of the postwar era, and it is filled with great artists who contributed a great deal to the music. The fact that Rooney was a drummer and does his own drumming adds a greater authenticity to the musical scenes. When Mickey Rooney solos on the drum kit with the same sort of unbridled exuberance he had exhibited in his musicals with Judy Garland at this same studio a dozen years earlier, he still seems like a man, not a boy. His screen persona had effectively left his Andy Hardy past behind and, as an actor, was ready to progress. Some of the songs are forgettable, but the jazz numbers featuring the top legends are solid. One song, "A Kiss to Build a Dream On," became a hit for Louis Armstrong and was nominated for a Best Song Oscar (it lost to "In the Cool, Cool, Cool of the Evening" from the Paramount feature *Here Comes the Groom*). Sometimes the music interrupts the flow of the action and becomes more of a distraction than an organic part of the narrative. The plot is so thin that it almost needs all the musical interludes just to get it to feature length. The story is sometimes predictable and dull, but Rooney is good throughout, and it is fun to see him do his own drumming. For all its shortcomings, the film is certainly unique.

Since *The Strip* did not garner much enthusiasm (the *New York Times* did not even bother to review it), and its box office netted no real profit, MGM didn't have anything on its agenda for a grown-up Mickey Rooney. Just as he had moved on from the character that made him a superstar, he was also no longer sought after by that studio.

Harry Cohn at Columbia felt differently. He was pleased with Rooney's work in *He's a Cockeyed Wonder* and continued to believe the actor still meant something at the box office. Producer Jonie Taps hired Rooney for a three-picture deal at Columbia for $75,000 per film. This was good money for the period, and while a veteran actor of Rooney's caliber should have probably been earning more at this point in his career, he was happy with the contract. Not only did he have a guaranteed three-picture deal for a set salary, but he was going to be working with his friends Richard Quine and Blake Edwards. The films would see Rooney exploring comedy, musicals, and heavy drama once again, which exhibited his versatility in a continued attempt to advance his career.

SOUND OFF

(Columbia, 1952)

Director: Richard Quine
Screenplay: Blake Edwards, Richard Quine
Producer: Jonie Taps. *Cinematographer:* Ellis W. Carter. *Editor:* Charles Nelson
Cast: Mickey Rooney (Mike Donnelly), Anne James (Lt. Coleen Rafferty), Sammy White (Joey Kirby), John Archer (Maj. Paul Whiteside), Gordon Jones (Sgt. Crockett), Wally Cassell (Tony Baccigalupi), Arthur Space (Barney Fisher), Dick Crockett (Boat Owner at Lake), Al Eben (Hymie), Helen Ford (Mrs. Rafferty), Mary Lou Greer (Evelyn), Robert Lowell (Guard), Boyd Morgan (Red), Marshall Reed (Captain Karger), Tony Taylor (Boy in Park), Joy Windsor (Crockett's Girl), Emil Sitka (Waiter)
Songs: "Sound Off" (music and lyrics by Willie Lee Duckworth; performed by the cast); "Home Sweet Home in the Army" (music by Al Rinker, lyrics by Tom Adair; performed by Mickey Rooney and the cast); "Blow Your Own Horn" (music and lyrics by Mickey Rooney; performed by Mickey Rooney); "Bugle Blues" (music by Lester Lee, lyrics by Bob Russell; performed by Mickey Rooney and the cast); "It's the Beast in Me" (music by Lester Lee, lyrics by Bob Russell; performed by Mickey Rooney); "My Lady Love" (music by Lester Lee, lyrics by Bob Russell; performed by the cast)
Released: May 18, 1952
Specs: 83 minutes; black and white

This comedy about army life was Mickey Rooney's first in a three-picture deal with Columbia Pictures, for which he would earn triple what he made at MGM for *The Strip*. The Metro movie helped fulfill his contractual obligation to that studio, where he would deliver three films for $25,000 per movie. The $75,000 he received for the Columbia films helped pay a lot of outstanding bills.

However, despite the money promised by this new three-picture deal, Rooney could not afford to wait around while Columbia finished preproduction on this movie and he could get to work. So he took a quickie job with indie producer Benedict Bogeaus in the low-budget western *My Outlaw Brother* (1951), which costar Robert Stack recalled as "a piece of Limburger."[1]

Sound Off is a typical army comedy with the occasional musical number. And while there is nothing particularly remarkable about the film and the songs are hit and miss, its comedy is entertaining and funny, as is Rooney's performance.

Mickey Rooney plays Mike Donnelly, a brash entertainer whose aggressive personality and need to always be "on" bleeds into his real life. When he is drafted into the army, he must learn to adapt to a regimen without being the center of attention.

All of the clichés are here. Rooney's character wisecracks and goofs off through his training, not taking it seriously. He has an angry sergeant, is smitten with a pretty girl who works on his base, and eventually gets into enough trouble to where he faces court-martial. Given thirty days to prove himself, Mike does a complete turnaround and spends the month being the best soldier he can be. Impressed, his superiors assign him to a special unit that entertains embattled troops overseas. Thus, the film concludes with his being placed in an area of the army where his abilities will do the most good.

It is easy to see how the script is tailored to Rooney's talents as well as his own experiences. Rooney himself had been assigned to a special unit in the service and spent it entertaining soldiers during World War Two. Rooney's own personality was known to fluctuate wildly from friendly and affable to aggressive and unsettling. Rooney was also an entertainer whose energetic need for attention off screen was legendary. And Rooney had recently put together a nightclub act showing off his talents. Part of the problem with his marital difficulties was due to his never settling into a niche at home and having to go out all night and be a part of the action. Rooney said in an interview,

> *Sound Off* was a fun picture. The songs were good, the comedy was funny, I was among friends, and I should have been having a good time. But I was going

> through a divorce and other personal problems when we made it, so I didn't have any fun. When I see the picture now, I am surprised I got through it.[2]

Rooney's performance shows none of the frustrations in his personal life that he alludes to. In fact, he handles the comedy, including the slapstick, with the same enthusiasm as Mike Donnelly, his character, does in the nightclub scenes. Performing a tossed salad routine in a club (getting into a tussle with a guy who, of course, ends up being Mike's sergeant once he is in the army), tossing and turning his first night trying to sleep on an army cot, bumbling through maneuvers, and adding a bit of soft shoe to a marching drill are among the comic bits Rooney performs.

One of the funniest scenes in this movie is when Mike goes AWOL and is pursued by his sergeant and another superior. The two men end up at the park, where they jump into boats without paddles and must paddle with their hands in what becomes a slow, clumsy chase. It is a very funny visual and nicely paced by director Richard Quine. Quine had been a friend to Rooney as far back as his MGM heyday and gave the actor a lot of creative control, listening to his ideas and implementing them when they were sound ways to improve the scene. Even one of the better songs on the soundtrack, "Blow Your Own Horn," was composed by Rooney himself. Richard Quine and Blake Edwards were still perfecting their comedy style at this point. This is one of Edwards's earliest screenplays, and it's interesting to watch the movie in hindsight.

Because *Sound Off* was a low-budget movie, it made a decent profit. Reports from period theater owners vary in their response to the movie. An exhibitor in North Carolina reported to *Box Office* that the film was "one of the biggest laugh hits that we have played in some time. Rooney is tops."[3] Meanwhile, a drive-in movie manager told the same magazine, "Mickey isn't as good as he used to be, as a good many people told me, but as long as he is in color you'll get a crowd."[4]

Sound Off was successful enough to please Columbia's head mogul Harry Cohn, so Quine and Edwards put together another colorful musical comedy set in the military for their next Mickey Rooney film. This one was set in the navy. A military backdrop continued to be a bit cliché for an actor with Mickey Rooney's successful background, but at this point in his career, he was in no position to quibble.

ALL ASHORE

(Columbia, 1953)

Director: Richard Quine

Screenplay: Blake Edwards, Richard Quine. *Characters:* Aurania Rouverol

Producer: Jonie Taps. *Cinematographer:* Charles Lawton Jr. *Editor:* Charles Nelson

Cast: Mickey Rooney (Francis "Moby" Dickerson), Dick Haymes (Joe Carter), Peggy Ryan (Gay Night), Ray McDonald (Skip Edwards), Barbara Bates (Jane Stanton), Jody Lawrance (Nancy Flynn), Jean Willes (Rose), Joan Shawlee (Hedy), Ed Fury (Tennis Player), Emil Sitka (Bartender), Fay Roope (Commodore Stanton), Rica Owen (Dotty), Patricia Edwards (Susie), Eddie Parker (Sheriff), Dick Crockett (Charlie), Frank Kreig (Barnaby), Ben Welden (Hugo), Gloria Pall (Lucretia), Joan Shawlee (Hedy)

Songs: "All Ashore" (music by Fred Karger, lyrics by Robert Wells; performed by The Cheerleaders vocal group over opening credits); "Heave Ho, My Hearties" (music by Fred Karger, lyrics by Robert Wells; performed by Dick Haymes, Ray McDonald, and sailors; reprised by Haymes and McDonald during "opera bouffe" dream sequence); "You're My Buddy, Buddy Boy" (music by Fred Karger, lyrics by Robert Wells; performed by Dick Haymes, Ray McDonald, and Mickey Rooney; reprised by Haymes, McDonald, and Rooney during "opera bouffe" dream sequence); "I Love No One But You" (music by Fred Karger, lyrics by Robert Wells; performed by Peggy Ryan, Ray McDonald, Mickey Rooney, and Dick Haymes); "Who Are We to Say" (music by Fred Karger, lyrics by Robert Wells; performed by Dick Haymes); "I'm So Unlucky" (music by Fred Karger, lyrics by Robert Wells; performed by Mickey Rooney); "I Sing to the Sky" (music by Fred Karger, lyrics by Robert Wells; performed by Barbara Bates and Mickey Rooney [in the "opera bouffe" dream sequence; operatic voices dubbed]); "I'm Sir Francis the Dragon" (music by Fred Karger, lyrics by Robert Wells; performed by Mickey Rooney [in the "opera bouffe" dream sequence; operatic voice dubbed]); "I Lay Down My Arms" (music by Fred Karger, lyrics by Robert Wells; performed by Mickey Rooney and Barbara Bates [in the "opera bouffe" dream sequence; operatic voices dubbed]); "Boy Meets Girl/Catalina" (music by Fred Karger, lyrics by Robert Wells; performed by Dick Haymes, Ray McDonald, Mickey Rooney, Peggy Ryan, Jody Lawrance, Barbara Bates, and beach party chorus)

Released: March 3, 1953

Specs: 80 minutes; black and white

Availability: DVD (Sony Choice Collection)

Sound Off enjoyed enough success that the same team—producer Jonie Taps, writer Blake Edwards, and director Richard Quine—tried another musical comedy set in the service, this time the U.S. Navy. *All Ashore* is as colorful and amusing as its immediate predecessor and once again allows Mickey Rooney to play comedy, including some good slapstick sequences.

Rooney, Dick Haymes, and Ray McDonald are three navy buddies on leave who hook up with girls and troublesome situations in what can be described as a low-budget version of *On the Town* (1949), a popular MGM musical. Haymes and McDonald are the sharper guys in this trio of friends, while Rooney plays the put-upon buddy who sacrifices his money and his watch (which gets pawned) and ends up playing fifth wheel when the other guys find girls and he has none. Some of the more amusing scenes in *All Ashore* feature Rooney tagging along on double dates, including caddying for them as they play golf and turning the corner behind them as they ride tandem bikes and Rooney drives on a bouncy scooter. Still, Rooney's character is essentially bullied by his "friends" throughout the movie and seems a little out of his element.

Much of the comedy is visual, and just as there is an offbeat chase scene in *Sound Off*, so is there one in *All Ashore*. In *Sound Off*, military superiors are chasing the Mickey Rooney character in a boat, but neither have oars, so they are paddling with their hands and getting nowhere. In *All Ashore*, Rooney's character finds himself in a girl's room, sneaks out a window, and is pursued by MPs, who chase him onto a playground area (Rooney goes down the slide backward, pushes a swing into the chin of his pursuer, etc.). Columbia had been home to the most slapsticky short comedies in Hollywood for nearly twenty years by the time *All Ashore* was filmed there, so fans of the Three Stooges, for instance, will likely recognize some of the sound effects utilized for the slapstick sequences in this movie.

As with most low-budget musicals, the songs are hit and miss, while there is an opera sequence that doesn't fit in too comfortably and disrupts the flow of the movie. However, Rooney was once again surrounded by friends, and these are friends who have real credentials in musical comedy. Besides Quine and Edwards, singer Dick Haymes and dancers Ray McDonald and Peggy Ryan (who later married, and then eventually divorced) offer their experience to the project, making it that much better. Ray McDonald had already scored big in Rooney's MGM film *Life Begins for Andy Hardy* (1941) as the tragic Jimmy Frobisher. McDonald would die tragically at the age of only thirty-nine from choking on his food while having dinner in a hotel room. Peggy Ryan lived many more years.

Perhaps the lack of a really great set of songs is one of the big reasons why this wasn't as big a hit as other service musicals (like *On the Town*). But watching McDonald and Ryan dance is definitely a highlight, and for what it's worth, the film makes great use of Technicolor and is very pretty to look at.

On its own terms, *All Ashore* is another happy musical comedy with a military background, and it is at least as pleasantly entertaining as *Sound Off* had been. And since it managed to turn a reasonable profit for Columbia, the investment in Rooney seemed justified. But the success of this film had only a marginal impact on Mickey Rooney's career. While his low-budget movies might turn a profit after enjoying some success in neighborhood theaters, they did little to allow Rooney to recapture any measure of the fame he had once enjoyed.

After completing *All Ashore*, Mickey Rooney was asked back to MGM to make the last movie necessary to fulfill his contract, and he once again earned only a third of what he was making at Columbia. But first, Rooney was asked by his friend Bob Hope to play a supporting role in Hope's Paramount comedy *Off Limits* (1953). Bob Hope plays a fight manager who gets drafted. Mickey Rooney plays a fellow soldier who has skill as a fighter and longs to become one. Rooney recalled,

> The producers didn't want me. The studio didn't want me. But Bob Hope knew I'd be good in the role so he insisted on me. I never forgot that. I also never forgot that he would always invite me to play in his golf tournaments, even when my life and career was at a low point and nobody wanted to work with me. He's a true friend.[1]

Bob Hope recalled in his book *The Road to Hollywood*,

> Paramount had some doubts about hiring Mickey for the role. He had a reputation for liking the nightclub life, and the studio was worried he would not prove reliable. I said, "Mickey is one of the most talented actors in this town." As I expected, Mickey was totally professional throughout the shooting. When *Off Limits* was released, the critics raved about the connection of Hope and Rooney.[2]

The success of *Off Limits* was helpful to Rooney, as Hope had a built-in audience that now noticed Rooney's strong work. And it was subdued in that *Off Limits* was a Bob Hope movie and thus it was Hope who did the big gags.

After completing the Hope film, it was back to MGM for Mickey Rooney to costar with Eddie Bracken for the first time (they would work together again on stage years later). *All Ashore* had shown Rooney working effectively as part of a team dynamic, and his pairing with Bracken showed him in that same capacity. While at the time it was essentially a coincidence, this would become worth notice in several more of Rooney's comedy films.

A SLIGHT CASE OF LARCENY

(MGM, 1953)

Director: Don Weis
Screenplay: Jerry Davis. *Story:* James Poe
Producer: Henry Berman. *Cinematographer:* Ray June. *Editor:* Ben Lewis
Cast: Mickey Rooney (Augustus "Geechy" Cheevers), Eddie Bracken (Frederick Winthrop Clopp), Elaine Stewart (Beverly Ambridge), Marilyn Erskine (Emily Clopp), Douglas Fowley (Mr. White), Robert Burton (Police Captain), Charles Halton (Willard Maibrunn), Henry Slate (Motorcycle Cop), Rudy Lee (Tommy Clopp), Mimi Gibson (Mary Ellen Clopp), Robert Foulk (Mr. Logan), Dabbs Greer (Gas Delivery Man), Ida Moore (Old Lady), Joe Turkel (Holdup Man)
Released: June 5, 1953
Specs: 71 minutes; black and white
Availability: DVD (Warner Archive Collection)

For the final film to fulfill Mickey Rooney's old contract, MGM put him in this low-budget comedy opposite Eddie Bracken. And, as with most of the films he was making at during this period, *A Slight Case of Larceny* did not help to advance Rooney's film career, but it has greater significance as we examine his filmography. The team dynamic that had been hinted at in *All Ashore* became a duo in this movie, with Rooney and Bracken complementing each other nicely. Rooney said in an interview,

> I did do a lot of comedies playing off another actor, and I worked well in that situation. But there were no plans to make me part of a regular comedy team. Eddie and I both started out as child stars and both had big careers in pictures in the 1940s. By the time we did this picture, we both needed money.[1]

Rooney and Bracken play Geechy Cheevers and Freddie Clopp, respectively, two army buddies who start their own filling station. When a big corporate-owned gas station moves in across the street and becomes a business rival, Geechy and Freddie siphon gas from their opposition to keep in business.

The dynamic here is especially interesting when we compare this comedy to the previous Columbia release, *All Ashore*. In that film, Rooney was the amiable patsy to his two sharper friends. In *A Slight Case of Larceny*, it is Rooney who is the aggressive, gregarious one, while Bracken plays along. Geechy is filled with razzle-dazzle ideas and schemes that he hopes will make him rich. While Freddie is fine with a wife, children, a comfy home, and a steady job as a mechanic, Geechy wants more. After having not seen his buddy since shortly after the war, Geechy visits Freddie at his job, gets him fired, and then talks him into mortgaging his house to buy his own gas station, where Geechy will also work. Geechy takes advantage of his buddy, but it never seems unscrupulous. He truly believes in his schemes and is solidly convinced that his ideas are what's best for his friend and for himself.

There is a romantic element when Geechy lays eyes on a pretty young woman who works for the rival gas station. She has no interest in this gregarious character at first, but Geechy eventually wears her down. There

Mickey Rooney, Eddie Bracken, and Henry Slate

is no real conflict, and it appears this element of the female character is merely MGM's excuse to give attractive starlet Elaine Stewart a showcase.

Some of the film's highlights include two fun slapstick sequences, including Geechy and Freddie's attempt to haul gasoline in an old pie wagon they have purchased. They fill it with gas for delivery, but the gas spills from the vehicle's roof as they haul it, with Freddie behind the pie truck's wheel. The truck's weight also causes it to sway, so Freddie must not only keep the windshield clean of gas, with wipers that don't work, but he must try to keep it straight and on the road. Soon its weight is such that it rolls ahead of Geechy in the tow truck and starts pulling the smaller vehicle backward. They readjust, and then the tow truck breaks free of the pie truck, as Freddie goes flying wildly down the road, with no brakes. It is a nicely edited sequence of visual comedy, and both Rooney and Bracken ham it up in delightful comic fashion. Rooney does a funny bit on a trampoline during a scene set at the beach. Annoyed at his girl cavorting with muscle men at the beach, Geechy tries to show off on the trampoline and simply bounces wildly until he plops into a hole in the sand, getting up dazedly with the help of the very men who aroused his jealousy.

Rooney and Bracken make a good team, and Rooney's recollection that they both had fallen from previous stardom is accurate. Bracken had settled into a niche as the nervous young man who found himself in outrageous comic situations, especially in the Preston Sturges classics *Hail the Conquering Hero* (1944) and *Miracle of Morgan's Creek* (1944), but he aged out of those parts and was getting less screen work by the 1950s. In fact, he left movies all together after *A Slight Case of Larceny* and concentrated on TV work and the theater. Years later, when Rooney's career had hit bottom, Bracken asked him to appear in a dinner theater show and it gave another surge to Rooney's career.

Most reviewers did not bother with *A Slight Case of Larceny*, and its short running time usually found it playing weekend matinees or as the lower half of a double feature. However, it holds up nicely as a pleasant low-budget comedy that showcases the talents of both actors.

Rooney was now free of MGM and returned to Columbia to do the third in his three-picture deal that netted him three times what Metro was paying him. Rooney again worked with Richard Quine and Blake Edwards, and the trio decided to leave comedy and instead film James Benson Nablo's serious drama about a car mechanic who gets mixed up with gangsters. This sounds like the same plot trajectory that would define one of Mickey Rooney's comedies of the period. But instead, *Drive a Crooked Road* turned out to be one of the actor's best films from this period.

DRIVE A CROOKED ROAD

(Columbia, 1954)

Director: Richard Quine
Screenplay: Blake Edwards. *Story:* James Benson Nablo. *Adaptation:* Richard Quine
Producer: Jonie Taps. *Cinematographer:* Charles Lawton Jr. *Editor:* Jerome Thoms
Cast: Mickey Rooney (Eddie Shannon); Dianne Foster (Barbara Mathews); Kevin McCarthy (Steve Norris); Jack Kelly (Harold Baker); Harry Landers (Ralph); Jerry Paris (Phil); Paul Picerni (Carl); Dick Crockett (Don); Jeffrey Stone (Wells); Peggy Maley (Marge); Patrick Miller (Teller); Mike Mahone, George Paul, and John Close (Police Officers); Irene Bolton, Diana Dawson, Linda Danson (Pretty Girls); Amzie Strickland (Bit)
Released: March 10, 1954
Specs: 83 minutes; black and white
Availability: DVD (Sony Choice Collection)

The third of Mickey Rooney's three-picture deal with Columbia, *Drive a Crooked Road* was made by the same team that had done *Sound Off* and *All Ashore*. However, this time they switched from lightweight musical comedy to heavy drama. Rooney plays Eddie Shannon, a quiet, unassuming guy who has no family, lives alone, and has only a few friends. He works as a garage mechanic and part-time race-car driver for local events, quietly going about his life and keeping to himself. He becomes smitten with a pretty female customer named Barbara, who shows some interest in him. He doesn't realize that she is merely luring him in so that Steve, her actual boyfriend, and his partner, Harold, can persuade Eddie into being their getaway driver for a heist.

Poster for *Drive a Crooked Road*

Rooney's subdued performance is especially effective and demonstrated almost immediately. His character quietly endures ribbing from the other mechanics for his humdrum lifestyle, and when he first sees Barbara, he offers the sort of careful double take that shows Eddie's immediate attraction. Rooney was a master at bombastic comedy and could have offered the sort of reaction that would get a laugh. But his brilliance as an actor allowed him to realize that his reaction must be subdued like his character. It is brief but one of the most telling highlights in the early part of the film. The structure of the movie effectively shows Eddie gradually falling for Barbara, initially finding it pretty much impossible that so beautiful a woman could be attracted to a short, plain, shy individual like himself. When he is ultimately convinced, there is little he wouldn't do for her. It is a surprisingly emotional story and heartbreaking to watch at times.

Barbara is wily, realizing that Eddie would never break the law. But when she presents the proposition to Eddie, she paints a picture of the two of them enjoying continued bliss when Eddie has enough money from this job to get a good race car and perhaps qualify in Europe. Eddie's sense of honesty won't allow him to agree, but his infatuation with Barbara overwhelms him. He phones her, stands outside her apartment building, and wrestles emotionally with his feelings. Rooney conveys all of this beautifully. He stammers timidly, his voice choking up, as he begs Barbara over the phone to see him. When he finally agrees and the criminals fill him in on the details, he sweats and fidgets as he attempts to retain his composure and somehow justify his decision. Along with being the getaway driver, Eddie must work on the getaway vehicle so that it is effective in the robbery. He is told that he isn't allowed to see Barbara until the robbery has been completed successfully. When the robbery is completed, he goes to see her but is told she has moved away.

There is a bit more complexity to the Barbara character than the usual lead female in noir dramas. She has feelings of remorse for her actions. And while she has no real love for Eddie, her conscience is more sensitive than the men with whom she's keeping company, and she feels a real sorrow for having tricked a lonely, innocent man into committing a serious crime. When Eddie goes to see the men and ask if they know where Barbara is, she comes out of a room and confesses everything to him—how it was all planned from the beginning, how he was simply hooked into being a getaway driver, and that she does not love him. "I'm so sorry Eddie," she says. "I'm so sorry I'm sick." The men feel that they must now murder Eddie, despite the protestations of Barbara. They attempt to kill him and make it look like a car accident, but he survives. Eddie returns, head bloodied, and shoots Steve while defending Barbara.

Richard Quine's direction keeps the film's taut pace consistent, while the script is both compelling and absorbing with well-drawn characters. Both Kevin McCarthy as Steve and Jack Kelly as Harold add the necessary amount of cool toughness and cynical cunning to their characters. McCarthy is great and even downright chilling at times. Foster and Rooney have excellent chemistry. The action takes a backseat to Eddie's plight. The heist is never the focus—it's Eddie's spiral into this life of crime.

The use of music is also very effective, even though this low-budget production relies on stock music provided by composer Will Beitel. The forlorn orchestrations enhance the overall somber mood of the narrative. A jazz score is used to back up Eddie's frustrated tossing and turning when he must decide whether to take the criminals up on their offer. There is even a scene where Steve turns up the volume on the phonograph so he doesn't have to hear Barbara crying.

Critics were pleased and impressed with *Drive a Crooked Road.* A reviewer who went by the initials O.A.G. stated in a *New York Times* review,

> The story is vaguely familiar, but the treatment of it by Blake Edwards as adapted by the director, Richard Quine, from James Benson Nablo's story, is refreshing. In a nutshell, two smooth, high-type thieves, Kevin McCarthy, Jack Kelly and their partner, Dianne Foster, plan to rob a bank. Miss Foster is assigned the job of seducing Mickey Rooney, a withdrawn, "lonely little animal," into the task of driving a hopped-up escape car and being the fall guy. Mr. Rooney is a talented mechanic and a budding race driver. When he is told the deal, he refuses, but his feelings for Miss Foster, and her pleadings, lead him on to a successful conclusion of the holdup. When he learns he has been a patsy for the group, his fresh new emotional values are rudely ruptured. The film closes quietly on a wrecked and pitiable figure being taken by the police. The source of the merit of the film is not hard to spot; it is Mr. Rooney's characterization of the lonely little mechanic with his dreams of driving in the great European sports car races. He deserves a special salute for his job. Without detracting from his accomplishment, it should be pointed out that the scenarist had a lot to do with the creation. Jack Kelly along with Kevin McCarthy and Miss Foster all contribute nicely to the total effect, but it is clearly Mr. Rooney's day. It is solid, minor productions such as this that should form the body of film output.[1]

Drive a Crooked Road started filming in October of 1953. A month earlier, Mickey Rooney was shaken by the sad news that Lewis Stone, the erstwhile Judge Hardy in the popular Andy Hardy series, had suffered a sudden heart attack and died. According to Allan Ellenberger at his Hollywoodland website,

> On the evening of Saturday, September 12, 1953, Stone and his third wife Hazel were watching television at their home at 455 S. Lorraine Boulevard when they heard a racket in the back yard. When he investigated, Stone found lawn furniture floating in the pool and glimpsed three or perhaps four teenage boys running towards the street. Stone gave chase despite his wife's warning not to exert himself. Upon reaching the sidewalk, Stone suddenly collapsed. A gardener, Juan Vergara witnessed the chase and summoned aid. Sadly the actor died of a heart attack on the sidewalk without regaining consciousness. Lewis Stone was 73. Within the hour, police took three boys, one of them 13 and the other two 15, into custody and booked them on suspicion of malicious mischief. They told officers that they previously had taken a swim in the pool and "thought it would be funny if they threw the furniture into it" because Stone had chased them before. After being booked at the Wilshire Station, they were lectured by police before being released to the custody of their parents pending possible Juvenile Court action.[2]

Recalling Lewis Stone in his 1965 book, *i.e.: An Autobiography*, Rooney stated,

> When Lew died, I lost a part of me that I can't set down. Mostly we were professional associates working together and respecting each other's abilities. He was a gifted professional and the real basis of our association was that professionalism. It was a strong basis. When people ask if I have any residuals in the Hardy series, I tell them, truthfully, my residual is having worked with Lewis Stone.[3]

THE ATOMIC KID

(Republic, 1954)

Director: Leslie H. Martinson
Screenplay: Benedict Freedman, John Fenton Murray. *Story:* Blake Edwards
Producer: Mickey Rooney. *Associate Producer:* Maurice Duke. *Cinematographer:* John L. Russell Jr. *Editor:* Fred Allen
Cast: Mickey Rooney (Blix), Robert Strauss (Stanley), Elaine Devry (Audrey), Bill Goodwin (Dr. Rodell), White Bissell (Dr. Pangborn), Joey Forman (Hospital MP), Peter Leeds (Bill), Hal March (Ray), Fay Roope (General Lawlor), Stanley Adams (Wildcat Hooper), Robert Emmett Keane (Mr. Reynolds), Peter Brocco (Comrade Mosley), Paul Dubov (Anderson), Robert Nichols (Bob), Dan Riss (Jim), Don Haggerty (Lieutenant), Ray Walker (Newspaperman)
Released: December 8, 1954
Specs: 86 minutes; black and white
Availability: DVD (Olive Films)

Again working in a team dynamic and playing lightweight comedy in a low-budget feature for a smaller studio, Mickey Rooney produced *The Atomic Kid* himself for his own company, along with his associate, Maurice Duke. Rooney's movie-producing venture with Duke would eventually prove unsuccessful, but with this first film, Rooney had high hopes as he continued to try to find his way back to the top where he'd been before his wartime service.

Robert Strauss plays opposite Rooney. Strauss had been nominated for a Best Supporting Actor Oscar the year before, but for a highly dramatic role in *Stalag 17*. However, Strauss had played comedy before, serving as comic foil to Jerry Lewis in the Martin and Lewis features *Sailor Beware* and *Jumping Jacks* (both 1952). Rooney and Strauss had met on the film *The Bridges at Toko-Ri*, which they had filmed before *The Atomic Kid*, although it was released later (and is discussed in the next chapter).

Strauss and Rooney play Stan and Blix, a couple of guys looking for uranium. The two of them immediately resonate as an effective team. Strauss is the big, overbearing leader, while Rooney is the compliant patsy. There is a great deal of silly slapstick at the outset. Stan and Blix are lost in the desert when the film opens. They find a house they believe to be deserted, get in through the window, and then scream and run when they see mannequins sitting at a table. The action is all pretty mechanical stuff, with one going through a door and slamming it on the other hurrying close behind and so on. The two play it for all its worth, with screaming, yelling, and wild double takes. As low comedy goes, the opening scenes effectively establish just what the viewer is to expect for the remainder of the movie.

Strauss has a very funny bit when his character finds a car and starts driving around the area, wondering why army men are chasing him. They catch up to him and indicate that he is on an atomic bomb test site and the

Robert Strauss and Mickey Rooney

house he was in is the target. Stan is safely in a trench with the army, wailing about his buddy Blix in the house. Blix is looking in vain for food, when he picks up the phone to call the time. He is told by a soldier that "the bomb is about to be dropped" and suddenly realizes the danger he is in. Blix ducks, closes his eyes, and puts his fingers in his ears as he prepares for the blast, a comical reaction that is amusingly done by Rooney. When the bomb goes off, Blix is believed to be killed, but when army personnel inspect the site, Blix comes crawling from the debris completely radioactive. He is taken to a laboratory, babbling rapidly like a cartoon chipmunk in a neat effect (it is explained that his metabolism has doubled). Blix is now radioactive, so the government keeps him under wraps and sees how they can somehow make use of this unusual development. Stan sees it as a possible moneymaking scheme, and calls himself Blix's manager. He makes arrangements to write Blix's story (gathering info while a Pulitzer Prize–winning author does the actual writing).

Rooney had recently married for the fourth time and his wife, Elaine, has the only female role in *The Atomic Kid*. She plays a nurse with whom Blix is smitten. In one of the film's funnier sequences, Blix ties some sheets together and escapes from his guarded room to meet with the nurse. He forgets to tie the sheets to a base, and ends up falling out of the window. Two government men are hired to keep him under surveillance, but he is allowed to escape. Blix finds the nurse in a casino, and his radioactivity causes each slot machine to hit the jackpot. There is a very funny visual as Blix walks past a row of slot machines, and they all start dispensing money onto the floor, resulting in pandemonium among the other casino patrons. Blix ends up back at the nurse's house, and when they kiss his radioactivity goes haywire and causes Blix to glow in the dark.

The Atomic Kid taps into the popular science-fiction phenomenon that was happening in 1950s movies as well as the atomic testing that was in the news. And while it initially gives Rooney the opportunity to play in a team dynamic with Robert Strauss, as the film develops, they play in separate scenes, with Blix pursuing the nurse, and Stan looking at opportunities to make money off his buddy's situation. Their team dynamic returns as the film concludes when one of the alleged businessmen Stan is working with turns out to be a spy. By now, Blix's radioactivity has worn off, but he manages to fake it and foil the spy's plans.

The film ends on a great gag that brings it all full circle. Blix and the nurse have eloped and are driving to San Francisco for a honeymoon. To avoid reporters, Blix takes all back roads. When he stops at a house for directions, he finds the door is open, looks inside, and discovers mannequins. He screams, goes back to his car, and speeds off as the film ends.

While *The Atomic Kid* is a simple, silly comedy, Rooney plays it perfectly. He expresses earnestness, engages completely in the low-comedy aspects of the script, and has no problem playing up the sillier scenes to bring them to the sort of outrageous level that makes them funnier. The film can be dismissed as pure corn, but it is the sort that comes off effectively because it is performed so well. None other than Steven Spielberg has cited this movie as being among his favorites;[1] he even has it playing on a movie marquee in *Back to the Future* (1985) when Michael J. Fox travels back in time and finds himself in 1955.

Critics naturally dismissed a low comedy such as this, but audiences thought differently. A theater owner in North Carolina reported to *Box Office* magazine,

> I've just finished drying my tears of laughter. This is the funniest thing in a long time. Good for a big laugh session. All enjoyed this, and Rooney is great. Especially timely with all the atomic tests now in progress.[2]

A low-budget film for a low-budget company, *The Atomic Kid* dealt with a topical premise, and its boisterous cornball comedy pleased audiences of the time. Only weeks later, the film Rooney had completed just before going into this one, *The Bridges at Toko-Ri*, was released.

THE BRIDGES AT TOKO-RI

(Paramount, 1954)

Director: Mark Robson
Screenplay: Valentine Davies, adapted from the novel by James Michener
Producers: William Perlberg, George Seaton. *Cinematographer:* Loyal Griggs. *Editor:* Alma Macrorie
Cast: William Holden (Lt. Harry Brubaker), Fredric March (Rear Adm. George Tarrant), Grace Kelly (Nancy Brubaker), Mickey Rooney (Mike Forney), Robert Strauss (Beer Barrel), Charles McGraw (Cdr. Wayne Lee), Keiko Awaji (Kimiko), Earl Holliman (Nestor Gamidge), Richard Shannon (Lt. Olds), Willis B. Bouchey (Capt. Evans), Nadine Ashdown (Kathy Brubaker), Cheryl Lynn Callaway (Susie), Dennis Weaver (Officer), Dickie Jones (Pilot), Corey Allen (Solider)
Released: December 17, 1954
Specs: 102 minutes; Technicolor
Availability: DVD (Warner Home Video)

Mickey Rooney had been getting leading roles in B movies since leaving MGM, and this film gave him a supporting part in an A picture. According to Rooney, his role in this Paramount release came about rather unusually. While traveling by plane from a nightclub engagement, Rooney found himself sitting near writer James Michener, who was about to start work on a film version of his novel about the Korean conflict. Michener and Rooney hit it off well, so Michener wrote a part for Rooney in the movie script.

The Bridges at Toko-Ri is one of the first U.S. movies set during the Korean War. The story centers on Lt. Harry Brubaker, whose heroics during World War Two result in his being beckoned from his civilian life to return to duty on an aircraft. Rooney portrays, as the *New York Times* review described, "a pint-sized tornado as a helicopter pilot who loves to clown and fight."[1] Despite it being a smaller role, Rooney stated in his autobiography that he was pleased with his part:

> I jumped at the chance of playing Mike Forney, a cocky little Irishman who always wore a derby hat and specialized in jumping out of choppers to save downed navy fliers. And I rather enjoyed the thought that Bill Holden and I would die heroes' deaths in the icy waters off Korea.[2]

While Rooney is not the leading actor, he does appear throughout the film, and his scenes always resonate. His character, Mike, is a hard-drinking, brawling sort despite his short stature. In fact, Rooney makes that part of the character's emotional response to situations. Mike, a flyer, once rescued the Holden character, Lieutenant Brubaker. Thus, Brubaker thinks nothing of traveling sixty miles to Tokyo while at liberty in order to bail the recalcitrant Mike out of jail for "taking on the whole town." He has not seen his wife and children in a year, but he leaves them to take care of this matter, and the wife understands. Even though he is playing a smaller supporting role, Rooney's enthusiasm and natural ability shine through effectively whenever he is on screen. And, as Rooney stated in his autobiography, he does get a death scene, as does leading man Holden.

This is a perfect part for Rooney, which makes sense seeing as how it was written for him. It's the showiest role in the movie, and he does a great job playing an over-the-top character without overexaggerating his performance. In fact, he steals just about every scene he's in and, outside of some fantastic battle sequences, is the highlight of the film. Apparently Michener based Rooney's character on a pilot named Duane Thorin, who was known for wearing nonregulation headwear.

The Bridges at Toko-Ri is a good movie, and it shows Rooney is capable of resonating in a supporting role in a major film. It also benefits from strong performances by Holden, Grace Kelly as his patient wife, Fredric March as an admiral, and Robert Strauss in a smaller role with the character name Beer Barrel, who adds some levity to the more dramatic stretches. As stated in the previous chapter on *The Atomic Kid*, Rooney and Robert Strauss met while working on *The Bridges at Toko-Ri*, but they share no scenes together in this movie. They did hit it off on the set, so when Rooney produced *The Atomic Kid* for his own company, he hired Strauss to play opposite him.

The Bridges at Toko-Ri won an Oscar for special effects and was also nominated for editing. It was a high-profile movie, grossing nearly $5 million at the box office. It was probably the biggest movie that Mickey Rooney had been in since *National Velvet* ten years earlier.

However, neither *The Atomic Kid* nor *The Bridges at Toko-Ri* had any real impact on Rooney's movie career, so he decided to give television a try. *The Mickey Rooney Show* (also known as *Hey, Mulligan*) ran during the 1954–1955 season. Produced by Maurice Duke for Rooney's own company, with scripts by Blake Edwards and direction by Richard Quine, *The Mickey Rooney Show* gathered a cast that also included John Hubbard, Regis Toomey, Claire Carlton, and Joey Forman (who often performed in nightclub engagements opposite Rooney). Rooney played Mickey Mulligan, a page at a TV studio who longs to get a shot at being an actor. The series, which is on DVD, offers the same sort of light, funny humor that can be found in Rooney's movie comedies of the 1950s.

The Mickey Rooney Show probably could have been a success, but it was scheduled at the same time as Jackie Gleason's show on another network. Gleason's ratings were very high, making Rooney's very low. The two men were friendly, and Gleason was known for calling Rooney and telling him that when his own show was in reruns, he made a point to watch Rooney's. Rooney recalls in his autobiography that the show still might have gotten a second season, but he attended a party held by the show's sponsor, Pillsbury, and felt he was treated in a condescending manner by the son (who kept calling him Charlie and insisting that he perform his act for everyone). Rooney feigned a stomachache and abruptly left the party, especially after the Pillsbury son stated, "We own you."[3]

In 1955, Maurice "Mo" Duke, via Rooney's production company, produced another feature, *The Twinkle in God's Eye*, in which Mickey played a minister who sets out to tame a rustic western town. And in early 1956, his company produced the film *Jaguar* starring Sabu, in which Rooney did not appear as an actor. Both films tanked at the box office. One exhibitor wrote of *The Twinkle in God's Eye*, "I'll bet they made it for TV and it flopped so they figured exhibitors would pick up the tab."[4] Still, despite 1955 offering little to discuss, in his autobiography Mickey Rooney singled out 1956 as being one of the worst years of his cinematic career. He was kept afloat with engagements in Las Vegas that his associate, Maurice Duke, had set up for him. Unfortunately, in a place like Vegas, Rooney would gamble away his earnings as fast as he could make them.

THE BOLD AND THE BRAVE

(RKO, 1956)

Director: Lewis R. Foster
Screenplay: Robert Lewin
Producer: Hal E. Chester. *Cinematographer:* Sam Leavett. *Editor:* Aaron Stell
Cast: Wendell Corey (Fairchild); Mickey Rooney (Dooley); Don Taylor (Preacher); Nicole Maurey (Fiamma); John Smith (Smith); Race Gentry (Hendricks); Ralph Votrian (Wilbur); Wright King (Technician); Stanley Adams (Master Sergeant); Bobs Watson; (Bob); Tara Summers (Tina); Diana Darrin (Lina); Sidney Clute, Mike Ragan (GIs in Card Game); John Mitchum (GI in Bar); Robert Easton (Tall Blonde GI); Pat Conway, Douglas Spencer (Sailors in Bar)
Released: April 19, 1956
Specs: 87 minutes; black and white
Availability: Streaming (Amazon Instant Video)

In 1955, Mickey Rooney's TV series ended after one season, and he produced two failed features through his own company, starring in one of them. But according to the actor's autobiography, he had even less to say about his 1956 output. Rooney refers to the three features he made that year—*The Bold and the Brave, Francis in the Haunted House*, and *Magnificent Roughnecks*—as "turkeys" and even dismissed the fact that he was nominated for a Best Supporting Actor Oscar for *The Bold and the Brave*. Only a few years earlier, Rooney was disinvited as a presenter at the Oscars, so his being nominated showed that Hollywood had not written him off completely.

The Bold and the Brave is not a particularly remarkable film, but it has some significance in Mickey Rooney's career not only because of the Oscar nomination. The story deals with three American soldiers in Italy during the Second World War. Wendell Corey plays a pacifist who doesn't believe in killing another man. Don Taylor portrays a man with strict religious beliefs about right and wrong, good and bad. Mickey Rooney stands out as a gambler whose wartime experience is centered on crap games.

This is a good role for Rooney during this part of his life. Gambling was indeed an addiction for the actor, and his character in this film has the same problem regarding responsibility and contribution when distracted by throwing dice. While the disparate personalities of the three main actors were supposed to make a point about war, about good versus evil, and about human relationships, the aesthetic success of the film centered on Rooney's performance. There is a craps game scene in the film that emerges as the highlight. Rooney recalled,

> We just improvised that scene, held a craps game and made jokes. It turned out to be the most popular scene in the picture and I got nominated for an Academy Award. I directed that scene too, but never got any credit for it. It was sort of a you do this then I'll do that type of direction, but Lew Foster let me go with it. The others responded and we had our scene.[1]

Along with directing this scene without credit, Rooney also cowrote the film's theme song along with Ross Bagdasarian, who would later achieve fame as David Seville, mastermind behind Alvin and the Chipmunks.

Rooney's work in *The Bold and the Brave* shows a great deal of enthusiasm, which is appropriate for the character he plays. Willy Dooley is a very energetic, positive guy, but not an ethical one. Although he is married, he has always cheated on his wife, even to the point of being too embarrassed to read some of his steamy love letters to his army buddies. However, although he ironically indicates he got married to avoid the draft, his attitude about army life is positive: "Three squares a day, nice drinkin' buddies, lotsa laughs, this is the life." When he is reminded about the dangers of wartime, he says, "If they don't like it they should check out," and, "There's a time to be scared and a time to have some laughs." Dooley has dreams. He wants to be a real go-getter when he gets back home to New Jersey. He plans to use his wartime gambling winnings to open an upscale restaurant in New York City and be his own maître d'. Of course, a character who exhibits his dreams in a war movie usually doesn't make it out alive. Once again, Rooney's character is killed by a grenade.

As war movies go, including a tardy look at World War Two from a movie made eleven years after it ended, *The Bold and the Brave* is no better than average and completely carried by Mickey Rooney. It showed that the actor could still maintain interest in a lackluster film with his charismatic screen presence. This led him to the recognition necessary to get an Oscar nomination (which he did not win) but did little to advance his movie career. Rooney continued to be a star in small pictures and a supporting player in larger movies.

Mickey Rooney scored triumphantly in an otherwise average war movie, and next decided to accept the lead in the next Francis the Talking Mule movie. Donald O'Connor left the series, but it continued to be a moneymaker for Universal Studios. The plan was to continue the series with Mickey Rooney as its star.

51

FRANCIS IN THE HAUNTED HOUSE

(Universal, 1956)

Director: Charles Lamont
Screenplay: Herbert Margolis, William Raynor from a character created by David Stern
Producer: Robert Arthur. *Cinematographer:* George Robinson. *Editor:* Milton Caruth
Cast: Mickey Rooney (David Prescott), Virginia Welles (Lorna MacLeod), James Flavin (Chief Martin), Paul Cavanaugh (Frazier), Mary Ellen Kay (Lorna Ann), David Janssen (Lieutenant Hopkins), Ralph Dumke (Mayor), Richard Gaines (DA), Richard Deacon (Jason), Dick Winslow (Sergeant Arnold), Charles Horvath (Malcolm), Timothy Carey (Hugo), Helen Wallace (Mrs. MacPherson), Edward Earle (Howard), John Maxwell (Edward Ryan), Glen Kramer (Ephraim), Hellen Bennett (Mrs. Hargrove), Phil Harvey (Roger), Anthony Joachim (Harry), Fred Nurney (Dr. Nelson), Olan Soule (Dr. Bentley), Paul Frees (Voice of Francis)
Released: July 20, 1956
Specs: 80 minutes; black and white
Availability: DVD (Universal Studios: *Francis the Talking Mule Complete Collection*)

As stated earlier, Rooney's own company had the option to film the first Francis the Talking Mule movie back in 1950, but the option dropped, and Universal picked it up and cast Donald O'Connor as Peter Sterling, who befriends, and is befriended by, the talking mule named Francis. The movie was such a hit, Universal continued to make Francis comedies, five more over the next five years, with O'Connor in the lead role, Chill Wills providing the mule's voice, and Arthur Lubin directing. O'Connor remained active outside the series, appearing in such films as *Singin' in the Rain* (1952) and *Call Me Madam* (1953). However, after *Francis in the Navy* (1955), O'Connor chose not to continue with the series, quipping in the press that the mule kept getting more fan mail. In January of 1956, Mickey Rooney was announced as taking Donald O'Connor's place as the male lead in the Francis the Talking Mule series at Universal. Chill Wills wanted too much money, so he was replaced by voice actor Paul Frees. Arthur Lubin chose not to continue with the series, so Charles Lamont directed. The series was still popular enough for *Francis in the Haunted House* to make $1.2 million at the box office.

Despite the surefire product and Rooney's flair for comedy, *Francis in the Haunted House* has none of the charm of the previous films and is really just a dull, pedestrian affair that relies on predictable situations and mechanical gags. Rooney plays a character who comes from wealth, trying vainly to help the police solve a series of murders with the help Francis is giving him. Rooney tries his best, but there is nothing substantial in the script to latch onto and make the film any more than mediocre.

Francis in the Haunted House is the least interesting film in the series. It feels like a completely separate movie from the others, thanks to the new

Dick Winslow, Mickey Rooney, David Janssen, and James Flavin

cast and director. For the majority of the film, it feels like Rooney's character is involved in one long gag in which he tries to get everyone else to believe he learned about the murders from a mule. It gets really old, really quickly.

The *New York Times* actually reviewed this throwaway, which shows the box office strength of the series. Although no reviewer is credited, the review stated,

> The mule and Mr. Rooney struggle to find a murderer in a medieval castle filled with foreboding corridors, movable walls, trap doors and dungeons. It's a valiant, tiresome struggle. Francis does make at least one interesting observation. This is to a befuddled district attorney: "You've been in politics twenty years. What's so strange about a talking jackass?" Still, one wonders how long Francis can continue. Perhaps Universal offers a clue in *Haunted House*. Francis gets laryngitis but recovers. Still, it was a bad case of laryngitis.[1]

Exhibitors reporting to *Box Office* called the film the worst of the series, that its appeal was strictly for youngsters, and that the novelty of the talking mule was wearing thin.[2]

Rooney followed up this film with a cheap production at Monogram studios, but *Magnificent Roughnecks* was the weakest of the three features the actor made in 1956. Despite another team dynamic (with Jack Carson), *Magnificent Roughnecks* offered a dull story about oil drillers who brawl over the affections of a pretty woman. It was ignored by both the press and the public. However, despite the doldrums of 1956, Rooney still was nominated for an Oscar for *The Bold and the Brave*, and that was a portent for a few more successful ventures in 1957.

BABY FACE NELSON

(United Artists, 1957)

Director: Don Siegel
Screenplay: Daniel Mainwaring. *Story:* Irving Shulman, Robert Adler
Producer: Al Zimbalist. *Cinematographer:* Hal Mohr. *Editor:* Leon Barsha
Cast: Mickey Rooney (Baby Face Nelson), Carolyn Jones (Sue), Cedric Harwicke (Doc Saunders), Leo Gordon (John Dillinger), Anthony Caruso (Hamilton), Jack Elam (Fatso), John Hoyt (Parker) Ted de Corsia (Rocca), Elisha Cook Jr. (Homer van Meter), Robert Osterloh (Agent Johnson), Thayer David (Connelly), Dabbs Grer (Agent Bonner), George E. Stone (Hall), Lisa Davis (Lady in Red), Emile Meyer (Mac), Dan Terranova (Miller), Murray Alper (Alex), Harry Antrim (Pharmacist), Tom Fadden (Postman), Duke Mitchell (Solly), Kenneth Patterson (Vickman), Gil Perkins (Duncan), Paul Baxley (Aldridge), Dick Crockett (Powell), Christopher Dark (Jerry)
Released: December 11, 1957
Specs: 85 minutes; black and white

Despite Mickey Rooney being dismissive of his 1956 output, he did manage to get an Oscar nomination for his appearance in *The Bold and the Brave*. That showed Hollywood was taking at least some interest in him. In 1957 he agreed to appear in a *Playhouse 90* television drama titled *The Comedian* about an abrasive comic whose personality drives people away offstage while he makes them laugh on stage. The project had been offered to many comedians, all of whom turned it down, until it landed on the desk of Rooney's manager, Red Doff. Doff thought it was a good role for his client, and Rooney agreed after reading the script himself. Rooney's performance in the television drama won rave reviews, and he sarcastically stated in his autobiography that critics suddenly noticed he was a good actor. Rooney was so effective in the role that when he was rehearsing a scene with Mel Tormé, Jack Benny wandered onto the set to visit, thought it was an actual argument, and tried to break it up. When told by an amused Rooney and Tormé that they were rehearsing, Benny fell down laughing. *The Comedian* would earn Rooney an Emmy nomination. Shortly after completing work on *The Comedian*, Rooney also starred in another television drama titled *Mr. Broadway* about the legendary George M. Cohan.

Next, Rooney did a cameo in his friend Richard Quine's military comedy *Operation Mad Ball* (1957), which starred Jack Lemmon, Ernie Kovacs, Kathryn Grant (later Mrs. Bing Crosby), Dick York, Arthur Hunnicut, and James Darren. In his few scenes, Rooney effectively stole the picture. His fast-talking, nuanced southern mannerisms, playing a corn-fed master sergeant, picked up the pace of the film every time he was on screen. A dance bit he did with the much taller Marilyn Hanold recalled the similar routine he performed with Dorothy Ford in *Love Laughs at Andy Hardy* eleven years earlier. While Rooney's role was small, *Operation Mad Ball* was a hit movie and many were delighted with his performance. In fact, one exhibitor reported to *Box Office* that his patrons complained that Rooney didn't have a bigger part in the film.[1]

With this renewed interest in his work, Rooney took the lead in *Baby Face Nelson*, an old-fashioned gangster drama to be directed by Don Siegel. Rooney's manager found the script for his client and contributed to the funding of the production. The film was a hit, grossing over a million dollars, which was quite good for a low-budget feature. FBI chief John Malone served as consultant on the movie, but J. Edgar Hoover did not like the finished film and felt it glorified crime and criminals in the same manner as the 1930s Warner Bros. gangster films with stars like Edward G. Robinson, Humphrey Bogart, and James Cagney.

The film's on-screen writing credits read, "Screenplay by Irving Shulman and Daniel Mainwaring, story by Irving Shulman"; however, a June 23, 1958, advertisement in *Hollywood Reporter* reads, "Through no fault of The Writers Guild of America, the writing credits on *Baby Face Nelson* are incorrect and we wish to correct them now: Screenplay by Daniel Mainwaring, story by Robert Adler."[2] The producers originally planned to cast Frank Sinatra as the lead. They also planned to remake the film in 1970 with Dustin Hoffman in the role, but no such film was ever produced.

Baby Face Nelson did not please the critics at the time. Most of them noted that the movie was mostly a fictionalized account of the real-life gangster. After the film's release, it was attacked by California Representative H. Allen Smith, who claimed that it contributed to juvenile delinquency. Red Doff, Rooney's manager, dismissed Allen's attack as an attempt to get attention for his reelection campaign, indicating that Los Angeles FBI Chief John J. Malone was a consultant during the film's entire production.

Despite these negative responses, *Baby Face Nelson* was a box office success and has since lived on to garner respectability. Partly this is due to it being an earlier film for director Don Siegel, whose directorial career is among the most respected in twentieth-century American cinema. Rooney offers a strong performance in the title role, playing an actual gangster who was small in stature in the same way as the actor. The movie was shot in only seventeen days, and Siegel masterfully works with the small budget, the short schedule, and Rooney's fierce, energetic performance. The result is an aggressive, effective B gangster drama. The supporting cast is strong, with Carolyn Jones a standout in a role similar to that which she would play opposite Walter Matthau in Elvis Presley's best movie, *King Creole* (1958).

Rooney offers none of his charm but exhibits all of his charisma in the role. He presents Nelson as rugged but unsure, cocky and rebellious, and, finally, psychotic and overbearing. The character devolves as he grows, and Rooney completely loses himself in the complexities of Nelson's personality. Set against the low-budget backdrop that director Siegel works within, *Baby Face Nelson* is a stirring portent to the director's masterpiece, *Dirty Harry* (1971), featuring Clint Eastwood as the quintessential outsider. Rooney is downright chilling at times, and the role gives him another opportunity to show his range as an actor. It's a nice throwback to those gangster films of the 1930s. Perhaps the film would have had a more lasting impact if it had been an A picture with a bigger budget.

The success of *Baby Face Nelson* came about after its release, while Rooney was busily filming another throwaway titled *A Nice Little Bank That Should Be Robbed*. But this pedestrian heist comedy is easily overlooked. Even moviegoers dismissed it as a witless farce, while critics ignored it completely. However, once *Baby Face Nelson* showed its box office success, Rooney felt comfortable enough to return to MGM and pitch an idea. The studio was now being run by a new group of people who were not active during the years of his massive success or when he prematurely ended his contract. They welcomed the actor who had a recent Oscar nomination, was newly nominated for an Emmy for his TV work, and appeared in a couple of box office hits. And Rooney's pitch? Bring back Andy Hardy as a grown man returning to Carvel with his own family. Rooney even guaranteed MGM that he'd reassemble the actors who'd appeared in the original series sans Lewis Stone, who had passed away. Now with more clout in the industry than he had enjoyed in over ten years, Rooney was given the OK by MGM executives to start putting together the first new Hardy family movie in a dozen years.

ANDY HARDY COMES HOME

(MGM, 1958)

Director: Howard W. Koch
Screenplay: Edward Everett Hutshing, Robert Morris Donley. *Characters:* Aurania Rouverol
Producer: Red Doff. *Cinematographers:* William W. Spencer, Harold E. Wellman. *Editor:* John B. Rogers
Cast: Mickey Rooney (Andrew "Andy" Hardy), Patricia Breslin (Jane Hardy), Fay Holden (Mrs. Emily Hardy), Cecilia Parker (Marian Hardy), Sara Haden (Aunt Milly Forrest), Joey Forman (Beezy "Beez" Anderson), Jerry Colonna (Doc), Vaughn Taylor (Thomas Chandler), Frank Ferguson (Mayor Benson), William Leslie (Jack Bailey), Tom Duggan (Councilman Warren), Jeanne Baird (Sally Anderson), Gina Gillespie (Cricket Hardy), Jimmy Bates (Chuck), Teddy Rooney (Andrew "Andy" Hardy Jr.), Johnny Weissmuller Jr. (Jim), Pat Cawley (Betty), Don "Red" Barry (Fitzgerald), Sydney Smith (Mr. Gordon)
Released: December 22, 1958
Specs: 80 minutes; black and white
Availability: DVD (Warner Archive Collection: *The Andy Hardy Film Collection: Volume 2*)

Enjoying some success on TV and in films and returning to a newly managed MGM for another shot at an Andy Hardy series, Mickey Rooney hoped that *Andy Hardy Comes Home* would enjoy the same success as the earlier films and perhaps start a new Hardy series. Rooney said in an interview,

> TV was full of shows about families that were obviously inspired by the Hardy pictures. *Leave It to Beaver* was the latest one. I caught a few episodes and

> was amazed at how similar they were to what we used to do. I figured it was time to come back as a grown-up Andy Hardy. That was my pitch to MGM and they liked it.[1]

After given the OK by the studio, Rooney began contacting the actors who'd appeared in the original series. Fay Holden, who played Mrs. Hardy, had done nothing other than a TV appearance since 1950 and considered herself semiretired, but she agreed to appear. Sara Haden, who played Aunt Milly, was still a working actress, so it was no trouble to secure her services. Rooney also wanted George Breakston to return to the role of Beezy Anderson, but although Breakston was still active, he was now a director and committed to helming the TV series *African Patrol.* His unavailability resulted in casting his stage partner Joey Forman in the role. Cecilia Parker, who played sister Marian, left movies for marriage and family back in 1942 before the original series had ended. It took some convincing, but Rooney did manage to talk her into appearing in the film.

The only person who turned Rooney down was Ann Rutherford. Rooney wanted grown-up Andy to now be married to child sweetheart Polly Benedict, who'd been played by Rutherford in the original series. She was still a working actress but refused to appear in the movie, telling Rooney that people never marry their childhood sweethearts. Thus, in this film, Andy is married to a woman named Jane, whom he met at work, and has two young children. Marian has a teenaged son, but her husband is not mentioned. Rooney's real-life son by Martha Vickers, Teddy, played Andy Hardy Jr.

Rooney's manager, Red Doff, produced, and Howard Koch was hired to direct. Rooney worked hard to make *Andy Hardy Comes Home* as charming and pleasant as the original series had been. However, after the novelty of seeing everyone back in their familiar roles has worn off, we are left with a rather dull feature that has none of the charm of the original series.

Andy is now a lawyer for an aviation firm and wants to bring a factory to his old hometown of Carvel. A greedy landowner, who did not live in Carvel during Andy's youth, tries to stop him from succeeding and manages to turn the townsfolk against him. Of course, this man's dishonesty is eventually revealed and Andy wins out. The plant will come to Carvel, and nearly every citizen in the small town follows the mayor to the Hardy home to let Andy know of his, and the town's, victory. Andy is then asked by the mayor to become the town's judge, stepping into the shoes of his late father (an interim judge is revealed to have moved on). The film ends optimistically with "To be continued . . ." flashing across the screen as Rooney, and MGM, hoped to rekindle the series again.

While the movie itself is unremarkable, there are some nostalgic elements that offer a bit of interest. A few heartfelt discussions take place in Judge Hardy's study, where the judge and Andy had their man-to-man talks in earlier episodes. The scenes between Andy and his son are pleasant, as he appears uncertain how to handle suddenly being in his father's shoes, giving advice instead of receiving it.

There are a few quick flashbacks as Andy recalls old flames played by Lana Turner, Judy Garland, and Esther Williams (but, oddly, not Polly Benedict, who had been his steady girl throughout the series). Judy Garland's character, Betsy Booth, was always a pal and never a romantic interest, so the film instead shows a kissing scene between Mickey and Judy from *Babes in Arms*, with the character name Betsy awkwardly dubbed in (as that was not Ms. Garland's character in the musical).

Some of the then-and-now bits are funny, such as when Andy goes to a malt shop and discovers he can't stomach the ice cream sundae he had consumed so effortlessly as a teenager. Others fall flat, such as when Marian's son and his teen friends listen to Andy's old 78s with disdain and then put on some of their own 45s. The problem here is technical. Andy would have listened to big band music, and that is not what is played on the soundtrack when the kids put on one of his records. When they put on their own, it isn't 1958 rock and roll by Elvis Presley or Chuck Berry, but some ersatz studio music that sounds more like big band than rock and roll. Stuffy middle-aged studio heads usually had no idea how to present generation-gap humor properly. The filmmakers behind this movie proved themselves woefully out of touch.

The really unfortunate thing about *Andy Hardy Comes Home* is that it was a box office flop that lost money for the studio. So the plans to make it into another series never went beyond this one comeback movie. As Rooney stated in his autobiography, "The public simply didn't care what had happened to Andy Hardy."[2] Not that family sitcoms of this sort weren't popular; they were, but on television. The movies series was a dying art by 1958. Popular series like *Ma and Pa Kettle* and *The Bowery Boys* were wrapping up, and TV was where one would find recurring characters in familiar settings and situations. Perhaps the movie could have told us more about what happened between the last Hardy film and this one—how Andy ended up being a lawyer in California (which doesn't seem like the career path Andy would have taken) and so on. Leaving that dozen-year gap in his life untold was a hindrance to this movie's success. Also, much of the appeal of the early Hardy movies was Andy's youth and enthusiasm, and that can't continue the same as before with him now grown up and a father.

Mickey Rooney closed out the 1950s with two more low-budget features—a remake of *The Last Mile* (1959) and a movie called *The Big Operator* (1959). Neither was a bad movie, but neither was successful. *The Big Operator* lost over a quarter million dollars at the box office. As he entered the 1960s, Mickey Rooney realized that he was not going to capture the enormous stardom that had now eluded him for over a decade.

EVERYTHING'S DUCKY

(Columbia, 1961)

Director: Don Taylor
Screenplay: Benedict Freedman, John Fenton Murray
Producers: Red Doff, Allen Baron, Merrill S. Brody. *Cinematographer:* Carl Guthrie. *Editor:* Richard Brockway
Cast: Mickey Rooney (Beetle McKay), Buddy Hackett (Ad Jones), Jackie Cooper (Lieutenant Parmell), Joanie Somers (Nina Lloyd), Roland Winters (Captain Bollinger), Elizabeth MacRae (Susie Penrose), Gene Blakely (Commander Kemp), Gordon Jones (Conroy), Richard Deacon (Dr. Deckham), James Milhollin (George Imhoff), Jimmy Cross (Drunk), Robert Williams (Duck Hunter), King Calder (Frank), Ellie Kent (Nurse), William Hellinger (Corpsman), Ann Morell (Wave), George Sawaya (Simmons), Dick Winslow (Froehlich) Alvy Moore (Jim Lipscott), Walker Edmiston (Voice of the Duck)
Released: November 16, 1961
Specs: 80 minutes; black and white
Availability: DVD (Sony Pictures Home Entertainment)

In his autobiography *Life Is Too Short*, Mickey Rooney recalls doing little of note from 1959 to 1979, although he appeared in nearly thirty movies during that twenty-year period. As he entered the 1960s, Rooney was doing as much television as he was theatrical films. And while he had been trying to recapture his prewar superstardom since returning from the service in 1946, by the end of the 1950s, he had completely settled into lead roles in B movies and supporting roles in A pictures. Rooney was also on his fifth wife, having divorced Elaine and married Barbara Ann Thomason, who did some acting under the name Carolyn Mitchell and with whom he eventually had four children.

In 1960, Rooney appeared in two weak films. In *The Private Lives of Adam and Eve* he played opposite Mamie Van Doran as a couple who dream themselves into the story of Adam and Eve (Mamie playing Eve, Martin Milner playing Adam, and Mickey portraying the Devil). The dream sequences are in color, while the other footage is in black and white. The film was codirected by Rooney and coproduced by his manager, Red Doff, and it featured Fay Spain, Mel Tormé, Tuesday Weld, Cecil Kellaway, and Paul Anka. It was a complete flop at the box office.

Rooney's old studio MGM released his second film of 1960, *Platinum High School*, which reteamed him with Terry Moore, with whom he'd costarred in *He's a Cockeyed Wonder* for Columbia ten years earlier. *Platinum High School* was inspired by *Bad Day at Black Rock* (1955), with Rooney investigating his son's mysterious death at a private school and being met with hostility by the townspeople. Although a low-budget B movie, *Platinum High School* lost nearly $300,000 at the box office.

One of the more noted appearances Rooney made during this period was in the cult favorite *Breakfast at Tiffany's* (1961), a popular film among the many fans of its star, Audrey Hepburn. Rooney stated in *Life Is Too Short* that he was ashamed of his role as a stereotypical kimono-wearing Japanese character; unfortunately, it is today one of his more well-known performances due to the popularity of the film itself. An argument could be made that Rooney's Mr. Yunioshi in *Breakfast at Tiffany's* is one of the most controversial characters in film history. The backlash didn't really start until decades after the film's release when sensibilities were more attuned to this sort of over-the-top portrayal of an ethnic group. Rooney and the cast and crew had fun with the role at the time of filming and really thought they were helping to play up the comedy side of the movie. Sadly it has ended up being an embarrassing aspect of both Rooney's career and what is otherwise a great movie. That same year, Rooney also had a small role in the gangster drama *King of the Roaring 20s: The Story of Arnold Rothstein* starring David Janssen, with whom Rooney had worked in *Francis in the Haunted House*, and Dianne Foster, Rooney's costar from *Drive a Crooked Road*.

Rooney's final film in 1961 is *Everything's Ducky*, a silly comedy made for children. *Everything's Ducky* is significant in Rooney's career for a few reasons. First, it is another attempt at a team dynamic. He and the bombastic Buddy Hackett make an effectively lowbrow comedy team. Second, the film shows him working effectively in a movie made almost exclusively for children. Finally, Rooney was revisiting lightweight service comedy, recalling earlier movies like *Sound Off* and *All Ashore*.

In *Everything's Ducky*, Rooney and Hackett are navy men who are assigned to take charge of a deceased officer's pet duck. They discover the duck not only has a mind of its own, but it can also talk. And while the premise is far-fetched and silly, it was made for the family trade and it succeeds at that level. In fact, one theater owner told *Box Office* that the film was "very funny and pleased our small fry Saturday audience."[1]

The comedy team structure between Rooney and Hackett seems to owe itself mostly to Bud Abbott and Lou Costello, who had a successful series

Buddy Hackett, Mickey Rooney, and friend

of comedy features during the 1940s and 1950s. By 1961, Costello had died, but his and Abbott's films had become TV staples. Also, the studio that distributed *Everything's Ducky*, Columbia, had released its old Three Stooges comedies to television and they were such a sensation that the Stooges were again making movies for the studio. Rooney is the overbearing straight man; Hackett is the comical patsy. That dynamic is utilized throughout the film, from one silly misadventure to another. Apparently during the filming of a barroom brawl sequence, the amateurs the studio hired as active extras overdid things a bit, and some people got hurt. Mickey Rooney was so angered, he walked off the set. This situation is said to be one of the reasons for the 1961 formation of the Stuntmen's Association of Motion Pictures, which is composed of trained, skilled professional stunt men and women.

Everything's Ducky boasts a good supporting cast, including Jackie Cooper appearing in a film with Mickey Rooney for the first time since *The Devil Is a Sissy* in 1936. Given the success of other talking-animal films and television shows of the time, and the great cast of character actors this movie has, it is a bit surprising that it ended up being so weak. The cast doesn't have any good material to work with, the dubbing of the duck's voice is awkward, and the film ends abruptly. What is most significant about this film is that it leads to the same comedy team dynamic between Hackett and Rooney that is utilized for Stanley Kramer's all-star comedy epic *It's a Mad, Mad, Mad, Mad World.*

REQUIEM FOR A HEAVYWEIGHT

(Columbia, 1962)

Director: Ralph Nelson
Screenplay: Rod Serling, based on his television play
Producer: David Susskind. *Cinematographer:* Arthur J. Ornitz. *Editor:* Carl Lerner
Cast: Anthony Quinn (Mountain Rivera); Jackie Gleason (Maish Rennick); Mickey Rooney (Army); Julie Harris (Grace Miller); Stanley Adams (Perelli); Madame Spivy (Ma Greeny); Herbie Faye (Bartender); Jack Dempsey (Himself); Muhammad Ali/Cassius Clay (Ring Opponent); Val Avery (Young Fighter's Promoter); Barney Ross, Rory Calhoun, William "Haystacks" Calhoun (Themselves); Michael Conrad (Thug); Lou Gilbert (Doctor); Nancy Cushman (Woman on Elevator); John Indrisano (Man Watching TV in Bar); Arthur Mercante (Referee); Angelo Rossito (Midget Wrestler); Fred Blassie (Wrestler)
Released: October 16, 1962
Specs: 87 minutes; black and white
Availability: DVD (Sony Pictures Home Entertainment)

Requiem for a Heavyweight began as a television drama written by Rod Serling of *Twilight Zone* fame. Broadcast in 1957, Jack Palance played a washed-up prizefighter trying to find his place in society after he can no longer fight. It won Serling an Emmy. David Susskind produced a feature-length version, with Serling writing the screenplay and the director of the television drama, Ralph Nelson, helming the movie. It was a strong, emotional drama with fine performances, but since this book concentrates on Mickey Rooney's work, his supporting role is the focus.

Rooney plays Army, a former fighter who now works in the corner of the fighter Mountain Rivera (Anthony Quinn), taking care of his cuts and administering basic first aid. He is also a friend of the fighter as well as the fighter's manager, Maish (Jackie Gleason). The three men live together and call themselves the Three Musketeers.

Rooney's character augments Gleason in relation to Quinn's fighter. While Army is earnest and supportive, Maish realizes that Mountain is past his prime, so he puts him in fights and bets against him. This has Maish mixed up with gangsters who rely on him when placing their own bets. Maish believes Mountain will lose within four rounds against a tough young fighter. Thus, he owes money to the mob when Mountain, in what would be his final fight, manages to go seven rounds. The gangsters put up $1,500 for Maish and money of their own, but since Mountain lasted longer than anticipated, Maish is now expected to pay back all of the money. He arranges with an exploitative promoter to put Mountain in the wrestling ring. Mountain refuses to be humiliated by wearing Indian headgear and dancing about the ring, but then discovers that if he doesn't, the mob will kill Maish. He also discovers that Maish had been betting against him for some time.

Army is different. While Maish is out creating a deal to use Mountain for more money, Army is traveling the various job opportunities so that Mountain can get some kind of work. Mountain is completely unable to function in society, knowing nothing except the fight game. Army stays with him, supports him, encourages him, and doesn't let him quit. At an employment office Mountain meets an attractive social worker who does her best to help him, but when she sets up a meeting for Mountain to work as an athletic director at a boys' camp, Maish takes him out and gets him drunk. Mountain shows up intoxicated at the interview and ruins his chances. Maish realizes that Mountain cannot make the money needed in a simple job at a boys' camp.

While Quinn and Gleason are central to the narrative and Rooney is clearly in support, Rooney still manages to resonate with his performance. Sometimes the dialogue overlaps—often Quinn's uninhibited performance threatens to overshadow everyone else in the scene—but Rooney remains focused and committed in every scene. In a card game between Maish and Army, even the *New York Times* noticed that Mickey Rooney "takes the honors hands down."[1] The review also stated,

> Mickey Rooney's delineation of the trainer is equally restrained, and while he does not have Mr. Gleason's opportunities he, too, is sad, defeated and sentient without being lachrymose.

Rooney maintains Army's devotion to Mountain completely, angry with Maish for "selling his soul on the street" and stating, "I love this kid like he's my own flesh and blood. If anything happens to him, well, just be careful Maish." Army is also unaware that Maish needs the money to repay a gambling debt from betting on Mountain to lose more quickly in his final fight. When Army discovers this as the film is concluding, he looks angrily at Maish and calls him "a lousy fink."

Rooney's finest moment in *Requiem for a Heavyweight* is at the very end. When Mountain swallows his pride and walks into the wrestling ring with full Indian headgear (and a wig with braids), holding a toy tomahawk, and starts dancing about the ring, the camera pans back to a close-up of Army standing outside the ring a few yards away with tears in his eyes. It is a very moving conclusion, and it is Rooney's expression that wraps the film so effectively.

Requiem for a Heavyweight is arguably the best film of the 1960s that Mickey Rooney appeared in. And even though it was only a small part, it was an effective one and his impact on the closing scene helped define the entire production. Rooney later recalled,

> It was a good picture with a great script by a great writer. I was already friends with Gleason, but I thought Quinn was really terrific. He wasn't sure how to play the fighter and talked to me, Gleason, the director, the writer Rod Serling, trying to figure out his approach to the character. There were a lot of ways to play it. Well, Quinn started talking to other fighters; older guys that were through fighting. He put the character together that way. I thought he did a wonderful job.[2]

However, not everyone was pleased with the way Quinn interpreted the fighter character. Anthony Quinn recalled in his autobiography *One Man Tango*, "I pushed Gleason's buttons at every turn. The slightest thing would set him off."[3]

Requiem for a Heavyweight wasn't Mickey Rooney's only experience with Rod Serling. Rooney also appeared on an episode of *The Twilight Zone*. The episode was titled "The Last Night of a Jockey" and telecast October 25, 1963. Rooney is the only performer in the entire program (not counting Serling's introduction and outro). He is a jockey currently being investigated for corruption. He is granted his wish to become bigger and starts rapidly growing. But this is all symbolic, as it is really a descent into stressed-out madness. Along with his work in *Requiem for a Heavyweight*, the episode is one of Mickey Rooney's finest performances of the 1960s.

IT'S A MAD, MAD, MAD, MAD WORLD

(United Artists, 1963)

Director: Stanley Kramer
Screenplay: Tania Rose, William Rose.
Producer: Stanley Kramer. *Cinematographer:* Ernest Laszlo. *Editors:* Gene Fowler Jr., Robert C. Jones, Frederic Knudtson
Cast: Spencer Tracy (Capt. T. G. Culpeper), Sid Caesar (Melville Crump), Milton Berle (J. Russell Finch), Ethel Merman (Mrs. Marcus), Mickey Rooney (Ding Bell), Buddy Hackett (Benjy Benjamin), Phil Silvers (Otto Meyer), Edie Adams (Monica Crump), Dorothy Provine (Emeline Marcus-Finch), Dick Shawn (Sylvester), Terry-Thomas (J. Algernon Hawthorne), Jim Backus (Fitzgerald), Barrie Chase (Sylvester's Girlfriend), William Demarest (Aloysius), Marvin Kaplan (Irwin), Arnold Stan (Ray), Jimmy Durante (Smiler Grogan), Ben Blue (Pilot), Alan Carney (Police Sergeant), Chick Chandler (Detective), Lloyd Corrigan (Mayor), Norman Fell (Detective), Paul Ford (Colonel Wilberforce), Stan Freberg (Deputy), Edward Everett Horton (Dinckler), Don Knotts (Motorist), Mike Mazurki (Miner), Bob Mazurki (Miner's Son), Zasu Pitts (Operator), Carl Reiner (Air Traffic Controller), Nick Stewart (Truck Driver), Sammee Tong (Laundryman), Jesse White (Radio Operator), Cliff Norton (Reporter), Buster Keaton (Jimmy), Eddie "Rochester" Anderson and Peter Falk (Cab Drivers), Sterling Holloway (Fire Chief), Joe E. Brown (Union Official), Doodles Weaver (Hardware Store Clerk), Tom Kennedy (Traffic Cop), Allen Jenkins (Cop), Stanley Clements (Detective), cameos by Jack Benny, Jerry Lewis, Leo Gorcey, and the Three Stooges (Moe Howard, Larry Fine, Joe DeRita)
Released: December 2, 1963

Specs: 154 minutes (edited), 174 minutes (restored video), 182 minutes (extended reedit), 192 minutes (original), 205 minutes (roadshow), 197 minutes (extended);[1] color.
Availability: DVD and Blu-ray (MGM Home Video).

There are two schools of thought regarding Stanley Kramer's epic comedy *It's a Mad, Mad, Mad, Mad World.* Some believe it to be a bloated, overlong, noisy mess. Others, such as this writer, find it to be relentlessly hilarious. Mickey Rooney has the former opinion:

> It was just too much. Every comedian in show business was crammed into that picture. It was too long, it was too loud, and it was just too much. And it wasn't fun to make. Comedians aren't a fun group to be around. We shot in the desert during the summer when the heat was miserable. That's all I want to say about that movie.[2]

Despite Rooney's misgivings, he remains consistently delightful in this wild slapstick satire on greed.

Stanley Kramer was known for heavy dramatic message movies like *The Defiant Ones* and *Judgment at Nuremberg*. He wanted to do something that was lighter and funny but still had a satiric point. The result is this epic comedy about a disparate group of people who witness a car going over a cliff; as the driver is dying, he reveals that there is $350,000[3] buried under a big W. The remainder of the film follows the various groups going through a series of outrageous slapstick difficulties while attempting to find the money.

While the film is jammed with familiar comedians in small roles (some only seconds long), Mickey Rooney has one of the principal roles as one of the people who witness the crash and hear about the treasure buried under a W. He and Buddy Hackett play a comedy team on their way to a club date. They get the idea to charter a plane and beat the others to the park where the W is supposed to be, and manage to talk a wealthy plane owner into transporting them. The plane owner (Jim Backus) is a carefree drunk who gets knocked out en route, so Mickey and Buddy must fly the plane themselves. They frantically try to keep the plane in the air while radioing to air traffic controllers, who attempt to talk them down safely. Rooney and Hackett get the chance in this movie to take that chemistry they clearly had in *Everything's Ducky* and really show it off after being given some solid comedic material to work with. They're both great and play off each other

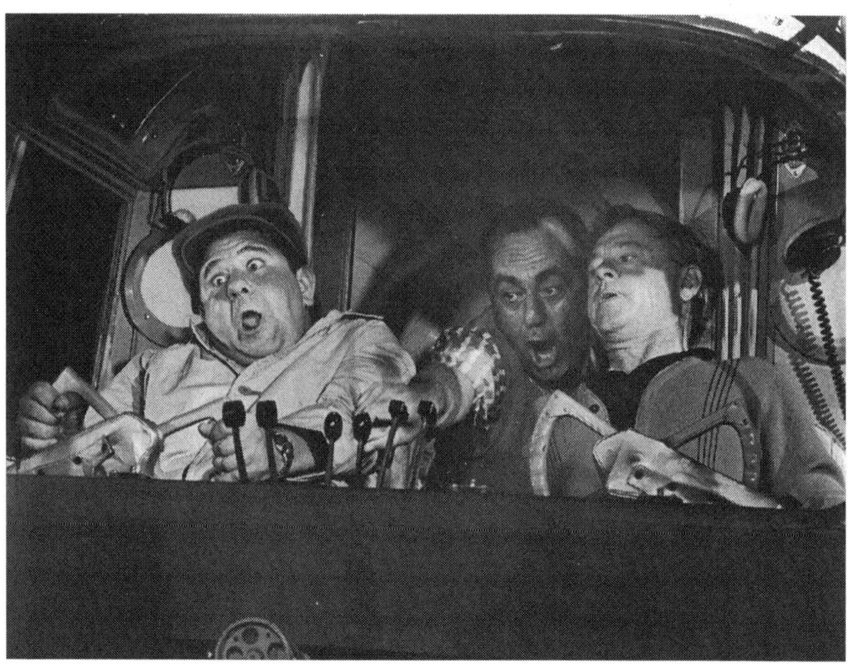

Buddy Hackett, Jim Backus, and Mickey Rooney

beautifully. And while they remained friends for the rest of their lives, they never appeared in a movie together again.

As this film is structured, each group's quest is shown as a separate vignette, and director Kramer edits between these in a cross-cutting manner to show their progress. All of the scenes are funny at different levels and are further enhanced by the various familiar faces in small roles and cameos that come up within each segment. The W turns out to be four trees that are structured in that shape.

If we were assessing *It's a Mad, Mad, Mad, Mad World* as a film, there would be a great deal to say about how it effectively uses comic excesses in order to make its point and remain entertaining. From a sociocultural perspective, the film was made just at the right time. Given wide release shortly after the assassination of President John F. Kennedy, Americans were hungering for comedy. The unbridled silliness and enormous production struck a chord with grieving America at the time, so despite a budget of nearly $10 million, the film made nearly $50 million at the box office.

According to Stanley Kramer, Spencer Tracy was already in very poor health at the time this movie was filmed and had a strict four-hours-per-day shooting schedule. Kramer stated,

> During the filming of Mad World with all the comedians, I think Spencer Tracy was in poorer health than I realized: he had bad color and no stamina whatsoever. But then, even though his lack of energy showed, I think he had his best time ever during the making of a film. The comedians worshipped him. Never before or since has a king had a court full of jesters who strove only to entertain him so that his majesty might say, "That was funny," or just laugh and smile. Milton Berle, Jonathan Winters, Buddy Hackett, Phil Silvers, Mickey Rooney—even the silent Sid Caesar—crowded about him and vied for his affection. They had it. And he talked about them to the very last; he loved them all.[4]

Despite Rooney's recalling that the set was no fun, Kramer recalls Rooney and Hackett breaking up Spencer Tracy with an off-color parody of *Boys Town*.

One significant thing regarding Mickey Rooney's participation in *It's a Mad, Mad, Mad, Mad World* was his salary. His new agent, Bullets Durgom, arranged that he get $125,000, which was the most he'd made for a movie in some time. Rooney's star had fallen significantly by the 1960s, and a dustup he had on live TV with host Jack Paar of *The Tonight Show* didn't help his employability. Durgom told Arthur Marx, "Kramer didn't want to pay it. But he wanted Mickey real bad, so after I found out he was paying that to the other comedians, I held out and finally he gave it to Mickey too."[5]

The success of Rooney's appearances in this film, *The Twilight Zone* on TV, and *Requiem for a Heavyweight* resulted in him once again being offered his own TV series. After finishing *It's a Mad, Mad, Mad, Mad World*, Rooney appeared on television in episodes of *Burke's Trial*, *Rawhide*, and *Combat*, among others. Doing as much TV work as film work, it was determined that Mickey Rooney could not only carry a TV series, but he was popular enough to attract viewers. The show was planned to be on at night and in a time slot where the competition was not so serious as *The Jackie Gleason Show* had been for Rooney's first series ten years earlier.

The show *Mickey* was scheduled for the 1964–1965 season, but despite good writers and supporting players, it was on opposite the very popular *Dick Van Dyke Show* and floundered in the ratings. However, the network was interested in continuing the show due to the popularity of one of Mickey's costars, Sammee Tong. Tong had many fans from his stint on TV's *Bachelor Father* a few years earlier, and the network considered him the real draw for the series. However, Tong was a gambler who owed the mob a lot of money. When unable to pay it back, rather than suffer whatever consequences, Tong committed suicide. He left behind a note that stated, "I have taken my own life. Nobody is to blame."[6] The series was cancelled after only a few episodes ran.

Rooney remained active on television, however, including playing George M. Cohan in a teleplay about the Seven Little Foys, featuring Eddie Foy Jr. as his own father and the Osmond Brothers as most of his brood. He also took a part in the beach movie *How to Stuff a Wild Bikini* (1965), which most feel spelled the end of the beach series. Bullets Durgom was unhappy with Rooney taking any role for whatever money he was offered, as it lowered his price and made it harder for Durgom to get his client top-paying jobs.

On the home front, Rooney was still married to his fifth wife, Barbara, who had borne him four children. She often balked at his filming overseas, realizing the temptation for infidelity was greater when he did so. However, when Rooney was in the Philippines filming *Ambush Bay*, his wife engaged in a bit of infidelity of her own.

AMBUSH BAY

(United Artists, 1966)

Director: Ron Winston
Screenplay: Marve Feinberg, Ib Melchior
Producer: Hal Klein. *Cinematographer:* Emmanuel I. Rojas. *Editor:* John F. Schreyer
Cast: Hugh O'Brian (1st Sgt. Steve Corey), Mickey Rooney (Sgt. Ernest Wartell), James Mitchum (Pvt. James Grenier), Peter Masterson (Sgt. William Maccone), Harry Lauter (Cpl. Alvin Ross), Tisa Chang (Miyazaki), Gregg Amsterdam (Cpl. Stanley Parrish), Bruno Punzalan (Ramon), Tisa Chang (Miyaki), Buff Fernandez (Tokuzo), Joaquin Fajardo (Koyamatsu), Jim Anauo (Reynolds), Tony Smith (Private George), Clem Stadler (Davis), Amado Abello (Amado), Juris Sulit (Midori), Max Quismudno (Max)
Released: September 14, 1966
Specs: 109 minutes; color
Availability: DVD (MGM Home Entertainment)

After his TV show was cancelled and after Mickey Rooney accepted a cameo in *How to Stuff a Wild Bikini* (1965), much to his agent's chagrin, the actor's next film was *Ambush Bay*. Shot in the Philippines, *Ambush Bay* followed a group of marines during World War Two on a secret mission. They must connect with a female spy, who will offer sensitive information about the enemy that could help a planned invasion. Rooney is effectively low key as a cynical veteran marine. However, his role is clearly in support of the film's star, Hugh O'Brian, who draws from his own real-life experience in the war to help define his role in the movie. He offers an outstanding performance, with Mickey Rooney's effective support helping to enhance the low-budget movie.

Despite a low budget, the action sequences are realistic and powerful. The marines deal with snipers, suicide warriors, mines, and other dangers. The film enjoyed good reviews, and Rooney's performance was singled out by critics. However, Rooney found the shooting of this film to be difficult and uncomfortable for the actors. He stated in his autobiography, "I had hated my time in the Philippines. The plot of *Ambush Bay* had us hacking our way through the worst kind of jungles on the island, fighting mosquitoes and drinking the local water."[1]

Still, Mickey Rooney is most effective in a rather offbeat role. O'Brian has the standout role as the leader, so Rooney, also playing a seasoned veteran, must register in the part while not overshadowing the leading man. In less-experienced hands it might have been a more challenging role, but Rooney pulls it off beautifully. Rooney's ability to convey a character beyond the written dialogue is especially discernible here. Just the look in his eye, the expression on his face, and his general manner exude all of the hardened seen-it-all competence of the marine veteran he is portraying. At thirty-five, Rooney was generally older than others in the unit. At least one, a quick replacement for an ailing soldier, has no combat experience at all. While O'Brian plays the leader, Rooney must co-lead through his support of the commander and his experience over the other soldiers involved in this mission. It is the same way Rooney the actor must support O'Brian as the film's leading man, while setting an example for the younger thespians in the ensemble cast.

While *Ambush Bay* is a good, albeit clichéd, movie, and Rooney is good in it, its inclusion in a book on the actor's essential films is mostly due to its directly affecting an area of his personal life that would impact his professional career. While Rooney was filming in the Philippines, he contracted an illness and returned home. This was exacerbated by problems he was having in his fifth marriage, as he discovered wife Barbara was having an affair. Rooney accepted a club date along with his partner Bobby Van, but in his autobiography *Life Is Too Short*, he says doesn't know how he got through it. His weight plummeted down to 116 pounds—frighteningly slim, even for a man who is short in stature like Rooney. He was checked into a hospital to recover.

While he was recuperating, Barbara visited him in the hospital frequently and they talked about their situation. Rooney had filed for divorce, asking for custody of their four children. They decided to give it another try, and she agreed to break off her affair. When she attempted to do so, her lover flew into a rage and shot her to death, then killed himself, with a gun registered to Rooney, which, ironically, he had given to Barbara for protection. Mickey's friends Sig Frolich, cowboy actor Don "Red" Barry, and his son Timmy all came to the hospital to be there when Mickey's doctor broke the news. Rooney first wanted to be sure the children were unharmed. They were in the home when this happened. He then collapsed into sobs.

In an interview with Emma Brockes for the *Guardian*, Michael Rooney, one of the children recalled,

> I don't remember a thing. I was about three or four. And my mum and my dad were going through a divorce. My mum was kind of seeing somebody on the side. But then my father and my mother decided to get back together, and the guy my mum was dating wasn't having it. So he took the very gun that my father gave my mother for protection and killed her in our house. Then killed himself. It was a murder suicide. We were in the house when it happened. But I don't remember a thing. We were scurried out and told we were going to see the movie *Mary Poppins*. It wasn't like, oh, your mother's dead upstairs. My grandparents adopted us, my mother's parents. It was stable after that. My grandparents taught me to rake the leaves in the backyard, clean up my room, all that stuff. And we went to regular schools. I think I was about 13 or 14 when I really understood what had happened. For years I thought my grandmother was my mother, because the transition was so smooth. And then my grandmother sat us down and told us why our mother was no longer around. She started showing us pictures of my mother. The way they did it was really good. [My father] told me that my mother was one of the most wonderful ladies he had ever met, that she was really nice, a caring person, she was wonderful with us and loved us all. At that point, I really needed to hear that.[2]

His wife's murder emotionally destroyed Rooney. Her best friend, Marge Lane, tried to help him, and he ended up rather hastily marrying her. They were married for only one hundred days and then divorced. Rooney would later claim he does not even remember their having been married.

This tragedy affected Rooney so deeply that his work also suffered. In fact, the year 1967 was the very first time no Mickey Rooney movie was released in a theater since 1945 when he was in the army. Rooney made a few TV appearances in 1967, but no theatrical film. His only theatrical release in 1968 was as part of Otto Preminger's all-star flop *Skidoo*. Then in 1969 as he was appearing with Dick Van Dyke in *The Comic*, Carl Reiner's look at silent movie comedy, Rooney got the idea that it might be time to reteam with Judy Garland.

THE COMIC

(Columbia, 1969)

Director: Carl Reiner
Screenplay: Carl Reiner, Aaron Ruben
Producers: Carl Reiner, Aaron Ruben. *Cinematographer:* W. Wallace Kelley. *Editor:* Adrienne Fazan
Cast: Dick Van Dyke (Billy Bright), Michele Lee (Mary Gibson), Mickey Rooney (Cockeye), Cornel Wilde (Frank Powers), Nina Wayne (Sybil), Pert Kelton (Mama), Steve Allen (Hmself), Barbara Heller (Ginger), Ed Peck (Edwin G. Englehardt), Jeannine Riley (Lorraine), Gavin MacLeod (1st Director), Jay Novello (Miguel), Craig Huebing (Doctor), Paulene Myers (Phoebe), Fritz Feld (Armand), Jerome Cowan (Lawrence), Isabel Sanford (Woman), Jeff Donnell (nurse), Carl Reiner (Al Schilling), Frank Biro (Fred), Maurice Dallimore (Faversham), Paul Frees (Narrator), Carter Harbaugh (Tommy), Scott James (Billy Jr.), Suzi Kaye (Amanda Lou Phipps), Mantan Moreland (Man Commenting on Funeral), Billy Barty (Actor), Geoff Edwards (TV Host), Mel Berger (Fatso)
Released: November 19, 1969
Specs: 94 minutes; color
Availability: DVD (Sony Choice Collection)

Carl Reiner recalled in his autobiography that when he was working with Dick Van Dyke on *The Dick Van Dyke Show*, Van Dyke would often state that he wished he was working during the era of Charlie Chaplin, Buster Keaton, and Laurel and Hardy.[1] Reiner also remembered contacting Laurel by phone when they wanted to have Van Dyke and Mel Berger portray Laurel and Hardy on an episode, and needed permission to do so. Laurel informed the shocked Reiner that he and the estate of the late Oliver Hardy did not own the rights to their image or likeness, so he could not grant them permission. Both of these events helped to inspire *The Comic,* in which Reiner looks at the rise and fall of a fictitious silent movie comedian named Billy Bright, played by Dick Van Dyke. Mickey Rooney has a supporting role as Cockeye, a cross-eyed comic who is Billy Bright's one loyal friend through all the ups and downs.

The idea of exploring the silent film era, the process of a slapstick comic who enjoyed great popularity but could not adapt well to talking pictures, is a great one. Superstars of the silent era were sometimes completely incapable of sustaining their careers effectively in sound films. A movie focusing on a fictitious comic with real talent who must find ways to redefine what had made him a success when the business he is in completely reinvents itself had great potential. Having someone with Carl Reiner's talent, insight, and frame of reference directing and co-writing the screenplay, and having Dick Van Dyke in the title role, made this project even more attractive. Unfortunately, the approach that Reiner chose resulted in a film that never did reach its potential.

The Comic is hardly a salute to the great silent screen comics. Billy Bright is presented as a difficult, womanizing egomaniac who is so dislikable that when, at the conclusion of the film, he sets his alarm to awaken in the middle of the night to catch one of his old movies on TV, it is not a moving scene. One can't feel sorry for a despicable man like Billy Bright. It's like they took the most scandalous aspects of every popular silent film star's life and combined them all in one person.

The film is said to be based on various aspects of Chaplin, Keaton, and Laurel. However, interestingly enough, it more closely resembles Mickey Rooney's career; bad decisions, the inability to advance in the film industry as he got older, womanizing, gambling, and alcoholism were all part of Rooney's life. But this does not seem intentional and is likely a simple coincidence.

Rooney's character is obviously inspired by Ben Turpin, a cross-eyed comedian whose screen career ran from the dawn of the twentieth century until his death in 1940. But the relationship between Bright and Cockeye is similar to the friendship W. C. Fields had with Tammany Young, who was a consistent companion, appeared in his films, and remained supportive through all of the comedian's ups and downs until Young's death in 1936. While Van Dyke is clearly the star of *The Comic*, Rooney's consistent presence and the loyalty of the character he exudes are strong ingredients that impact the narrative effectively. He is easily the best part of the movie. Pauline Kael put it best in her review, stating that Rooney "creates a character out of almost nothing and lives it on the screen so convincingly that you fully expect to see him again after the movie is over."[2] However, despite the valiant effort of all involved, *The Comic* was a box office flop. Van Dyke told Larry King, "Very few people saw that movie, but we're proud of it."[3]

It was around the time he was filming *The Comic* that Mickey Rooney got the idea to get back together with Judy Garland to open an acting school and perhaps eventually create a chain of such schools with their names attached. Garland had also fallen on hard times, had problems with drugs and alcohol, and Rooney felt they could both recover from their demons with this venture. Rooney and Garland had reunited on TV a few years earlier, reminiscing about their MGM years and then re-creating one of their classic dances from their movie *Girl Crazy*. The program was well received and now, once again at a very low point in his career, Rooney thought that perhaps this venture could make a difference in his and Garland's careers, the two of them once again dancing side by side and inspiring young performers with their veteran status.

Rooney approached Garland with his usual enthusiasm, telling her his idea, offering the details he had worked out in his head, and saying that they really needed to be together again, like the old days. In the midst of his pitch, Rooney reminded Judy Garland of an incident when they arrived at Grand Central while fourteen thousand excited fans were waiting. When Rooney finally took a breath, Garland spoke. "Mick it isn't that way anymore," she said. "We were the toast of the town then."[4] Rooney was adamant, so Garland said she would think about it. Rooney recalled in his autobiography that it was only a few months later when he was playing golf and saw a cart with a single passenger heading toward him. Rooney's intuition told him that it was bad news. He was right. The man in the cart approached him and stated that they had just heard on the radio that Judy Garland had died. Rooney recalls collapsing to the ground, sobbing uncontrollably, and hurting his hands as he punched the ground screaming, "Why? Why?" Judy's children considered asking him to speak at the funeral, but Rooney admitted he couldn't have handled it. He attended, stood in back, and left quietly without fanfare. Rooney recalled in his autobiography,

> I understood what she was feeling. So, in fact, did many of her fans. They, too, would have understood. And they would have been far more loving with her than she was to herself.[5]

As Mickey Rooney entered the 1970s, the world of MGM stardom, classics like *Boys Town*, and popular entertainment like the Hardy family series or the musicals with Judy Garland seemed so long ago, as if they never happened.

PULP

(United Artists, 1972)

Director: Mike Hodges
Writer: Mike Hodges
Producer: Michael Klinger. *Cinematographer:* Ousama Rawi. *Editor:* John Glen
Cast: Michael Caine (Mickey King); Mickey Rooney (Preston Gilbert); Lionel Stander (Ben Dinuccio); Lizabeth Scott (Princess Betty Cippola); Victor Mercierca (Prince Cippola); Nadia Cassini (Liz Adams); Al Lettieri (Miller); Dennis Price (Mysterious Englishman); Amerigo Tot (Sotgio); Leopoldo Trieste (Marcovic); Robert Sacchi (Jim Norman; the Bogeyman); Giulio Donnini (Typing Pool Manager); Luciano Pigozzi (Clairvoyant); Mary Caruana (Mae West); Anna Pace Donnella (Jean Harlow); Tondi Barr (Gloria Swanson); Werner Hasselmann, Louise Lambert (Tourists in Restaurant)
Working title: "Memoirs of a Ghostwriter"
Released: November 5, 1972
Specs: 95 minutes; color
Availability: DVD (MGM Home Video)

Before engaging in the movie *Pulp*, Mickey Rooney was approached by Norman Lear to appear in the pilot of a TV show he was planning about a bigoted middle-aged man trying to cope with the changes in the culture as well as a liberal son and daughter-in-law. Challenging the norm for what was feasible on TV, the central character, Archie Justice, would loudly proclaim his prejudices, racial and otherwise, as part of the dialogue. After reading the script, Rooney turned the project down and warned Norman Lear about taking a chance on such edgy material. The show eventually premiered in 1971 as *All in the Family* with Carroll O'Connor in the role of Archie Bunker. The show was a hit, became a classic, and eventually reached iconic status. Rooney never regretted turning it down. Tony Randall also wanted Rooney to play the Oscar Madison role on TV's *The Odd Couple*, based on the Neil Simon play. Randall had toured with Rooney in the play and enjoyed working with him. Of course the role went to Jack Klugman. So, Rooney went back to movies. And for his next movie venture, he accepted a role in a film that was also edgy and outrageous, maybe as much as the *All in the Family* project, but in different ways.

Michael Caine and Mike Hodges enjoyed great success with *Get Carter* (1971), so they teamed up for this seriocomic story about Mickey King, a pulp fiction writer who writes sexually inspired novels under pseudonyms like Guy Strange and Les B. Han. Mickey is asked to ghostwrite a famous retired movie actor's autobiography, but just who he is to represent is shrouded in secrecy. Intrigued, Mickey takes the job and is flown to a remote island to meet with his client (the film was shot on the isle of Malta). Rooney portrays Preston Gilbert, a former star of gangster films who is now dying of cancer and wants to reveal all in an autobiography. Preston believes his sordid life would best be served by a writer like Mickey. However, because Preston spent a lot of time rubbing elbows with actual mobsters, the prospect of a tell-all book has made him a target of former associates in high places who do not want their secrets revealed.

When *Pulp* was made, the vintage Hollywood films of the 1930s and 1940s were enjoying a nostalgic renaissance. Festivals featuring the movies of Humphrey Bogart, W. C. Fields, the Marx Brothers, and Mae West were popular in revival houses in the bigger cities, and even found their way into smaller towns' theaters. Actors like these were the rage on college campuses. Thus, a lot of newer movies were homages to older ones, including *Pulp*. Caine is the sort of cynical, sarcastic leading man as Humphrey Bogart was in films like *The Maltese Falcon* (1941) and *The Big Sleep* (1947). It is his performance that anchors *Pulp* and makes it worth watching.

However, in a book on Mickey Rooney's films, it is Rooney's performance that we must give the most attention. Rooney approaches the character with unbridled enthusiasm, his Preston Gilbert a loud, overbearing sort who grandstands in every situation. Even in a restaurant, Preston dons a waiter's jacket and starts comically serving a couple of tourists, spilling wine all over them and making a scene in the guise of entertainment. There are aspects of Rooney the actor's noted personality traits abounding in the Preston Gilbert character, and thus, writer-director Hodges wanted him for the role. Rooney did not accept immediately, which is puzzling because he certainly needed the work, so Elisha Cook Jr. was also considered (which would have been a neat touch, as Cook had been in *The Maltese Falcon*). Although Caine plays a pulp writer, he carries himself as a something of an ersatz private eye, getting deeper and deeper into a cesspool of crimes, murders, and ugly characters. It begins upon his arrival in Malta, where he finds a dead body in a bathtub before he even meets Rooney's character. In fact, Rooney himself is killed off midway through the movie.

Rooney plays Preston with all bells and whistles, defining the character's boisterous nature, his self-aggrandizing, by shouting the dialogue and flailing his arms with blatant gestures. It is not a case of Rooney overacting. He obviously perceives Preston as the type of character who would carry himself about in this manner. When he stands in his briefs and dances in front of a mirror, he clearly admires himself. As he barks orders at underlings, he believes himself to be a much larger and imposing presence than his diminutive stature presents. Perhaps Rooney is drawing from elements of a lot of "big men" he'd known during his long career, defining the character of Preston along those lines. But while he is a part of the movie, Rooney draws our attention away from every other actor, including Michael Caine.

While he doesn't have a great deal of footage, Mickey Rooney registers strongly in the role and makes a difference as to the rhythm of each scene. Unfortunately, *Pulp* is not a particularly good film. It meanders a lot and takes a lot of time revealing important plot points. Most characters don't register at all. But, for the nostalgic factor, it is good to see Lizabeth Scott in her first theatrical film since appearing with Elvis Presley in *Loving You* (1957). *Pulp* would be her final movie. Acting veteran Lionel Stander is also good as a gravel-voiced henchman, a part he'd been playing since the 1930s, adding a touch of authenticity to the proceedings.

In his autobiography *What's It All About?* Michael Caine indicates how much he enjoyed working with older actors he'd grown up seeing at the movies, and recalls working with Rooney on this film as being quite an experience. Caine found Rooney to be very warm and friendly, offering advice to the younger actor to save his money. Rooney had been working for decades, had been the top movie star in the nation for years, and was now, at the time of this film, completely broke. Caine recalled that Rooney used to tell him "the filthiest jokes with every four-letter word imaginable."[1]

Mickey Rooney makes no mention at all of *Pulp* in his autobiography *Life Is Too Short*, so he likely thought little of it. But it is an essential part of his filmography due to it being one of the few interesting performances he offered during what can probably be described as the doldrums of his career. He was married to his seventh wife, Carolyn, who was only twenty-three years old, not even born when Mickey Rooney was enjoying success as the number one movie star in the country. Rooney was also spending more time doing guest spots on TV. He managed to secure a few small parts in movies during the 1970s, but often in lackluster vehicles. In one particularly bizarre film, *The Manipulator* (1971), Rooney plays a crazed former makeup man in Hollywood who kidnaps and imprisons a woman and rants at her for the feature film's running time. While one might be impressed with Rooney's ability to play such a role, the film itself is particularly unsettling and unenjoyable. He also appeared in the G-rated low-budget flop *The Godmothers* (1973), which reunited him with Billy Barty from the Mickey McGuire comedies. On TV, he fared better doing guest spots on various popular shows. At this time his most noted TV work was probably voicing Kris Kringle in *Santa Claus Is Coming to Town* (1970), which became a yuletide perennial.

As the 1970s continued, Rooney did some other feature voice-overs, including the Scarecrow in *Journey Back to Oz* (1974), and a few more appearances on TV and in low-budget films, but despite nostalgia for the era when he was the biggest star, his current work did not register with the public. This was borne out in a 1977 issue of the Sunday *Parade* supplement, syndicated in many newspapers. In a section called "Ask Them Yourself" where people can write in and ask a celebrity a question, someone asked Mickey Rooney, "Whatever happened to you?" At that time, Rooney had two major films coming out: *The Domino Principle* starring Gene Hackman and the Walt Disney feature *Pete's Dragon*. He mentioned those movies, stating, "I'm still very much around."[2]

PETE'S DRAGON

(Walt Disney Productions, 1977)

Director: Don Chaffey
Screenplay: Malcolm Marmorstein. *Story:* Seton I. Miller, S. S. Field
Producers: Jerome Courtland, Ron Miller. *Cinematographer:* Frank V. Phillips. *Editor:* Gordon D. Brenner
Cast: Helen Reddy (Nora); Jim Dale (Dr. Terminus); Mickey Rooney (Lampie); Red Buttons (Hoagy); Shelley Winters (Lena Grogan); Sean Marshall (Pete); Jane Kean (Miss Taylor); Jim Backus (The Mayor); Charles Tyner (Merle); Gary Morgan (Grocer); Jeff Conaway (Willie); Cal Bartlett (Paul); Walter Barnes (Captain); Al Checco, Henry Slate, Jack Collins (Fishermen); Robert Easton (Store Proprietor); Roger Price (Man with Visor); Robert Foulk (Sea Captain); Ben Wrigley (Egg Man); Joe Ross (Cement Man); Kim Diamond, Rocky Bonfield (Dancers)
Songs: "I Saw a Dragon" (music and lyrics by Al Kasha and Joel Hirschhorn; sung by Mickey Rooney, Helen Reddy, and Ensemble); "It's Not Easy" (music and lyrics by Al Kasha and Joel Hirschhorn; sung by Sean Marshall and Helen Reddy); "Passamashloddy" (music and lyrics by Al Kasha and Joel Hirschhorn; sung by Jim Dale, Red Buttons, and Ensemble); "Candle on the Water" (music and lyrics by Al Kasha and Joel Hirschhorn; sung by Helen Reddy); "There's Room for Everyone" (music and lyrics by Al Kasha and Joel Hirschhorn; sung by Helen Reddy, Sean Marshall, and Ensemble); "Every Little Piece" (music and lyrics by Al Kasha and Joel Hirschhorn; sung by Jim Dale and Red Buttons); "Brazzle Dazzle Day" (music and lyrics by Al Kasha and Joel Hirschhorn; sung by Helen Reddy, Sean Marshall, and Mickey Rooney); "Bill of Sale" (music and lyrics by Al Kasha and Joel Hirschhorn, sung by Shelley Winters, Charles Tyner, Gary Morgan, Jeff Conaway, and

Helen Reddy); "Finale: I Saw a Dragon/Brazzle Dazzle Day" (music and lyrics by Al Kasha and Joel Hirschhorn; sung by Helen Reddy, Sean Marshall, Mickey Rooney, and Company)
Released: November 3, 1977
Specs: 128 minutes; Technicolor
Availability: DVD and Blu-ray (Disney)

In 1977 Mickey Rooney had meandered with little success on TV and in movies, had divorced his seventh wife, and was married to his eighth (and last) one, Jan. Rooney also appeared in two high-profile movies in 1977. One was Stanley Kramer's *The Domino Principle* featuring Gene Hackman as a troubled Vietnam vet who finds himself in and out of jail and mixed up with the wrong people. When he finally is sentenced to a long prison term for murder, he is visited in his cell by an important man, who arranges for him to leave prison if he agrees to kill again. Mickey Rooney plays Hackman's cell mate in prison, and the two have some interesting and fun dialogue exchanges. However, Rooney had obviously come a long way from Andy Hardy with dialogue like "Maybe we can score a couple of eighteen-year-olds and play hide the weenie all night long" in response to the privileges Hackman seems to be enjoying while in prison. While the movie was not particularly well received, reviewers gave kudos to Rooney for his strong performance.

Pete's Dragon could not be more unlike *The Domino Principle*. A big, colorful, wholesome Disney musical, *Pete's Dragon* was a hit with the family trade and with children, despite not being one of Disney's best movies. In his book *The Disney Films* Leonard Maltin states,

> The story is perfect Disney fodder: an orphan boy named Pete flees from his cruel guardians and comes to a Maine fishing town, where he's taken in by a young woman who lives in a lighthouse with her father. The lonely youngster's best friend turns out to be a dragon named Eliott, which causes Pete to be pursued by a number of people who want to exploit the animal. Unfortunately, the film has more than its share of problems. First, it is too long. There are a couple of agreeable songs, but not one that might be remembered after the film is over. But *Pete's Dragon* does have one major asset: the animated title character designed by Ken Anderson and brought to life with verve and humor by Don Bluth and his crew.[1]

As far as Mickey Rooney's contribution is concerned, *Pete's Dragon* is something of a triumph. It is good to see Rooney singing big production numbers again and responding to the choreography with energy and commitment. It is actors like him, Red Buttons, and Jim Dale who keep *Pete's Dragon* going as well as it does, because despite a good singing voice, Helen Reddy has only fair acting skills. Janet Maslin pointed out in her *New York Times* review,

> *Pete's Dragon* is full of performers who nicely detract attention from one another's weaknesses. Sean Marshall doesn't sing well, but Helen Reddy does, so she often accompanies his vocals. Miss Reddy is serviceable but undistinguished as an actress—she has a tendency to behave as if she were a very bright light bulb in a very small lamp—but she so often finds herself in the company of Messrs. Rooney, Dale or Buttons that her scenes work well.[2]

For the most part, the actors in *Pete's Dragon* are great; they just don't always have the best material with which to work. The songs are decent but not memorable (although, surprisingly, the music was nominated for Best Song and Best Score Oscars). There's often too much going on in the movie; cut out the not-so-necessary characters and plot lines and it could easily have been a ninety-minute film rather than one that runs over two hours.

The Disney studio acquired the rights to this story in 1955 with the intention of filming it for TV, having just launched the Disneyland anthology program. The idea was for the dragon to never be seen. The story was shelved until 1975 when it was again dusted off for what would eventually become this production. Mickey Rooney appears to be no more significant than any of the other actors hired for this movie and is barely mentioned in any of the reviews, other than the fact that he appears in the movie.

Director Don Chaffey must have noticed that Mickey Rooney fared well in family entertainment, because he cast Rooney in *The Magic of Lassie* the following year. Rooney was billed second after James Stewart in a cast that also included Pernell Roberts, Stephanie Zimbalist, Alice Faye, Gene Evans, and Mike Mazurki. It would be Rooney's only movie during 1978.

In 1979, Rooney was contacted by Francis Ford Coppola about appearing in another movie that Coppola was helping to produce. Rooney would be playing an old, retired jockey. The film would be based on Walter Farley's novel *The Black Stallion*.

61

THE BLACK STALLION

(United Artists, 1979)

Director: Carroll Ballard
Screenplay: Melissa Mathison, Jeanne Rosenberg, William D. Wittliff, based on the novel by Walter Farley
Producers: Francis Ford Coppola, Fred Roos, Tom Sternberg. *Cinematographer:* Caleb Deschanel. *Editor:* Robert Dalva. *Music:* Carmine Coppola
Cast: Kelly Reno (Alec Ramsey); Mickey Rooney (Henry Dailey); Teri Garr (Alec's Mother); Clarence Muse (Snoe); Hoyt Axton (Alec's Father); Michael Higgins (Neville); Ed McNamara (Jake); Dogmi Larbi (Arab); Kristen Vigard (Becky); Don Hudson (Taurog); Tom Dahlgren (Veterinarian); Daniel Henning (Danny); John Burton, John Buchanan (Jockeys); John Karlsen (Archeologist); Frank Cousins (African Chieftain); Marne Maitland (Drake Captain); Cass-Olé (The Black Stallion)
Released: October 17, 1979
Specs: 118 minutes; color; widescreen; released in 70mm and 35mm
Availability: DVD (20th Century Fox Home Video)

The Black Stallion was a popular novel written by Walter Farley in 1941. It spawned six sequels. But it was not until the late 1970s, when Francis Ford Coppola purchased the rights to the story, that it was considered for a motion picture adaption. Coppola hired Carroll Ballard to direct despite Ballard's only directorial credit being an Oscar-nominated short subject, *Harvest*, ten years earlier. Ballard had been a classmate of Coppola's at UCLA. Despite Ballard's inexperience, *The Black Stallion* is beautifully directed and one of the most artistic family films ever to be conceived in the Hollywood mainstream.

The story deals with a young boy named Alec, who is on a ship with his father. Alec is quite taken by a beautiful Arabian horse that is stabled on the ship. There is an explosion on board, and the horse escapes and jumps overboard as the ship is engulfed with flames. Alec also escapes as the ship sinks. He and the horse are together on a deserted island, so Alec befriends and tames the animal, and they are soon rescued. Once back home, Alec meets old trainer and former jockey Henry Dailey. The two of them team up to train the stallion as a racehorse with Alec riding as a "mystery jockey," complete with mask, so as not to reveal his age.

The opening scenes, before Mickey Rooney appears in the role of the trainer, are presented with very little dialogue. We see very large, sweeping shots of the boy running and swimming with the horse, director Ballard using the widescreen image to its greatest effect by surrounding the movement of the characters with colorful negative space. While not quite a montage, Ballard offers a series of sequences that present the time and space of the narrative without dialogue or narration. We see the boy and horse responding to each other tentatively, gradually connecting, and finally a relationship is formed where the boy rides the horse, and it is protective of him. When a rescue team finds them, Alec must keep the stallion from attacking the men. Once they are home, the horse chases the garbage collector out of the yard like a veritable watchdog, attempting to protect the boy.

Mickey Rooney has a large role in a very big movie here. And it could not have been better casting. Rooney later recalled,

> I had played a jockey in a lot of movies,[1] and always connected well with the horses. So I really felt comfortable on this picture. And sometimes when you're on a movie, you get a feeling that it is something special. I had that feeling while we shot this one. I knew we had something. I think it is one of the best pictures I ever made.[2]

The scenes between Alec and Henry show the development of a human relationship just as Alec had made his connection with the horse. At the same time, Henry must connect with the stallion as the two of them train the animal to battle the fastest horses in the world. Director Ballard continues to offer scenes without dialogue, showing the evolving effort of the trainers and the progression of the horse as it continues to get faster. These are interspersed with scenes between Reno and Rooney that have dialogue (mostly from Rooney), as the older man offers advice regarding how to properly ride a horse, work with him, train him, and respond to him effectively. While Alec had managed to do a lot of this instinctively, Henry helps him to better understand and refine his approach.

The characters of both Alec and Henry are as instinctive as the direction is calculated. Rooney shows once again that he is a master at exhibiting a firmness of character with pure honesty whose emotions are all completely on the surface. The depth of his character is not hidden or gradually revealed. He is very much a genuine, honest character who believes in what he is doing and feels the dream he shares with the boy about the horse is a perfectly attainable goal. There is some element of naïveté in this approach, but it is conveyed so honestly that it is completely effective. Even the scene where Henry comes to convince Alec's skeptical mother to allow the boy to ride the horse in an important race utilizes this approach. Teri Garr, as the mother, brilliantly wavers between a clear refusal to allow her child to engage in something so dangerous and the emotional connection to Alec that allows her to understand its importance.

The Black Stallion was among the most critically acclaimed movies of 1979. Janet Maslin wrote in the *New York Times*, "Mr. Rooney lends humor and humanity to the proceedings, and he fits surprisingly well into Mr. Ballard's careful scheme."[3] Michael Bowen of the *Boston Globe* stated, "Generations from now, when people talk about horse movies, they won't be talking about *National Velvet* or *My Friend Flicka*, they'll be talking about the majestic beauty of Carroll Ballard's *The Black Stallion*."[4] However, Roger Ebert was less impressed with Mickey Rooney's appearance in this film. In his review, he indicated, "The presence of Mickey Rooney, who plays the trainer, is welcome but perhaps too familiar. Rooney has played this sort of role so often before (most unforgettably in *National Velvet*) that he almost seems to be visiting from another movie. His Academy Award nomination for the performance is probably a recognition of that."[5] There are a lot of similarities between this film and *National Velvet* and between the roles Rooney played in both films (a photo of him in *National Velvet* is even displayed among Henry's personal effects in the movie). This does not diminish the impact his performance has here. Mi in *National Velvet* is decidedly more cynical, whereas Henry puts all his faith into Alec and the horse without any hesitation.

While most critics pointed out the beauty of the film's opening scenes, few responded as favorably to how well Ballard filmed the final race. The director carefully edits between shots of Alec's face astride the stallion, close-ups of the hooves running powerfully, medium wide shots that show the expanse and utilize the negative space, and longer shots that indicate how far ahead the stallion is of the others. That, along with Carmine Coppola's stirring music score, makes this sequence an emotional triumph. The horse's victory concludes the film with a swirl of celebrating that is once again presented without dialogue.

After a lifetime of making movies, decades of struggle attempting to reclaim some level of the respect and stardom he'd once had and subsequently lost, Rooney finally came back with a truly triumphant performance in this big-budget movie. *The Black Stallion* took two years to produce, amid a lot of problems at many levels, but none of these involved Rooney. In fact, he shot his scenes after these troubles had subsided. The budget for the film was in the neighborhood of $3 million but reached nearly $5 million by the time of completion. It made nearly $40 million at the box office, won an Oscar for editing, and was nominated for its music score; Mickey Rooney was nominated as Best Supporting Actor.

The Black Stallion came out just as Rooney began appearing on Broadway in the triumphant burlesque musical comedy *Sugar Babies*. Rooney later recalled,

> When they first called me about it I thought it was a lousy idea. Who wants to see burlesque? That stuff is dead! Well I finally got talked into doing it, and it is one of the best decisions I ever made. For once![6]

Sugar Babies opened on Broadway at the Mark Hellinger Theatre on October 8, 1979, and closed on August 28, 1982, after 1,208 performances. It was nominated for ten Tony awards, including Best Musical, and Rooney was nominated for Best Performance by a Lead Actor in a Musical. Rooney said,

> My face was on the cover of magazines because of *Sugar Babies* so when my son Timmy called and said, "Congratulations, Dad," I thought he was talking about that. Then he tells me I am nominated for an Oscar for *The Black Stallion*. I almost fainted![7]

A Tony nomination and an Oscar nomination was a great way for Mickey Rooney to conclude the 1970s. Now in the midst of a full comeback, Mickey Rooney was able to weigh his options as he entered the 1980s.

EPILOGUE

From *Bill* to *Night at the Museum*, and an Honorary Oscar in Between

THE BILL MADE FOR TELEVISION MOVIES

The success of *The Black Stallion* on the movie screen and *Sugar Babies* on the Broadway stage led Mickey Rooney to *Bill*, a TV movie about the real-life Bill Sackter, a man with special needs who spent most of his life in an institution but was eventually released to live with a family and expand his limitations. It was telecast on CBS December 22, 1981, and won Mickey Rooney both an Emmy award and a Golden Globe for his performance.

Bill Sackter was seven years old when, after taking a mandatory intelligence test, he was classified as "subnormal" by the state of Minnesota and institutionalized. He never saw his mother or siblings again (his father died that year). After forty-four years Sackter was relocated to a halfway house and worked various jobs to support himself. While working a temporary assignment as a handyman at a country club, he was befriended by Barry and Bev Morrow, who eventually became his legal guardians. They moved to Iowa where Bill successfully ran a campus coffee shop. Rooney's challenge for the role was to successfully convey the complex Bill character, who was dismissed as "mentally retarded" in his day but had perceptions that were sometimes discernible and deeper than what examinations as early as 1920 would have uncovered.

Rooney was in full comeback mode when *Bill* aired in 1981. *The Black Stallion* was a huge hit, and Rooney was prominent in the audience at the

Oscar ceremonies (he lost to Melvyn Douglas, his old costar from *Captains Courageous*, who won for *Being There*). As indicated in the previous chapter, Rooney was on the cover of many top magazines promoting the Broadway hit *Sugar Babies*, for which he earned a Tony nomination. He was once again considered a star in the entertainment mainstream, and his classic films were just now being rediscovered as the new home video market of VHS and Betamax tapes started to open up. His gentle, honest portrayal of Bill Sackter only strengthened this latter-day recognition and respect. Rooney's brilliant acting ability never left him. It was always evident, even in the most wrongheaded productions during the period where he "couldn't get arrested."[1] Nobody was noticing, but Rooney never stopped being a great actor. Now that he was once again being noticed, his fine acting given more challenging roles, he rose to the occasion and began winning awards and acclaim. The success of *Bill* resulted in a sequel, *Bill: On His Own* (1983). Bill Sackter died that year. The *Bill* films offer some of Mickey Rooney's finest acting. He takes a role that could have been overexaggerated and instead gives a very genuine, moving performance. The films are both very simple, and it's Rooney who really drives them and makes them memorable (the sequel is less memorable, but he's still great in it).

Due to his success in *Bill*, Rooney tried another TV series, *One of the Boys*, for the 1982–1983 season. The show also starred Dana Carvey and Nathan Lane. When it was cancelled, Rooney was disgruntled and vowed to never appear on a TV series again. Television series comedy had not been Rooney's area. He accepted shows that were quickly cancelled, and turned down or missed out on series that became lasting hits.

A LONG OVERDUE HONOR

In 1983, Mickey Rooney was told by the Academy Awards that he'd be honored with a lifetime achievement award at their next ceremony. On April 11, Rooney proudly accepted the award and offered an emotional speech where he remembered to thank deceased stars like Judy Garland, Lewis Stone, Wallace Beery, Spencer Tracy, and Fay Holden (the beloved Ma Hardy died in 1973).

However, as Rooney ventured on in the 1980s, his comeback and renewed interest did not amount to anything further. He would continue to tour with *Sugar Babies*, but did little on TV or in feature films. His only 1984 credit was a Yuletide TV movie titled *It Came upon a Midnight Clear*. In 1985 his sole credit was a voice-over in a Care Bears animated movie.

He did little in 1986, nothing in 1987, a couple of TV spots in 1988, another voice-over in 1989, and closed out the '80s in the feature comedy *Erik the Viking*.

The comeback that included an Oscar nomination, a Tony nomination, an Emmy, a Golden Globe, and a special Oscar seemed to be over in a scant four years. The rest of the 1980s was uneventful, and during the 1990s Rooney resigned himself to taking whatever roles he was offered. This kept him active in movies and on TV, but some of the choices were hardly worthy of his talents. There is nothing to be said about *Silent Night, Deadly Night 5* (1991), which was released directly to video, or his cameo in the low-budget throwaway *Maximum Force* (1992). He did return to TV for a series based on *The Black Stallion*, called *The New Adventures of the Black Stallion*, which ran for three seasons on the Family Channel (1990–1993). He kept active doing TV guest spots and appearances in movies, but nothing truly of note for the remainder of the decade. Mickey Rooney found more success away from film and TV during the 1990s. He wrote his autobiography *Life Is Too Short* in 1991. He toured in Stephen Sondheim's *A Funny Thing Happened on the Way to the Forum* and returned to Broadway in *The Will Rogers Follies*. He toured Canada in the play *The Mind with the Naughty Man* and played the Wizard in a stage version of *The Wizard of Oz* at Madison Square Garden. In 1994, he wrote a novel about a child star, *The Search for Sunny Skies*. However, despite making millions throughout his long career and enjoying a $65,000 weekly salary while doing *Sugar Babies*, Rooney continued to gamble away his money and declared bankruptcy in 1996.

MICKEY IN THE TWENTY-FIRST CENTURY

As Mickey Rooney entered the twenty-first century, he tried to earn extra money touring in a musical comedy act with his wife, Jan Chamberlin, first called "Mickey Rooney's One Man One Wife Show" and later retitled "Let's Put on a Show." However, by 2005, Rooney claimed he was once again broke. Fortunately, he soon received an offer for another big movie that would pay him more than $200,000 to appear in a small role. It would be his first big movie since *The Black Stallion*.

Rooney was touring with his eighth wife, Jan, whom he had married in 1978, when he was offered a role in a feature film titled *Night at the Museum*. The movie was going to feature many stars, including Ben Stiller, Owen Wilson, Paul Rudd, Ricky Gervais, and Robin Williams. Rooney and Dick Van Dyke were to play janitors. Rooney had a small role but in a big-budget film that cost over $100 million to make and grossed nearly $600 million at the box office. He received a much-needed $250,000 for his small role, in which he played a tough veteran janitor always willing to fight. Seeing the eighty-six-year-old Rooney playing something of an extension of his Whitey Marsh character from *Boys Town* was one of the many fun elements of the feature, which spawned two sequels.

During the Christmas season of 2007, Rooney appeared as Baron Hardup in *Cinderella* on the British stage. In 2008, he was rather prolific on TV and in movies, playing small roles in five different productions. Rooney was on hand for the first sequel to *Night at the Museum*, but his part in *Night at the Museum: Battle of the Smithsonian* (2009) was cut due to time constraints before the film was released. After a cameo in the 2011 film *The Muppets*, Rooney was back for *Night at the Museum: Secret of the Tomb* (2014). Director Shawn Levy spoke about Rooney to Bryan Alexander in *USA Today*:

> Mickey Rooney was 93 when he shot his final scene as the diminutive night security guard Gus in *Night at the Museum: Secret of the Tomb*. "Yes, he was in a wheelchair, and yes, sometimes I had to cue a line for him," says Shawn Levy, "But Mickey was so energetic and so pleased to be there. He was just happy to be invited to the party."
>
> Levy says Rooney never counted on his showbiz pedigree to earn the Gus role for the original *Night at the Museum* in 2006. He auditioned for the part. "This is in an industry now where, if someone has a two-episode arc on a CW show, they don't want to ever audition," Levy says. "So the fact that this legend came in and actually showed what he could do to get the part, that's kind of remarkable and awesome. And it speaks to a love of the work. Mickey really wanted to be in this." Rooney triumphed, and the part was written around him co-starring with fellow night guards played by Dick Van Dyke and Bill Cobbs.[2]

Rooney's final years were, sadly, not all about this sort of productivity and positive attention. In 2011, the ninety-year-old alleged that he was a victim of elder abuse, naming Christopher Aber, one of his wife Jan's sons from a previous marriage. Although he was separated from his eighth wife in 2012, he had been married to her longer than all seven of his other marriages combined. On March 2, 2011, Rooney spoke at a special U.S. Senate committee meeting regarding legislation to thwart elder abuse. Rooney's attorneys claimed that Aber "threatens, intimidates, bullies and harasses Mickey" and refused to reveal the actor's finances to him, "other than to tell him that he is broke."[3]

Rooney had a restraining order issued to Christopher Aber and his wife, but eventually they made a confidential settlement. Rooney adopted Jan's other son, Mark, who cared for him during his final years.

Mickey Rooney died in his sleep on April 6, 2014, at the age of ninety-three. He had just completed filming his scenes for B. Luciano Barsuglia's *Dr. Jekyll and Mr. Hyde* (2015) a few weeks earlier. At around the same time, Rooney updated his will, disinheriting everyone except Jan's son Mark, who had been caring for him. Despite the millions he made in his career, the $65,000 per week he was paid while doing *Sugar Babies*, and the $250,000 he received for *Night at the Museum*, Mickey Rooney's estate was worth only $18,000 when he died. Out of that he owed back taxes and medical bills. Eulogizing him at the time of his death, a film critic from *The New Yorker* stated,

> His live-wire expressiveness spoke of the can-do, will-do spirit that may have encouraged Depression-weary audiences with a dose of practical optimism, but the enforced razzle-dazzle showed only one side of his persona (and perhaps warped his personality). Rooney, in his more matter-of-fact (if less heralded) performances, holds the screen with a seemingly effortless intensity.[4]

But it was longtime friend and fellow former MGM child star Margaret O'Brien who summed it up best when she told the press upon Rooney's passing, "He could do anything."[5]

NOTES

PROLOGUE

1. Not shoe polish as has been reported elsewhere.
2. Albert Herman (1887–1958) directed everything from short comedies, to B westerns, to television episodes in a career that spanned four decades.
3. *Mickey's Circus* was released September 9, 1927.
4. Personal interview with the author. August 10, 2001.
5. Personal interview with the author.
6. Mangum, John. *A Midsummer Night's Dream* (complete): Felix Mendelssohn." www.hollywoodbowl.com.
7. Personal interview with the author.
8. Personal interview with the author.
9. Personal interview with the author.
10. Cooper, Jackie. *Please Don't Shoot My Dog: The Autobiography of Jackie Cooper.* New York: William, Morrow, and Company, 1981.
11. *Private Screenings*. Turner Classic Movies interview broadcast October 2, 2006.
12. Rooney, Mickey. *Life Is Too Short*. New York: Villard Books, 1991.
13. Personal interview with the author.

CHAPTER I

1. Cooper, Jackie. *Please Don't Shoot My Dog: The Autobiography of Jackie Cooper.* New York: William, Morrow, and Company, 1981.

2. Nugent, Frank S. "'The Devil Is a Sissy' Moves into the Capitol—Two New Films at the Rialto and Palace." *New York Times*, October 17, 1936.
3. Personal interview with the author. August 10, 2001.

CHAPTER 2

1. A famous family vaudeville act featuring Eddie Foy (1856–1928) and his seven children, of which Bryan (1896–1977) was second oldest.
2. Personal interview with the author. August 10, 2001.
3. Personal interview with the author.
4. Rooney, Mickey. *Life Is Too Short*. New York: Villard Books, 1991.

CHAPTER 3

1. Rooney, Mickey. *Life Is Too Short*. New York: Villard Books, 1991.
2. *Variety* staff. "A Family Affair." *Variety*, December 31, 1936.
3. Nugent, Frank. "A Family Affair." *New York Times*, April 20, 1937.
4. Personal interview with the author. August 10, 2001.
5. Hay, Peter. *MGM: When the Lion Roars*. Atlanta, Turner Publishing, 1991.

CHAPTER 5

1. Personal interview with the author. August 10, 2001.
2. Nugent, Frank. "Captains Courageous." *New York Times*, May 12, 1937.
3. *Variety* staff. "Captains Courageous." *Variety*, May 14, 1937.
4. Personal interview with the author.

CHAPTER 6

1. Personal interview with the author. August 10, 2001.

CHAPTER 7

1. Personal interview with the author. August 10, 2001.
2. Tucker, Sophie. *Some of These Days: The Autobiography of Sophie Tucker*. New York: Doubleday, 1945.
3. Tazelaar, Marguerite. "Thoroughbreds Don't Cry." *New York Herald-Tribune,* December 5, 1937.

CHAPTER 8

1. Personal interview with the author. August 10, 2001.
2. "What the Picture Did for Me." *Motion Picture Herald*, May 14, 1938.
3. Thompson, Howard. "You're Only Young Once." *New York Times*, January 3, 1938.

CHAPTER 9

1. Personal interview with the author. August 10, 2001.
2. Nugent, Frank. "Love Is a Headache." *New York Times*, January 28, 1938.
3. Personal interview with the author.

CHAPTER 11

1. *Variety* staff. "Hold That Kiss." *Variety*, May 10, 1938.
2. Personal interview with the author. August 10, 2001.

CHAPTER 12

1. Hay, Peter. *MGM: When the Lion Roars*. Atlanta: Turner Publishing, 1991.

CHAPTER 13

1. *Variety* staff. "Love Finds Andy Hardy." *Variety*, July 13, 1938.
2. "What the Picture Did for Me." *Motion Picture Herald*, November 12, 1938.

CHAPTER 14

1. Davidson, Bill. *Spencer Tracy: Tragic Idol*. New York: E.P. Dutton, 1988.
2. Curtis, James. *Spencer Tracy: A Biography*. New York: Knopf, 2011.
3. Green, Irving. "30,000 Crowd Streets to View Film Pageantry." *Omaha World-Herald*, September 8, 1938.
4. Reports that Spencer Tracy's Oscar was accidentally labeled Dick Tracy, like the comic strip detective, are apocryphal.
5. Personal interview with the author. August 10, 2001.
6. Personal interview with the author.

CHAPTER 15

1. Crisler, B. R. "Stablemates." *New York Times,* October 21, 1938.
2. "What the Picture Did for Me." *Motion Picture Herald*, January 7, 1939.

CHAPTER 16

1. Personal interview with the author. August 10, 2001.
2. "Out West with the Hardys." *Box Office*, June 24, 1939.
3. "What the Picture Did for Me." *Motion Picture Herald*, January 28, 1939.

CHAPTER 17

1. Nugent, Frank. "The Adventures of Huckleberry Finn." *New York Times*, March 3, 1939.
2. Rooney, Mickey. *Life Is Too Short*. New York: Villard Books, 1991.

CHAPTER 18

1. Personal interview with the author. August 10, 2001.

CHAPTER 19

1. Personal interview with the author. August 10, 2001.
2. Eyman, Scott. *Lion of Hollywood: The Life and Legend of Louis B. Mayer*. New York: Robson, 2005.
3. Eyman, *Lion of Hollywood*.
4. Nugent, Frank. "Andy Hardy Gets Spring Fever." *New York Times*, July 19, 1939.
5. *Variety* staff. "Andy Hardy Gets Spring Fever." *Variety*, July 22, 1939.

CHAPTER 20

1. Role originally intended for actor Bobs Watson, hence the character name.
2. Cut from the film after President Roosevelt's death in 1945 and considered lost for years, but eventually a 16mm print of the scene was found and restored on the DVD.

3. Fowler, Jack. Mickey Rooney Obituary. *National Review*, April 7, 2014.
4. Personal interview with the author. August 10, 2001.
5. Personal interview with the author.
6. Personal interview with the author.
7. *Variety* staff. "Babes in Arms." *Variety*, September 20, 1939.
8. Nugent, Frank. "Babes in Arms." *New York Times*, October 20 1939.
9. "The Exhibitor Has His Say: *Babes in Arms.*" *Box Office*, January 1940.
10. Due to revivals and continued rereleases, *The Wizard of Oz* would earn nearly a quarter billion dollars by 2014.
11. Personal interview with the author.

CHAPTER 21

1. Crowther, Bosley. *The Lion's Share: The Story of an Entertainment Empire.* New York: Dutton, 1957.
2. Nugent, Frank. "Judge Hardy and Son." *New York Times*, January 18, 1940.

CHAPTER 22

1. Agee, James. "Cinema: Success Story." *Time*, March 18, 1940.
2. *Ghosts on the Loose* (1943), made after the act was renamed the East Side Kids.
3. Personal interview with the author. August 10, 2001.
4. Nugent, Frank. "Young Tom Edison." *New York Times*, March 15, 1940.
5. "The Exhibitor Has His Say: *Young Tom Edison*." *Box Office*, May 1940.

CHAPTER 23

1. Personal interview with the author. August 10, 2001.
2. "What the Picture Did for Me." *Motion Picture Herald*, November 23, 1940.
3. Agee, James. "Andy Hardy Meets a Debutante." *Time*, July 22, 1940.
4. *Variety* staff. "Andy Hardy Meets a Debutante." *Variety*, July 3, 1940.

CHAPTER 24

1. Willie is played by Larry Nunn, whose daughter Terri Nunn was the lead singer of the group Berlin, which had a hit record with "Take My Breath Away" (1986).
2. Nugent, Frank. "Strike Up the Band." *New York Times*, September 30, 1940.
3. *Variety* staff. "Strike Up the Band." *Variety*, September 18, 1940.

CHAPTER 26

1. Personal interview with the author. August 10, 2001.
2. Personal interview with the author.
3. Personal interview with the author.
4. Crowther, Bosley. "Men of Boys Town." *New York Times*, April 11, 1941.
5. *Variety* staff. "Men of Boys Town." *Variety*, April 15, 1938.

CHAPTER 27

1. Pryor, Thomas. "Life Begins for Andy Hardy." *New York Times*, August 22, 1941.

CHAPTER 28

1. Pryor, Thomas. "Babes on Broadway." *New York Times*, January 1, 1942.
2. "The Exhibitor Has His Say: *Babes on Broadway*." *Box Office*, July 1942.

CHAPTER 29

1. Crowther, Bosley. "The Courtship of Andy Hardy." *New York Times*, April 10, 1942.

CHAPTER 30

1. Rooney, Mickey. *Life Is Too Short*. New York: Villard Books, 1991.

CHAPTER 31

1. Crowther, Bosley. "So Long Andy: The Latest Hardy Family Picture Bids Adieu to That Bumptious Boy." *New York Times*, February 21, 1943.
2. "The Exhibitor Has His Say: *Andy Hardy's Double Life*." *Box Office*, March 1943.

CHAPTER 32

1. William Saroyan had once worked as a telegraph boy.
2. Personal interview with the author. August 10, 2001.

3. Crowther, Bosley. "The Human Comedy." *New York Times*, March 3, 1943.
4. "The Exhibitor Has His Say: *The Human Comedy*." *Box Office*, June 1943.
5. "The Exhibitor Has His Say."

CHAPTER 33

1. Personal interview with the author. August 10, 2001.
2. Agee, James. "Girl Crazy." *Time*, December 27, 1943.
3. *Variety* staff. "Girl Crazy." *Variety*, December 4, 1943.
4. Strauss, Theodore. "Girl Crazy." *New York Times*, December 3, 1943.

CHAPTER 34

1. "Easy to Love" was written in 1936 and had been intended for an earlier Hardy film. The ballad was set for Judy Garland to sing in *Life Begins for Andy Hardy* (1941), but this song, along with three other Garland vocals, was cut from the film. Judy's prerecording of the Porter classic can be found on the Rhino CD "Judy Garland: Collectors' Gems from the M-G-M Films."
2. "The Exhibitor Has His Say: *Andy Hardy's Blonde Trouble*," July 1944.

CHAPTER 35

1. Personal interview with the author. August 10, 2001.

CHAPTER 36

1. Personal interview with the author. August 10, 2001.
2. Crowther, Bosley. "Love Laughs at Andy Hardy." *New York Times*, January 8, 1947.
3. Not to be confused with the 1932 Warner Bros. film with the same title, which starred James Cagney and was about auto racing.

CHAPTER 38

1. Leigh, Janet. *There Really Was a Hollywood*. New York: Doubleday, 1984.
2. Marx, Arthur. *The Nine Lives of Mickey Rooney*. New York: Stein and Day, 1986.

CHAPTER 40

1. Rooney, Mickey. *Life Is Too Short*. New York: Villard Books, 1991.
2. Personal interview with the author. August 10, 2001.

CHAPTER 41

1. Crowther, Bosley. "The Fireball." *New York Times*, November 10, 1950.

CHAPTER 42

1. Crowther, Bosley. "He's a Cockeyed Wonder." *New York Times*, October 20, 1950.
2. Rooney, Mickey. *Life Is Too Short*. New York: Villard Books, 1991.

CHAPTER 44

1. Stack, Robert, with Mark Evans. *Straight Shooting*. New York: Macmillan, 1980.
2. Personal interview with the author. August 10, 2001
3. "The Exhibitor Has His Say: *Sound Off*." *Box Office*, November 1952.
4. "The Exhibitor Has His Say."

CHAPTER 45

1. Personal interview with the author. August 10, 2001.
2. Hope, Bob, with Bob Thomas. *The Road to Hollywood: My Forty-Year Love Affair with the Movies*. New York: Doubleday, 1977.

CHAPTER 46

1. Personal interview with the author. August 10, 2001.

CHAPTER 47

1. O.A.G. "Drive a Crooked Road." *New York Times*, April 3, 1954.
2. Ellenberger, Allan. "Lewis Stone's Death and Funeral." Hollywoodland website, www.allanellenberger.com.
3. Rooney, Mickey. *i.e.: An Autobiography*. New York: Putnam, 1965.

CHAPTER 48

1. McBride, Joseph. *Steven Spielberg: A Biography*. London: Faber and Faber, 1997.
2. "The Exhibitor Has His Say: *The Atomic Kid*." *Box Office*, March 1955.

CHAPTER 49

1. Crowther, Bosley. "The Bridges at Toko-Ri." *New York Times*, January 21, 1955.
2. Rooney, Mickey. *Life Is Too Short*. New York: Villard Books, 1991.
3. Rooney, *Life Is Too Short*.
4. "The Exhibitor Has His Say: *The Twinkle in God's Eye*." *Box Office*, August 1957.

CHAPTER 50

1. Personal interview with the author. August 10, 2001.

CHAPTER 51

1. *New York Times* staff. "Francis in the Haunted House." *New York Times*, July 21, 1956.
2. "The Exhibitor Has His Say: *Francis in the Haunted House*." *Box Office*, January 1957.

CHAPTER 52

1. "The Exhibitor Has His Say: *Operation Mad Ball*, " *Box Office*, June 1958.
2. Advertisement. *Hollywood Reporter*, June 23, 1958.

CHAPTER 53

1. Personal interview with the author. August 10, 2001.
2. Rooney, Mickey. *Life Is Too Short*. New York: Villard Books, 1991.

CHAPTER 54

1. "The Exhibitor Has His Say: *Everything's Ducky*." *Box Office*, June 1962.

CHAPTER 55

1. Weiler, A. H. "Requiem for a Heavyweight." *New York Times*, October 17, 1962.
2. Personal interview with the author. August 10, 2001.
3. Quinn, Anthony. *One Man Tango*. New York: HarperCollins, 1995.

CHAPTER 56

1. The various running times are for different versions released on VHS, DVD, Blu-ray, the original theatrical run, and various theatrical reissues. Some versions include an overture and an intermission (the features mock news reports as to how the chase is progressing).
2. Personal interview with the author. August 10, 2001.
3. While it may not seem like a lot of money in the twenty-first century, that amount in 1963 would be in the neighborhood of $3 million today.
4. Kramer, Stanley. *It's a Mad, Mad, Mad, Mad World: A Life in Hollywood*. San Diego: Harcourt, 1997.
5. Marx, Arthur. *The Nine Lives of Mickey Rooney*. New York: Stein and Day, 1986.
6. "Sammee Tong Is Found Dead. Pill Bottle Found near Actor's Body." *Los Angeles Times*, October 27, 1964.

CHAPTER 57

1. Rooney, Mickey. *Life Is Too Short*. New York: Villard Books, 1991.
2. Brockes, Emma. "Murder in Tinseltown." *Guardian*, October 17, 2005.

CHAPTER 58

1. Reiner, Carl. *My Anecdotal Life*. New York: St. Martin's Press, 2003.
2. Kael, Pauline. *Deeper into Movies*. New York: Little, Brown and Co., 1973.
3. "Dick Van Dyke Discusses His Career in Entertainment." *Larry King Live*. Aired September 22, 2000.
4. Rooney, Mickey. *Life Is Too Short*. New York: Villard Books, 1991.
5. Rooney, *Life Is Too Short*.

CHAPTER 59

1. Caine, Michael. *What's It All About?* New York: Random House, 1992.
2. "Ask Them Yourself." *Parade*, May 22, 1977.

CHAPTER 60

1. Maltin, Leonard. *The Disney Films*. New York: Crown, 1984.
2. Maslin, Janet. "Pete's Dragon." *New York Times*, November 4, 1977.

CHAPTER 61

1. Rooney played a jockey in *Down the Stretch* (1936), *Thoroughbreds Don't Cry* (1937), *Stablemates* (1938), and *National Velvet* (1944).
2. Personal interview with the author. August 10, 2001.
3. Maslin, Janet. "The Black Stallion." *New York Times*, October 13, 1979.
4. Bowen, Michael. "The Black Stallion." *Boston Globe*, February 7, 1980.
5. Ebert, Roger. "The Black Stallion." *Chicago Sun-Times*, October 17, 1979.
6. Personal interview with the author.
7. Personal interview with the author.

EPILOGUE

1. Personal interview with the author. August 10, 2001.
2. Alexander, Bryan. "Mickey Rooney Gives One Final 'Museum' Moment." *USA Today*, December 17, 2014.
3. Feinberg, Scott. "A Star Is Burned: Mickey Rooney's Final Days Marred by Bizarre Family Feud." *Hollywood Reporter*, April 9, 2014.
4. Brody, Richard. "The Natural: Farewell Mickey Rooney." *The New Yorker*, April 7, 2014.
5. McCartney, Anthony. "Iconic Actor Mickey Rooney Dies at 93." *Miami Herald*, April 7, 2014.

BIBLIOGRAPHY

BOOKS

Agee, James. *Agee on Film.* Boston: Beacon Press, 1966.

Anger, Kenneth. *Hollywood Babylon.* New York: Simon and Schuster, 1965.

Blottner, Gene. *Columbia Noir.* Jefferson, NC: McFarland, 2015.

Caine, Michael. *What's It All About?* New York: Random House, 1992.

Cooper, Jackie. *Please Don't Shoot My Dog: The Autobiography of Jackie Cooper.* New York: William, Morrow, and Company, 1981.

Crowther, Bosley. *The Lion's Share: The Story of an Entertainment Empire.* New York: Dutton, 1957.

Curtis, James. *Spencer Tracy: A Biography.* New York: Knopf, 2011.

Davidson, Bill. *Spencer Tracy: Tragic Idol.* New York: E.P. Dutton, 1988.

Eyman Scott. *Lion of Hollywood: The Life and Legend of Louis B. Mayer.* New York: Robson, 2005.

Frank, Gerold. *Judy.* New York: Da Capo Press, 1999.

Hannsberry, Karen Burroughs. *Bad Boys: The Actors of Film Noir.* Jefferson, NC: McFarland, 2008.

Hay, Peter. *MGM: When the Lion Roars.* Atlanta: Turner Publishing, 1991.

Hope, Bob, with Bob Thomas. *The Road to Hollywood: My Forty-Year Love Affair with the Movies.* New York: Doubleday, 1977.

Kael, Pauline. *Deeper into Movies.* New York: Little, Brown and Co., 1973.

Kramer, Stanley. *It's a Mad, Mad, Mad, Mad World: A Life in Hollywood.* San Diego: Harcourt, 1997.

Leigh, Janet. *There Really Was a Hollywood.* New York: Doubleday, 1984.

Maltin, Leonard. *The Disney Films*. New York: Crown, 1984.
Maltin, Leonard. *The Great Movie Shorts*. New York: Crown, 1972.
Marill, Alvin H. *Mickey Rooney: His Films, Television Appearances, Radio Work, Stage Shows, and Recordings*. Jefferson, NC: McFarland, 2004.
Marx, Arthur. *The Nine Lives of Mickey Rooney*. New York: Stein and Day, 1986.
McBride, Joseph. *Steven Spielberg: A Biography*. London: Faber and Faber, 1997.
Neibaur, James L. *The Bob Hope Films*. Jefferson, NC: McFarland, 2004.
Okuda, Ted. *The Monogram Checklist*. Jefferson, NC: McFarland, 1987.
Quinn, Anthony. *One Man Tango*. New York: HarperCollins, 1995.
Reiner, Carl. *My Anecdotal Life*. New York: St. Martin's Press, 2003.
Rooney, Mickey. *i.e.: An Autobiography*. New York: Putnam, 1965.
Rooney, Mickey. *Life Is Too Short*. New York: Villard Books, 1991.
Stack, Robert, with Mark Evans. *Straight Shooting*. New York: Macmillan, 1980.
Tucker, Sophie. *Some of These Days: The Autobiography of Sophie Tucker*. New York: Doubleday, 1945.
Tyler, Don. *The Great Movie Musicals*. Jefferson, NC: McFarland, 2010.
Walker, Alexander. *Elizabeth: The Life of Elizabeth Taylor*. Revised ed. New York: Atria Books, 2011.

Articles

Agee, James. "Cinema: Success Story." *Time*, March 18, 1940.
Alexander, Bryan. "Mickey Rooney Gives One Final 'Museum' Moment." *USA Today*, December 17, 2014.
Berkvist, Robert. "Ann Rutherford, Studio Film Sweetheart, Dies at 94." *New York Times*, June 12, 2002.
Brody, Richard. "The Natural: Farewell Mickey Rooney." *The New Yorker*, April 7, 2014.
"Eddie Mannix Ledger." Margaret Herrick Library, Center for Motion Picture Study, Los Angeles.
Feinberg, Scott. "A Star Is Burned: Mickey Rooney's Final Days Marred by Bizarre Family Feud." *Hollywood Reporter*, April 9, 2014.
Fowler, Jack. Mickey Rooney Obituary. *National Review*, April 7, 2014.
Green, Irving. "30,000 Crowd Streets to View Film Pageantry." *Omaha World-Herald*, September 8, 1938.
Hollywood Reporter. Advertisement regarding screenwriters for *Baby Face Nelson*. June 23, 1958
Los Angeles Times. "Sammee Tong Is Found Dead. Pill Bottle Found Near Actor's Body." October 27, 1964.
McCartney, Anthony. "Iconic Actor Mickey Rooney Dies at 93." *Miami Herald*, April 7, 2014.
Oliver, Myrna. "Maurice Duke; Colorful Movie Producer." *Los Angeles Times*, November 2, 1996.
Parade. "Ask Them Yourself." May 22, 1977.

REVIEWS

Agee, James. "Andy Hardy Meets a Debutante." *Time,* July 22, 1940.
Agee, James. "Girl Crazy." *Time*, December 27, 1943.
Bowen, Michael. "The Black Stallion." *Boston Globe*. February 7, 1980.
Crisler, B. R. "Stablemates." *New York Times*, October 21, 1938.
Crowther, Bosley. "The Bridges at Toko-Ri." *New York Times*, January 21, 1955.
Crowther, Bosley. "The Courtship of Andy Hardy." *New York Times*, April 10, 1942.
Crowther, Bosley. "He's a Cockeyed Wonder." *New York Times,* October 20, 1950.
Crowther, Bosley. "The Fireball." *New York Times*, November 10, 1950.
Crowther, Bosley. "The Human Comedy." *New York Times*, March 3, 1943.
Crowther, Bosley. "Love Laughs at Andy Hardy." *New York Times*, January 8, 1947.
Crowther, Bosley. "Men of Boys Town." *New York Times,* April 11, 1941.
Crowther, Bosley. "So Long Andy: The Latest Hardy Family Picture Bids Adieu to That Bumptious Boy." *New York Times*, February 21, 1943.
Ebert, Roger. "The Black Stallion." *Chicago Sun-Times*, October 17, 1979.
Maslin, Janet. "The Black Stallion." *New York Times*, October 13, 1979.
Maslin, Janet. "Pete's Dragon." *New York Times*, November 4, 1977.
New York Times staff. "Francis in the Haunted House." *New York Times*, July 21, 1956.
Nugent, Frank. "The Adventures of Huckleberry Finn." *New York Times*, March 3, 1939.
Nugent, Frank. "Andy Hardy Gets Spring Fever." *New York Times*, July 19, 1939.
Nugent, Frank. "Babes in Arms." *New York Times*, October 20, 1939.
Nugent, Frank. "Captains Courageous." *New York Times*, May 12, 1937.
Nugent, Frank S. "'The Devil Is a Sissy' Moves into the Capitol—Two New Films at the Rialto and Palace." *New York Times*, October 17, 1936.
Nugent, Frank. "A Family Affair." *New York Times*, April 20, 1937.
Nugent, Frank. "Judge Hardy and Son." *New York Times*, January 18, 1940.
Nugent, Frank. "Love Is a Headache." *New York Times*, January 28, 1938.
Nugent, Frank. "Strike Up the Band." *New York Times*, September 30, 1940.
Nugent, Frank. "Young Tom Edison." *New York Times*, March 15, 1940.
O.A.G. "Drive a Crooked Road." *New York Times*, April 3, 1954.
Phillips, William. "The Human Comedy." Review of William Saroyan's novel. *Nation*, March 1943.
Pryor, Thomas. "Babes on Broadway." *New York Times*, January 1, 1942.
Pryor, Thomas. "Life Begins for Andy Hardy." *New York Times*, August 22, 1941.
Strauss, Theodore. "Girl Crazy." *New York Times*, December 3, 1943.
Tazelaar, Marguerite. "Thoroughbreds Don't Cry." *New York Herald-Tribune,* December 5, 1937.
Thompson, Howard. "You're Only Young Once." *New York Times*, January 3, 1938.
Weiler, A. H. "Requiem for a Heavyweight." *New York Times*, October 17, 1962.
Variety staff. "Andy Hardy Gets Spring Fever." *Variety*, July 22, 1939.

Variety staff. "Andy Hardy Meets a Debutante." *Variety*, July 3, 1940.
Variety staff. "Babes in Arms." *Variety*, September 20, 1939.
Variety staff. "Captains Courageous." *Variety*, May 14, 1937.
Variety staff. "A Family Affair." *Variety*, December 31, 1936.
Variety staff. "Girl Crazy." *Variety*, December 4, 1943.
Variety staff. "Hold That Kiss." *Variety*, May 10, 1938.
Variety staff. "Love Finds Andy Hardy." *Variety*, July 13, 1938.
Variety staff. "Men of Boys Town." *Variety*, April 15, 1938.
Variety staff. "Strike Up the Band." *Variety*, September 18, 1940.

EXHIBITOR COMMENTS

Box Office. "The Exhibitor Has His Say." A column that offers exhibitor comments about audience reaction and response at their theaters. Used for the following films:

Andy Hardy's Blonde Trouble, July 1944 issue
Andy Hardy's Double Life, March 1943 issue
The Atomic Kid, March 1955 issue
Babes in Arms, January 1940 issue
Babes on Broadway, July 1942 issue
Boys Town, June 1938 issue
Everything's Ducky, June 1962 issue
Francis in the Haunted House, January 1957 issue
The Human Comedy, June 1943 issue
Operation Mad Ball, June 1958 issue
Out West with the Hardys, June 1939 issue
Sound Off, November 1952 issue
The Twinkle in God's Eye, August 1957 issue
Words and Music, January 1949 issue
Young Tom Edison, May 1940 issue

Motion Picture Herald. "What the Picture Did for Me." A column that offers exhibitor comments about audience reaction and response at their theaters. Used for the following films:

Andy Hardy Meets a Debutante, November 23, 1940
Love Finds Andy Hardy, November 12, 1938
Stablemates, January 7, 1939
Out West with the Hardys, January 28, 1939
You're Only Young Once, May 14, 1938

ONLINE SOURCES

Aleperti, Cliff. "*The Human Comedy* (1943) Starring Mickey Rooney." www.immortalephemera.com.

Brockes, Emma. "Murder in Tinseltown." *Guardian*, October 17, 2005. www.theguardian.com/stage/2005/oct/17/theatre.

Ellenberger, Allan. "Lewis Stone's Death and Funeral." Hollywoodland website, www.allanellenberger.com.

Internet Movie Database, www.imdb.com.

Johnson, Jim. Andy Hardy Fan Site, www.andyhardyfilms.com.

Johnson, Jim. Judy Garland Database, www.jgdb.com/index.html.

Mangum, John. "*A Midsummer Night's Dream* (complete): Felix Mendelssohn." www.hollywoodbowl.com.

Nolte, John. "Treasures from the Warner Archives: 'The Human Comedy' (1943)." Breitbart.com.

Turner Classic Movies, www.tcm.com.

Wikipedia, www.wikipedia.org.

INTERVIEWS

Larry King Live. "Dick Van Dyke Discusses His Career in Entertainment." Aired September 22, 2000.

Private Screenings. Turner Classic Movies interview broadcast on October 2, 2006.

Rooney, Mickey. Personal interview with the author. August 10, 2001.

INDEX

ABOUT THE AUTHOR

James L. Neibaur is a film historian who has written hundreds of articles, including over forty essays for *Encyclopedia Britannica*. He is also the author of numerous books, including *The Fall of Buster Keaton: His Films for MGM, Educational Pictures, and Columbia* (2010); *Early Charlie Chaplin: The Artist as Apprentice at Keystone Studios* (2011); *The Silent Films of Harry Langdon: 1923–1928* (2012); *Buster Keaton's Silent Shorts: 1920–1923* (coauthored with Terri Niemi, 2013); *The Charley Chase Talkies: 1929–1940* (2013); *The Elvis Movies* (2014); *James Cagney Films of the 1930s* (2014); *The Clint Eastwood Westerns* (2015); and *Butterfly in the Rain: The 1927 Abduction and Murder of Marion Parker* (2016).

GARY PUBLIC LIBRARY
3 9222 03233 6468